Infoculture

Stephen Vincent

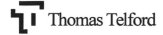
Thomas Telford

Published by Thomas Telford Publishing, Thomas Telford Ltd, 1 Heron Quay, London E14 4JD

First published 1998

Distributors for Thomas Telford books are
USA: ASCE Press, 1801 Alexander Bell Drive, Reston, VA 20191-4400, USA
Japan: Maruzen Co. Ltd, Book Department, 3-10 Nihonbashi 2-chome, Chuo-ku, Tokyo 103
Australia: DA Books and Journals, 648 Whitehorse Road, Mitcham 3132, Victoria

A catalogue record for this book is available from the British Library

ISBN: 0 7277 2597 1

Typeset by Gray Publishing, Tunbridge Wells
Printed in Great Britain by Redwood Books, Trowbridge, Wiltshire

Foreword

Although they have often been at the origin of human improvements, civil engineers are often considered traditional people. Our European schools of engineering are among the oldest universities in the world and our working procedures remain quite conventional.

The civil engineer's profession can, probably more than any other, benefit from the practice of data processing and information technologies, in design as well as management or procurement. With Stephen Vincent, you will enter into a dazzling world and get an optimistic view of the future.

François Gérard Baron
President of the European Council of Civil Engineers

Preface

I hope that you will enjoy reading this book. My mission is to dispel some of the haze of myths and mysteries that the new technology wizards have cast around the developing wonders of Information Technology.

I don't believe in artificial boundaries or classifications, so I don't have a profile of the ideal reader. My background is in the construction industry, but my interest is to see technology working for us, rather than against us, in all aspects of all of our lives.

I plan to take you on a voyage, from where we are today to where we could be going in the future. Enjoy the journey!

Stephen Vincent
Islamabad, November 1997

Contents

1 The information revolution

Introduction

We all live within an infrastructure of transport systems, water and food supplies, cities and settlements. Most of us don't stop to think about it – it just exists, and develops to suit our needs.

In the back of our minds, we each have our own personal understanding of where food comes from, of how cars work, of why money exists, and of all of the other components of knowledge which enable us to survive in this complex world.

But now something has changed, is still changing, and challenges us either to understand it or to be left behind by those who do. Are the people who really understand 'information technology' just the garage mechanics of our new information age computer 'vehicles', there to serve the public at large, or are they wizards and magicians with the power to control us all?

The big problem seems to be that whereas the motor car developed over many years, so that we could gradually extend our knowledge year by year, computers seem to change every month, every week, even every day. The capabilities of modern personal computers were hardly dreamt of a few years ago!

I started my career as a civil engineer, intent upon improving the world by building roads and water supplies and cities. How perceptions change! Now construction is seen by many people as environmentally damaging and unsustainable. Yet we all want water when we turn the tap on, and empty roads to drive on! I digress...

Now I find myself in a vortex of changing knowledge and understanding – the world of information technology. Here, perceptions change every day – a good investment yesterday is a white elephant today. How can the average person keep pace?

1

Just when I thought I was beginning to understand technology, along came culture, or more correctly 'culture change'. The way we live, the way we work, how we think and the things that we do are all changing to cope with the breakneck pace of modern life, adapting to a consumer-driven media-saturated society.

Hence the title of this book: *Infoculture*. Here is a classic chicken and egg situation. Is our culture changing in response to the bombardment of new ideas from computer and communication technology, or is technology responding to new thinking about the way we would like to live?

In my mind, the two are inextricably intertwined. Computers make new concepts possible. Communications allow the media to explain these new possibilities to people. People generate new thinking and new opportunities, which drive technology forward again. Information technology is as much a part of our future as the motor car, so let's understand it a little better.

Understanding information technology

So what is 'information technology'? Is it just an easy catch-all phrase to describe all of the wonderful new technology which many of us don't fully understand?

The real question is: how much do we really need to understand? There is no need to understand how the engine works to drive a car, or the complexities of the technology hidden inside a television to enjoy watching one. A computer is just another box with a switch on it, which carries out tasks to assist us in our daily lives, like a microwave or a washing machine.

Unfortunately, drawing the analogy with the motor car, computers are still at a fairly early stage of their development. People who drove vintage cars had to check the oil and water every day, change tyres quite often, and have a fairly good idea of how the engine worked to know what to do when the car would not start.

As cars developed, this became generic knowledge. If you understood how one car worked, you understood most others. Nowadays, there is little need to know more than the controls to drive the car. I have difficulty finding the lever to open the bonnet of my car; understanding how the engine underneath it works is simply unnecessary.

This book is devoted to identifying the general knowledge which everyone should know, without all of the jargon and tedious detail. I have also tried to rise above most of the daily changes to see the more enduring long-term principles which will stay relevant for a few years. Car designs may have changed a great deal, but the controls to drive them have been the same for decades.

But first, what is the 'Information Superhighway' which has been mentioned so often on the television and in the newspapers, and is it the same as the 'Information Society' that politicians talk about in Europe? Are these meaningful terms which we will all be using in the future, or just passing buzzwords which will all be forgotten in a few years' time?

The following is a personal interpretation, as are many of the descriptions which follow later in this book. However, as with all things, what really matters is what people perceive things to be rather than the clinical and clear-cut world of the scientist. Unfortunately most people who design computer systems are scientists, and nowadays most people who use them are not. Hence the root of a communication problem.

The Information Superhighway

In the 1980s, the future of information technology became, to a large extent, a race between the USA, Japan and Europe to produce more complex, faster operating, more miniaturized and cheaper 'chips', or integrated circuits, which many people knew would become the building blocks of the computers of the future. An integrated circuit just meant packing a fantastic amount of electronic circuitry into a very small component package, and there are many different types. It appeared that whoever led this field would reap the benefits of the new industrial age of manufacturing electronic artefacts.

As successful technological progress was made in manufacturing electronic components, it became possible to look forward to new visions of how we might live and work in the future. The suggestion that vast amounts of information might be stored in electronic form in the future started to look a real possibility. This information might encompass anything – all of the books in the library, all of the files in the office, all of the films ever made – at some time in the future.

Communications started to become an issue. How would everyone gain access to all of this information?

The possibilities for communicating with each other also started to develop rapidly. Video conferencing had been restricted to the realm of large corporations and international organizations because of the high costs involved. Through various technical advances it became imaginable that within a few years costs would reduce to the point where the use of

3

video telephones could become an everyday business and domestic occurrence, much as fax machines have become an everyday working tool in the 1980s and 1990s.

Hence the concept of the 'Information Superhighway' was born. Just as the telephone has made the world a much smaller place over the last generation, making it possible for people to talk to each other almost anywhere in the world whenever they want to, the Information Superhighway will allow all forms of new technology to communicate with each other whenever they need to, wherever they happen to be.

The telephone was fairly easy to understand. Each telephone has a handset with a microphone and an earphone. In its most basic form, this is just connected by two wires to another telephone; then two people can talk. Telephone exchanges and the dial or numbered buttons on the telephone instrument itself just enable different telephones to be connected to each other on demand.

The Information Superhighway is a very much more sophisticated and complex means of communication. Rather than just connecting telephone handsets together, it connects computers and electronic equipment together.

In the past, computers and other equipment were mainly designed to operate as independent units, each with its own independent purpose, connected together by human beings operating switches, reading printouts and typing at keyboards to coordinate the activities of different machines. Today the opportunities for connecting systems directly together to eliminate unnecessary human effort and make new forms of communication possible are much better understood. Natural commercial selection – where people prefer to purchase equipment which can be connected more easily – has combined with an immense, but mostly unseen, effort to develop international standards for intercommunication, which now mean that many types of equipment can communicate with each other more easily. This could be viewed as similar to, but much more complex than, standardizing electronic mains voltage and electric plugs throughout the world.

There are many aspects of this new international intercommunication which go far beyond the original principles of the telephone system. Rather than just connecting two computers together, it is becoming an everyday occurrence to connect many computers or other pieces of equipment together simultaneously. The volumes of information transferred over very short periods of time may be immense. Many different connections may be made and disconnected, even over just a few seconds. The whole pace of this electronic dialogue is unthinkably fast and diverse.

4

So, enough marvelling at all this new technology. What is the Information Superhighway? Is it an electrical cable, an optical fibre, a radio transmission, a satellite communication, or something else?

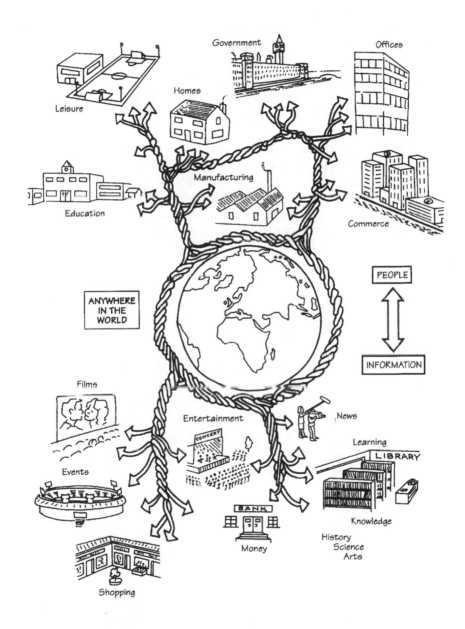

Figure 1.1. The Information Superhighway.

Let us take a step back and try to draw a parallel. Imagine a world full of people all needing to travel to meet other people. They can all travel by different means. Some might walk, drive by car, or take a bus, train, boat or aeroplane; there are many different ways that they can travel to their meetings. Electronic messages are like these people. They all need to get to places, but they can travel by different methods. In effect, what the Information Superhighway does is to provide a standardized international travel agency, which chooses the best method of travel, issues the ticket and then checks along the way to make sure that everyone gets to their destination. More than that, it does the equivalent of enabling everyone to speak the same language, anywhere in the world. Quite some achievement!

The type of connection to the Superhighway determines the level of service provided. Connection through an ordinary telephone line (more about this later) is like a local taxi service, while a high bandwidth optical fibre link is more like having a private airport that can land a Jumbo jet.

comparison of Telephone & fibre optics

The effect of implementing this Information Superhighway is to enable much greater freedom of communication between people and information, and between people and people. Figure 1.1 attempts to illustrate the opportunities that the Information Superhighway will provide when it is fully implemented. People, using computers, advanced interactive televisions or other future communications devices, will all be able to connect to the Superhighway, whether they are at home, at an office, in industry or commerce, in government, at leisure, in education or anywhere else. As well as being able to communicate with anyone else, the Superhighway will also give access to an immense range of information: libraries of knowledge; entertainment through television programmes, films, music and interactive games; learning from schools, colleges and universities; clubs and leisure activities; financial services and banking; and anything else which anyone has decided to make available in electronic form. The boundaries between such things as work, entertainment, leisure and education are likely to become much less distinct.

The need to implement the Information Superhighway has been given particular prominence in the USA, where the widespread availability of such facilities is seen as an essential component of the commercial world of the future. For instance, if every home is sufficiently well equipped to view films interactively at home, choosing any particular film and watching it whenever anyone wishes, there is considerable potential for an extensive entertainment industry to use this technology, both providing the means to view films in this way and making new films specifically for this new consumer market.

So far, I haven't said anything about the Internet. As I am writing this book, the Internet is the closest thing to this Information Superhighway of the future that is currently in existence. It embodies many of the principles required, but is still in many ways in its infancy, overloaded in parts by exceptional growth in demand, yet flexing its muscles as people experiment with the immense potential of its technology. More about this in Chapter 5.

dis·adv of net

The Information Society

Meanwhile, in Europe, the concept of the 'Information Society' of the future has been steadily developing. If we accept that the new information and communication technologies are inevitably going to become a much more fundamental part of our lives in the future, we can then start to prepare ourselves for the effects which these changes will have upon everything that we do.

If we can communicate with anyone, anywhere, at any time, where would we prefer to be, and when would we like to be in different places? Will many people prefer to work most of the time from home, to be closer to their families and leisure activities? If they do, what form will the office of the future take? Perhaps more of a meeting place than a production centre.

How will we be educated? The prospect of continually changing and developing jobs and careers leads towards the concept of continuous learning throughout our working lives, rather than just for limited concentrated periods, which in the past were mainly when we were quite young – at school and at university. In the future it may become normal to expect to change the course of one's career several times throughout a working lifetime, preparing for each change through new forms of interactive learning from home.

How will we buy goods and services? Will there still be shops as we know them today, or will most goods be ordered through electronic catalogues brought to us in the comfort of our living rooms?

What forms of leisure will we pursue? As our leisure time increases, will we be satisfied with a diet of television, films and music, or will we be looking for new forms of entertainment through interactive multimedia exploration, virtual reality games and other new ideas?

The Information Society is all about considering the answers to these and many other questions, and trying to understand what will happen to each aspect of our lives. If we anticipate changes, we can prepare for them, and attempt to minimize any detrimental effects. The Information

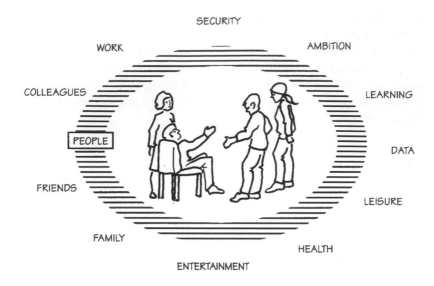

Figure 1.2. The Information Society.

Society is about people (Figure 1.2), and about understanding how to achieve a balance between the effects of advancing technology and the needs of the individual.

The Information Revolution

A high-level view, held by many people in Europe, is that we are currently in the middle of changes which will revolutionize all of our lives as much as the Industrial Revolution led to extensive changes in people's lives over a century ago.

The Industrial Revolution was not properly recognized until a number of years after it had happened. It is very difficult to see such changes when they are happening; only with the benefit of looking back over history is it possible to fully understand changes that have taken place.

So, are we really in the middle of a dramatic 'Information Revolution'?

Certainly, the pace of change is very rapid at the moment, and similar changes in perception about the future are occurring in different parts of the world almost simultaneously. Personal computers have suddenly become much cheaper and more readily available all over the world, and enthusiasts of all nationalities are steadily pushing forward the frontiers of what can be achieved using the Internet.

But these changes are still in the realm of the enthusiast, of the person who understands and wants to utilize the new technology, rather than the average person in the street. Changing patterns of employment may be more the result of international trade, giving access to lower cost manufacturing facilities in other countries, than a direct impact of information technology.

Information and communications technologies do seem to have become the enablers of change. The free market responds fairly rapidly to commercial opportunities when they occur. If the new technologies fulfil their early promise of reducing commercial costs through new working practices, and at the same time give individuals greater freedom and opportunity, it will be difficult to resist the pressures for change. A revolution seems inevitable. By the end of this book you may be in a better position to draw your own conclusions.

Cost of change [handwritten annotation]

Where are we today?

So, how far have we got? Advertisements in newspapers and magazines often include an Internet 'Web' address. Is this an early manifestation of the Information Society? Debatable. Many firms, and people, are experimenting with the possibilities of the new information age, but in the late-1990s this is still mainly the world of the enthusiast.

For many firms electronic mail (more about what this terminology means later) has become an essential component of daily working practice. But unlike the telephone or the fax, not everyone has an e-mail address yet. Hence most industries have to operate in a hybrid mode, using both standard couriers, mail, telephone and fax *and* the new electronic methods of communication where particular firms have the necessary facilities and there is a clear commercial advantage in doing so. For the moment at least, the early manifestations of the Information Superhighway are in many ways an extra complication in the communications jungle, rather than a simplification.

Meanwhile, though, the proportion of individuals and firms with access to new electronic forms of communication is increasing steadily every month. The Internet is having the most dramatic effect, mainly as a result of the ability to connect to it (with some limitations) through an ordinary telephone line. Internet service providers have appeared in almost every country in the world, with fierce competition on prices and services driving the cost of connection to quite low levels in some countries, for instance in the UK. In other countries, where services are limited, a significant premium may be charged, but the service is available and is still generally much cheaper than other forms of communication.

Cost!

Cable television, through optical fibres or other high-speed connections to individual houses, is opening up the possibility of new, faster
communications to homes and businesses. High-speed data lines are
gradually becoming cheaper for businesses. The next stage of this new
information infrastructure is evolving of its own accord through
commercial initiatives and activities in many countries, ready for the
future.

The information available on the Internet, although unbelievably
extensive, is still very variable in quality. Some firms and individuals have
created remarkably informative and interesting 'pages' on the 'World-
Wide Web' of information on the Internet, while others are still in the first
stages of experimentation. Rather surprisingly, this 'web' of information
is really quite easy to use, requiring a little more knowledge than just
turning on the television, but probably rather less than is required to
program the average early 1990s video recorder (Chapter 5).

Just as an illustration of what is possible today, I am actually in
Pakistan as I am writing this book. Using electronic mail, I am
communicating every day with colleagues, friends, family, firms and
experts all over the world, some of whom may be unaware that I am not
actually sitting in England. Over the past few weeks I have communicated with people in many countries in Europe, Africa, Asia and the
USA just as easily as if they had been here in Pakistan. With a connection
to the World-Wide Web, I have been checking the specifications of
electronic equipment in Japan, looking at prices in shops in the UK and
USA, and e-mailing friends to ask their opinions without even leaving my
desk here.*

*www
dis-adv*

But sometimes the e-mail messages do not reach their destination for a
couple of days, sometimes the connection to the Internet is so slow that I
resolve to get up very early in the morning to use it before all of the other
users here log on, and often I cannot find exactly the information I am
looking for. A number of times I have had to resort to using the fax
machine instead.

As the technology becomes more reliable and available, the human
components of the system become a more important link in the chain.
Most people open conventional postal mail when it arrives every day,

---

*In fact, the whole production of this book has made extensive use of electronic
communication. The manuscript was sent to the publisher in England by e-mail from
Pakistan. It then travelled in electronic form from the publisher to the sub-editor, and
onwards to the typesetter. The whole typeset book, complete with illustrations, was
returned to the author by e-mail, and the final proof corrections were sent back to the
publisher again by e-mail.

and read a fax as soon as it arrives. Many people do not check their electronic mail on a regular basis. There is not a general understanding of any etiquette, or standard behaviour, associated with the use of the Internet, except among the regular enthusiast users.

We are getting there, but there is still some way to go.

A glimpse of the future

In order to illustrate some of these rather abstract notions, let us consider an example of how technology might change the way things happen in the future.

This fictional story of the future starts in a small market town in the UK, with a population of average people, a few years in the future. Most people in the town have access to the latest form of the Information Superhighway at home. Anyone who does not have direct access at home can use public communication facilities at the local library.

Let us suppose that the home of the future is very similar to the home of today, except that the traditional television set has been replaced with a new interactive information communication unit. As well as acting like a conventional television set, this unit can also interrogate all of the millions of pages of information available on the Internet, show films selected interactively whenever requested, receive and send messages, much like letters, electronically (e-mail), and act as a video telephone to talk to other people or participate in conferences or discussions. There may be similar units in other rooms in the house, and almost everyone has such a unit at work.

There are still newspapers, television stations and radio stations, and places to distribute news and express opinions. Most of these, though, are now accessed through this new communications unit.

Recently, a whole series of news items and articles have concentrated on problems associated with living and working in the local town. Most people still commute to other towns. There is a shortage of local work, and many people spend a lot of their time travelling. As people's leisure time increases, a shortage of local sports and leisure facilities has become evident. Everyone has got used to the heavy trucks which drive through the centre of town, but they really would rather do without the noise, pollution and danger to pedestrians that they cause. There is also a lack of places for children to play safely in the evenings and at weekends. Something needs to be done – see Figure 1.3.

Hence, while talking about this one evening, a group of ordinary forward-thinking people decide that it is time to take matters in hand.

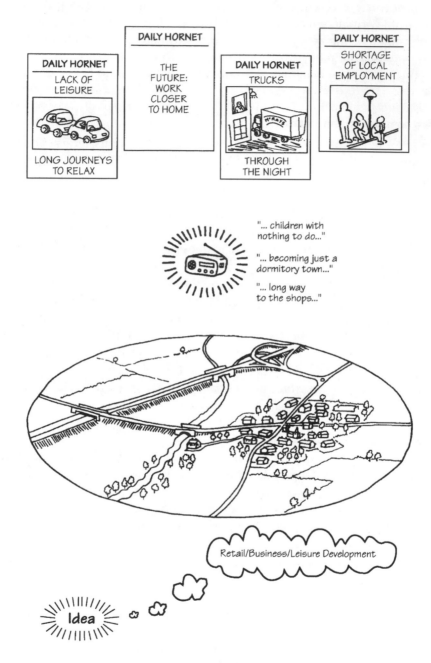

Figure 1.3. The window of local opportunity.

In the past, this would always have been the responsibility of the local council, with access to expertise and experience, or to commercial enterprises seeing an opportunity and deciding to take a risk in the hope of a commercial return.

But the council has tried to find solutions many times before, without success. There is always someone with a valid environmental or social objection to almost every scheme that they try. Our society has become too complex for straightforward solutions. The environmental and social mistakes of the past have made everyone sensitive to the problems that changes cause, and few seem to have the vision to make sacrifices in the hope of improving the situation of other people.

Commercial enterprises cannot see enough potential for a return on their investment to bother trying. The town is too small for there to be enough business, and the objections that the council has encountered to new schemes make them wary that any development plans will be blocked. Why should they bother when there are better opportunities elsewhere?

The first step towards finding a solution is to create an atmosphere in which it could happen. Information technology can help start the process. Someone, or several people, becomes bold enough to put forward the suggestion that some form of new development is needed. Perhaps a combined retail, business and leisure development tailored to local needs. But where could it be built, who will pay for it, who can design it, who will build it and who will operate and own it in the future?

Perhaps communication can come to the rescue. Rather than setting up an office or making someone's own home the focus of future communication, a unique electronic address is created in 'cyberspace' (just a convenient term for the Internet, the Information Superhighway and every other component of the new information infrastructure). At this address, some form of initial idea or suggestion is presented, just like putting up a poster on a public notice board.

Next, the media get interested. An article in a newspaper. An interview on the radio. Maybe a short item on the regional television news – and in each case the unique electronic address is included to form the focus of future activity.

This electronic address will become much more than just a place to display a poster. It is more like an electronic office and meeting room. Anyone can connect to it from their home or office communications unit, read the idea, and then send their own opinion or alternative suggestion. They could offer help, raise objections, recommend people who might assist, discuss ideas with other people through video conferencing and read the correspondence from other people, adding to the debate.

The original idea might die rapidly through valid objections, or it might develop and grow to encompass new ideas and tend towards a consensus that something needs to be done, and perhaps metamorphose into a number of alternative locations and forms for the development needed.

Of course, the individuals participating in this debate are likely to be much better informed than the average person is today. Through the communications unit, anyone can look for examples of similar schemes elsewhere, published in electronic form; they can check rules, regulations, standards and working practices in the comfort of their living room, consult conservation groups and the electronic libraries of environmental specialists, and offer constructive improvements or criticisms in their contributions to the debate.

If a realistic proposal starts to emerge, perhaps the local council will add its support to developing the idea further. If the community begins to see the benefits, perhaps the idea really is commercially viable, and some financial backing can be found. Anyone can look back through the history of the debate and the opinions expressed to develop their own understanding of what might be possible.

Perhaps the project could happen...

2 Technology trends

A brief history of computing

Before racing too far into the future, let us pause to take a brief look at the past, and at the present, and try to see the patterns of changes and trends in information technology which are going on around us.

The idea of creating computational machines to extend the calculating abilities of the human mind dates back as far as 1642, when the French scientist, mathematician and philosopher Blaise Pascal devised the first mechanical adding machine. In the nineteenth century, Charles Babbage worked out the principles of the modern digital computer with his design for a mechanical computer, but the machine was never completed.

A viable method of creating a real computer first became possible as a result of the development of the vacuum-filled glass radio valves used in early radio sets in the 1940s and 1950s. These early computers consisted of a room full of circuitry with many valves. Each valve generated a lot of heat and a considerable ventilation plant was needed to keep the room cool. These computers were programmed in early, quite limited forms of computer language, and were capable of little more than a modern programmable calculator.

Then came the transistor-based computers, and the advent of almost three decades through the 1960s, 70s and 80s when almost every major firm had a large, centralized, air-conditioned computer room full of cabinets, switches, tape drives, printers, miles of cable, and other associated paraphernalia. Every machine needed to be tended by a whole entourage of computer operators, programmers, keyboard operators and associated managers, and many were operated twenty-four hours a day in order to gain the full benefits from the large investments involved.

This was the heyday of computer giants like IBM and ICL, feeding a continuous demand for more computer power and greater storage capabilities for developing technical and business applications for these wondrous new machines. Almost every component steadily became smaller, cheaper and faster, as transistors were combined into integrated circuits, tape drives were replaced by disk drives, and new programming languages made ever more complex applications feasible.

The original forms of input to a computer are unthinkably laborious to us now. After the paper tape of the first computers, most computers were using punched cards by the early 1970s. Each card, like a long index card, contained just eighty letters or numbers, and any serious use of a computer required a whole deck of these cards at least several inches thick. Every card had to be punched by typing on a special machine, and any typing error meant that the card had to be discarded and retyped.

These great machines were designed mainly for 'batch' operation. A computer program was loaded into the computer's memory, which then processed a series of data records, either as punched cards or from a computer tape, and the output was normally in the form of a computer printout, on rather awkwardly sized continuous folded paper.

This all now seems about as relevant as understanding how a steam engine works! However, to understand some of the problems that we have implementing computer systems today, it may be useful to remember that the older generation of people now managing and supervising much of our contemporary world of work formed their initial understanding of the capabilities, limitations and risks of using computer systems during these early years of mainframe computer systems. The younger generation now taking forward the next stage of the Information Revolution has no memory of those early difficult years.

From those early computers there developed progressively smaller, faster and more powerful mainframes. Then along came the personal computer. The idea of a complete self-contained computer (at first rather expensive and not very powerful) on an individual's own desk rapidly gathered momentum. Just at the right time, methods of operating a computer, such as typing directly onto the screen, became much easier, prices came down, capabilities increased, and the rest, as they say, is history.

Slightly surprisingly, although IBM created the original 'IBM PC' (personal computer) from which most modern designs developed, it was other firms who really saw the potential of this new market and have gained much of the resulting commercial benefit. The concept of an IBM PC 'clone', or compatible PC, was born fairly early in the history of the modern PC. A compatible PC was originally one that behaved just like a real IBM PC from the outside, but inside might be rearranged to enable cheaper mass production by a competing manufacturer.

Many other designs of computer set out to compete for the personal computer market before the IBM PC came along, but almost all of them fell by the wayside as the IBM PC and compatible PCs dominated the international market, except for one notable exception: the Apple Macintosh. The Apple Macintosh managed to maintain a significant minority share of the market through the use of a more intuitive interface with the computer user. Although more expensive than the cheap, mass-produced IBM compatibles, certain groups of users were quite happy to pay a small premium for this improved interface, particularly those involved in graphic design, artwork and publishing, where more natural and creative control of the computer's capabilities is essential.

The evolution of computers is shown schematically in Figure 2.1.

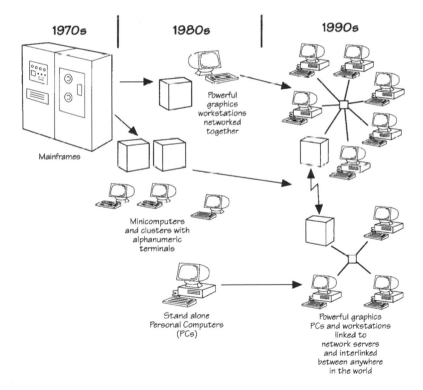

Figure 2.1. A simplified view of the evolution of computers through recent decades.

A perspective in time

We seem to be regularly bombarded with fantastic new developments in technology, but are they all really as new and unexpected as the advertisers would like us to believe? Although the time taken to design and manufacture any product is steadily reducing, it does still take a finite time to develop from an idea into a physical and marketable product. So all of the products just arriving in the shops today were actually designed a little time ago, and the products we will buy next year are already being planned and designed.

Successful manufacturers therefore need to have a clear idea of exactly what technology is going to be available when, so that their products will make use of the most advanced and most cost-effective components. The facilities to manufacture specialized components, especially computer chips, take significant time and investment to set up.

Most advances in technology, therefore, are the result of a considerable period of planning and development, and are actually part of measurable and predictable trends. So, to the people deeply involved in manufacturing for the future, life is not so full of unexpected surprises as it might seem.

Does anyone really understand it all?

But how many people really understand the whole range of technology changes taking place? As technology becomes more complex, people specialize in small areas of it to stay within the limitations of human comprehension.

A century or more ago, a well-educated person had an immense range of knowledge, and knew the basics of all of the main areas of knowledge in both the arts and the sciences . As the extent of human knowledge and understanding has multiplied exponentially over the last few decades, it has become almost impossible for anyone to maintain a full, balanced range of contemporary knowledge.

The need to comprehend knowledge on a selective basis inevitably leads to extensive gaps in the understanding of any individual. For instance, if someone doesn't need to understand how a computer works in order to use it, there is no need to acquire this knowledge or to attempt to keep it up to date. However, a complete lack of such knowledge places the individual at a disadvantage when discussing the purchase of a new computer with a salesperson.

The next few sections give a rather subjective view of some of the many trends of changes in the technologies of the information age. This is not an exhaustive encyclopaedia of facts and figures, more a taster of some of the background knowledge behind the myths and the folklore of modern technology.

Processing power

Processing power has always been one of the fundamental parameters considered when purchasing any type of computer. Every few months, a new processor chip appears, with yet greater processing capabilities. At first it justifies a premium price; then the prices of existing chips are reduced and the market settles down ready for the next release.

There seems to be a little way to go yet. The real problem here is that there is no right time to buy. Whatever you buy today will be out of date in six months' time. It really is very important to understand this, and not to be disappointed when more powerful and cheaper computers appear a few months after your purchase. Always justify a purchase in terms of value to you today. Don't imagine that the cost benefits and competitive advantages evident today will still be the same in a year's time – they won't.

Despite predictions for many years that parallel processing computers will offer even more dramatic advances in computer power, they are still only seen in significant numbers in specialized high-performance computers, rather than in the extensive personal computer market. Parallel processing just means doing lots of things at the same time, rather than one at a time in sequence. Future breakthroughs in this area could increase processing power by yet another order of magnitude, perhaps to generate even more complex and realistic virtual landscapes for the computer games of the future.

Memory and storage

Computers need to remember things, just like human beings, and every new software application requires yet more storage to operate effectively. When I started using computers, in the 1970s, most of the data for my programs was stored on magnetic tape. Over the years, along came ever more sophisticated methods of storage, until today the portable personal computer that I am writing this book on has many times the storage capacity of some complete computer facilities in the 1970s.

In simple terms, memory is of two types: (a) disks, compact discs (CDs) and various other forms of long-term storage which can best be imagined as rather like the filing cabinets in an office from which data has to be fetched to use it, and (b) more immediate working space (RAM chips – more explanation in Chapter 4), which can most easily be compared with the size of the desk that you are working at in the office – the larger the desk the more files you can have accessible on the desk at once.

All forms of storage and memory have been increasing in capacity and reducing in cost at a breathtaking pace over the last few years. For instance the price of the most common RAM chips has recently reduced by a whole order of magnitude in less than two years. Nevertheless, most major firms in the computer manufacturing industry still seem to be successfully in business, so production costs (or profits!) must have actually come down by these remarkable factors. There is no immediate sign of reaching a limit to this trend either – as long as computer software continues to demand such high amounts of storage, computer users will look to upgrade and extend their computers.

Software and Windows

Software breathes life into the logical and mechanistic world of computer hardware, just as a railway timetable turns a stationary collection of trains and railway track into an operational and living transport service.

The earliest software enabled scientists to carry out complex scientific calculations which it had been unrealistic to attempt by hand. The corporate mainframes of the 1980s were justified to a large extent by the steadily increasing demands of financial management to categorize and quantify everything about how a business operated.

Then the potential to computerize everything else started to take off. Word processing soon became a necessity rather than a luxury, using the computer for any form of computation became normal rather than unusual, and an immense software industry rapidly grew to try to satisfy the insatiable demand for new software applications. And then, with the development of the personal computer, vast new markets for endless diverse products opened up. In business, many people discovered the power of spreadsheets to manipulate tables of numbers and information in new ways. They gained the opportunity to type their own reports as they wrote them, draw their own diagrams and figures, maintain their own database of contacts, and use many other applications.

After a period of internal anarchy in many major firms, when different departments and individuals just 'did their own thing' to gain personal or localized advantage, a more reflective and objective approach naturally led towards the integration of all forms of software together into integrated office packages linked between computers through corporate communications networks. Another complexity for the software industry to generate revenue from!

And then, of course, there are the leisure and education market-places. Computers were no longer a massive investment that had to be operated twenty-four hours a day on business-critical tasks – an individual unit was steadily coming down to the same order of cost as the office desk and furniture that an individual needed at work, or the equipment in a well-equipped kitchen, or the furniture in the living room. Every well-equipped school now needs at least one room full of computers. Many university students regard their computer as being as essential to their studies as my calculator was when I was at university, or the slide rule I used at school, a few years ago! All these provide more opportunities for the software vendors.

Computer games have become big business, with breathtaking three-dimensional virtual worlds in which to explore and do battle. Every new development is more sophisticated than the last. First came computer graphics, then high-quality sound effects and voices, controls and dials, which allow the individual to become completely engrossed in this unreal world. It is interesting to observe that while business applications must inevitably develop in a cautious and methodical manner, because businesses, and often lives, depend on them, the developers of computer games have much more freedom to push computers to their operational limits in the search for new effects and experiences.

Somewhere, intertwined with most of this modern software, is Microsoft Windows, and its associated 'mice' or pointing devices. Xerox actually invented the idea, at their Palo Alto Research Center, but it was Apple who implemented it first on their Macintosh computers, where it became a major reason for their success. Digital Equipment Corporation and other major manufacturers implemented their own versions, but the place where it has really taken a decisive hold is with Microsoft on the ubiquitous PC. Every serious piece of commercial software now aims to be able to operate under the latest version of Windows.

Other trends are evident behind the scenes to the informed observer. By the early 1990s, methods of storing large databases of information had stabilized around the principles of relational databases, based on mathematical principles to structure methods of storage. In the 1970s many people dabbled in directly programming the company computer themselves. Nowadays, programming is a job for the specialist, with a proper training in analytical techniques.

The future of computer software is a little less predictable than that of computer hardware, because it is all about the direct and immediate application of human intelligence. New discoveries and standards can be accepted and applied almost overnight. Expect surprises!

Printers, plotters and scanners

Printer technology has also advanced in leaps and bounds in recent years. The old centralized line printers, with their special sized, continuous, ruled and punched down the edges paper have little relevance to the world of the PC. Those difficult to photocopy, unwieldy to store, and often faint and poorly printed pages of computer printout have inevitably been progressively superseded by laser and inkjet printers distributed all over the office, printing much closer to the person who needs the pages.

Inkjet printers have brought colour printing within the reach of everyone. As well as the small printers available for the individual's desk or the family computer at home, there are large format inkjet printers which can print colour drawings, maps, photographs and graphics at a small fraction of the cost of older printing techniques. For convenience and ease of use, the old plotters, moving coloured pens over the surface of a sheet of paper, have become obsolete in a very short space of time in the face of this new competition.

The challenge now is to create even higher resolution, lower cost printing and plotting machines so that anyone can print whatever they want, whenever they want, wherever they want at a reasonable price. New ideas are already working their way towards commercial production.

Scanning is another technology which has suddenly moved from being a specialized, costly, external bureau activity to new machines which even the domestic user can contemplate buying. It is no longer very expensive to scan a colour photograph or diagram into a computer, to include it in a document or edit it without having to redraw it completely. Typed and printed pages can be fed into a computer from the scanner, where the latest software recognizes the letters and converts the document from a picture of the page into words that can be edited using a word processor. With larger versions of the same machines, drawings and maps can be captured as computerized pictures, allowing them to be retrieved at any desk without handling real paper or to be overlaid with extra information electronically.

Multimedia, images and sounds

A rapidly developing new dimension of computer use is the expanding multimedia industry. At some moment in relatively recent years, a whole series of technologies reached reasonable maturity and price thresholds were crossed, bringing multimedia facilities to the average domestic computer.

The main technologies involved are: storage compression techniques, which store still pictures, video clips and high-quality sound in relatively small amounts of computer memory and disk space; high-speed processors and the standardization of methods to decompress this data in real time; high-quality computer displays; windows and hypertext (or hypermedia) which make accessing all this information as intuitive and easy as pointing to the goods in a display cabinet when out shopping; the arrival of the data compact disc, the CD-ROM; high-quality sound synthesis and sound generation techniques; and of course a lot of ingenuity and insight on the part of software designers to see the opportunities for using it all.

Multimedia is quite an interesting example of what I would call a 'technology leap'. The World-Wide Web on the Internet is another closely connected one. In each case, so many new technologies and inherent complexities are involved, when viewed through the eyes of the scientist, that one would expect an immense amount of learning and knowledge to be needed to use it effectively. In fact, quite the reverse is true. Everything dovetails into a coherent package which anyone can operate with just a little common sense and hardly any preparatory training.

Display technology is also moving on in leaps and bounds, just as domestic audio went through the hi-fi revolution a decade or two ago, with everyone coming to expect much higher standards of sound reproduction at a reasonable cost. Ordinary portable computers have colour displays; standard computer displays can show full-colour pictures at a reasonably high resolution. Large flat screens, with television and computer screens hanging on the wall like a picture, will soon be readily available. Display projectors, which project a computer display onto the wall like a slide projector, are steadily improving in resolution and decreasing in cost.

Intelligence and neural networks

Many of us will remember the apparent promise of artificial intelligence, pushed forward by major research programmes in the 1980s, where intelligent computers were going to make all of our lives so much easier. What became of it all?

Perhaps the researchers discovered that intelligence is not quite as logical and straightforward as many people thought. There was a great movement to reduce any decision making to a series of rules, the idea being that, given any question, the human mind could only apply logical rules to arrive at an answer. Immense rule bases were evolved, and the immensity and complexity of human decision making processes became much better understood.

There have been some interesting changes of emphasis in artificial intelligence research over the years. Initially, researchers seemed to be trying to emulate the human mind, for instance trying to create a computer program to take the main design decisions for an engineering project. The obvious intention was to improve the quality of design, by taking perfect decisions based on extensive knowledge and experience every time. This has all sorts of dangers. It assumes perfection – hence nobody needs to learn or develop new methods any further. It eliminates the need to train new human minds with proper understanding because the computer can do it all (the ultimate extension of the current generation's tendency to delegate arithmetic calculation abilities to an inert pocket calculator). A slightly worrying cul-de-sac!

However, real human minds soon got to grips with this problem and realized that the main potential for artificial intelligence, certainly in design decision making, is as the intelligent assistant. A human being must still take ultimate responsibility for any decision, but the intelligent computer is more like having an elder statesman looking over everyone's shoulder all of the time, the voice of experience pointing out where problems have occurred elsewhere, and always available to ask for assistance or to help to consider the effects of a decision. Just think of it: the company's most senior and experienced experts in every field, all sitting around you (and around everyone else as well), taking an individual interest in improving the quality of your work. Fantastic! But this is a little less glamorous than creating intelligent humanoid robots, and it will take quite a few years to come to fruition, so artificial intelligence has retreated from the limelight of media attention.

Then along came, among other things, 'neural networks' – computer programs trying to emulate directly the way that the nerve cells in the human mind work. This is an interesting idea, and a refreshing alternative to the methodical, logical, clinically correct digital machinery of conventional computers. In simple terms, a neural network is educated by showing it the correct sets of output answers for given sets of input values. From learning these, it can then guess the likely answers for other sets of input values. A neural network can conjecture results without necessarily being correct, just like a human being. An answer can be roughly right, or it might sometimes be completely wrong. But so far we are only talking of very simple problems: just a small number of virtual nerve cells compared with the millions in the human brain. Useful results may take a few years!

Voice recognition and artificial speech

Something much closer to immediate widespread application is voice recognition. Voice recognition systems have existed for many years, but the early systems had serious limitations. A particular system could only recognize one person's voice, and had to be 'trained' to that person's voice by repeating certain words to the computer or recognizer several times to learn standard qualities of the voice. Then it could only recognize a very limited range of words, perhaps just a few dozen, and there was always a high possibility of confusion between similar sounding words. And all this was also rather expensive.

Why can human beings who have never met before understand each other so easily, yet computers get so confused with even the simplest words and phrases? A decade of intensive international research is close to providing commercial products much closer to everyday communication needs.

Just imagine how you might communicate with a computer which can reliably recognize just a few hundred words. Instead of typing at the keyboard, or fiddling with the mouse, for all those day-to-day tasks, you could just tell the computer what you want it to do. Phrases such as 'check my e-mail', 'set the video recorder to record the news' or 'find the spreadsheet I was working on yesterday' could initiate a whole sequence of commands while you are still actually doing something else, without touching the keyboard or having to find the relevant button in the window on a computer screen.

But what about much more extensive word and phrase recognition, such as dictation directly into the computer, stored as words for editing and transmission? With the widespread use of speech recognition, keyboard skills may become less relevant to the ordinary user, opening up the opportunity of using a computer to a wider range of people. It will, though, take a number of years to evolve intuitive interfaces that understand enough to be useful, even if the perfect recognition of words was to become generally available tomorrow, so the computer keyboard and mouse are with us for a few years yet! Most software developers are only just getting to grips with the full potential of Windows-based systems, let alone thinking of the as yet undefined interfacing possibilities offered by voice recognition.

What about computer-generated speech? Modern computer games seem to be talking to our children all the time, so why doesn't all computer software do the same?

Of course, computer games have a fixed repertoire of words and phrases, and effectively just use a library of pre-recorded phrases and sounds which are triggered at the appropriate moments by the software. Generalized speech synthesis is a little bit more demanding. We have all heard the mechanical voices of early computer speech generators, and these have been refined and improved to add more tonal quality. An ordinary multimedia PC, using only inexpensive software, can already attempt to read any document, with relatively few grammatical errors, resorting to spelling unrecognized words and speaking unusual grammar. Improved voice quality, with a choice of the type of person that we imagine to be speaking, will soon become an everyday possibility.

Databases and digital archiving

One of the grand concepts of the computer world has always been to reduce all information to electronic form and then give up using paper. Hence in recent years we have been bombarded with a proliferation of computerized archiving and storage systems, all holding out the hope of demolishing the paper mountains steadily growing in many offices, and giving immediate unconstrained access to these vast stores of information.

The idea is becoming closer to reality, but once again there is quite a way to go. Yes, we now have low-cost computer storage, high-speed scanners, networks to access the data, and hence most of the paraphernalia needed to implement such a system. But we must beware of implementing a system based upon today's methods of working without considering the deeper implications of changing working practices, and hence information requirements and flows, which we may see during the next decade. Read the rest of this book first, and form your own opinions – don't always believe the salespeople!

Communications and networks

The whole world of communications technology is also hurtling forward at breakneck speed. Data transfer speeds and methods of interconnecting computer systems together which looked as though they were science fiction a few years ago are now an everyday part of our lives. Whether we like it or not, information upon which the way we live our lives depends, from our bank accounts to the orders for the products which will be on the shelves next time we go shopping, is winging its invisible way around us all of the time.

The future of information technology is so dependent upon, and intertwined with, communications technology, that the term ICT, information and communications technology, is supplanting IT (information technology) in some people's list of abbreviations. Communications technology does also have a life of its own, in telephone communications, television transmission and other related industries, which has helped to make communications a desirable focus for major financial investments throughout the world. The fabric of the Information Superhighway is steadily taking shape.

Most communications still seem to be based upon physical connections between points, but for any significant scale of improvement we will require communication through optical fibres rather than the copper wires of the old telephone lines. The rate at which data can be pushed through copper wire is also increasing though, so electrical wires, which are easier to install and connect locally than optical fibres, will probably still be evident in our offices and homes for a few years to come.

Microwave links and transmissions via satellites in space still have their applications as well, allowing almost instant connections between places far apart without the expense and effort of installing an optical or electrical cable.

Mobile phones have added a new dimension to communications, allowing conversations and data transmission within defined areas, at reasonable cost, without any physical connection. For the moment though, the rate at which data can be transmitted over the current generation of mobile phones is limited to being slightly lower than the capabilities of even an ordinary telephone line, and there are practical constraints on what is actually possible at these connection speeds.

Networking is best looked upon as the packaging which turns the basic resource of telecommunications links into structured and organized methods of exchanging and integrating information and resources between computers. In the past, there were a number of different types of networking system which were not compatible with each other, but the globalization of communications has now standardized the interfaces between networks so that almost any computer network can communicate with any other.

One of the benefits of computer networking software is that it insulates the computer itself from any dependence upon a particular type of hardware. The networking software takes care of any differences between communications through telephone lines, optical fibres or any

27

other type of telecommunications link; to the computer it doesn't matter. This has the added benefit that the computer can take advantage of the latest communications technology as soon as it is available, without any need for reprogramming or upgrades except in the network software itself.

Computer modems, the devices which translate between the electrical world of the computer and the world of sounds on the telephone line, have become faster and faster and cheaper and cheaper. It is difficult to see how they can actually get much faster on ordinary telephone lines.

Networking

Computers everywhere

Turning our attention closer to home, we only have to take a look at a major shopping centre or the daily newspaper to see that something has changed. Computers have become as readily available as washing machines! No longer are the computer shops all in obscure parts of town and industrial areas, where they used to serve the world of corporate accounts and businesses, selling equipment well beyond the financial reach and technical understanding of the average citizen. Now the computer shops are competing for the best retail sites in town. Supermarkets and department stores sell computers alongside food and clothes. Computers have become a commodity. The computer shops are stacked high with computers, printers and software. This is not occasional trade – they are all hoping to sell large numbers.

The same trend is being repeated in many countries around the world. Personal computer parts have become standardized, and can be imported anywhere in the world. Assembling a PC requires only standard technical skills, so locally assembled computers are also appearing all over the world. If local shops can build computers, they can also repair them, so another link in the commercial chain is becoming established: a long-term infrastructure to repair and maintain personal computers for the domestic market. There will probably be more business in upgrades than repairs, though, for the next few years.

A long way to go!

This has not been an exhaustive review of the current state of technology – that would be a significant volume in its own right. The Information Revolution is not just about any single well-defined technology, but about a whole series of interlinked fields of development. Each field is developing at a different pace, serving different markets and with different horizons.

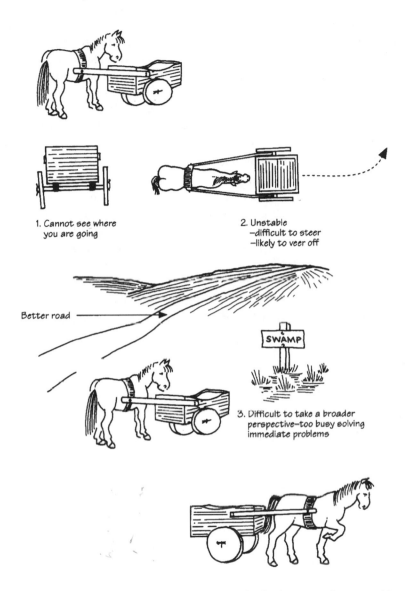

1. Cannot see where you are going

2. Unstable
   —difficult to steer
   —likely to veer off

Better road

SWAMP

3. Difficult to take a broader perspective–too busy solving immediate problems

Figure 2.2. The dangers of technology push: the horse and cart problem.

The Information Revolution is only becoming possible as a result of all of these things happening at once. Some technologies are leading the way, dragging others along behind to keep up, some are carving out secure niches for themselves, and others are highly dependent upon the success of associated products.

But this is by no means anywhere near the end of the story. There is a long, long way to go yet. We have to look forward to another decade or two at least of continual progress and change, where products will be superseded in only a few years, and successful new ideas will take hold and become commonplace in the space of only a few months, challenging everyone to invest more in staying up to date.

It is intriguing to reflect that it was the world of business that generated the initial demand for computers and provided the market-place for early developments. However, as costs have come down and performance has increased, it is now the potential demand of the domestic home computer market which is driving forward improve-ments in graphics, multimedia, low-cost networking and other benefits which make computers easier to use, and hence more attractive to the average householder. Business users will, in turn, reap the benefits of these improved capabilities.

This chapter has only looked at trends in technology. Technology is only one component of our future Information Society, and perhaps one of the easiest to analyse and describe. The next few chapters will look closer at how we use information technology and how it works, so that we can look forward to the wider implications for people in their worlds of work and leisure.

Traditions in construction

But first, let us go back to considering our project in a rural market town, which we started to think about at the end of the first chapter.

Any new project has traditionally been designed and constructed by the construction industry, which has well-established ways of working and thinking. Figure 2.3 illustrates some of the main elements of a traditional project.

First of all, there nearly always needs to be a client. This might be a government department, a local council or a commercial developer, but it must be an organization that has access to the money to build the project for it to be taken seriously by everyone concerned; otherwise the project is unlikely to happen and even talking about it is a waste of time and effort.

Ideas and proposals have to be generated at meetings. Lots of people need to travel to the same place, at the same time, to discuss what needs to be done. They must agree a mutual way forward, and they all go away with their own tasks to complete ready for the next meeting. Everyone's time costs money, since they could be doing something else to earn

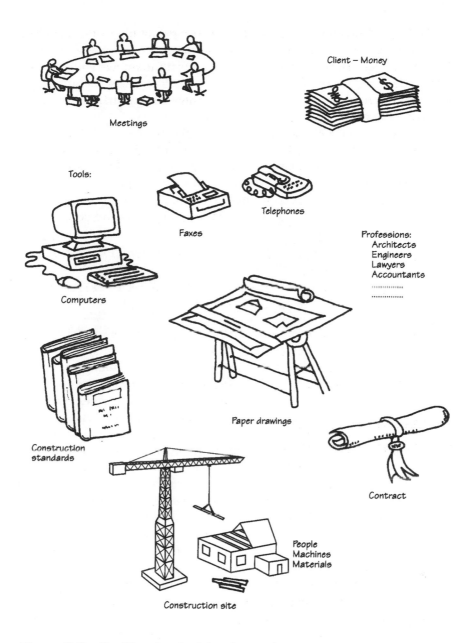

Figure 2.3. Traditional project development.

money if they were not at this meeting. Hence meetings must be short and efficient, without wasting a lot of time on considering hypothetical alternatives, details or complexities.

31

All of the people involved have a whole range of tools available to help them in their tasks. They have computers to carry out analyses, to write reports and letters, and maybe to visualize what the project will look like. They also have telephones and fax machines to contact each other for informal discussions and to update each other on any changes that they find necessary.

A project requires a whole range of specialist professional skills, which must all be recruited into the team from different firms, and which must work together in cooperation. There must be architects to make sure that the project will suit the human purposes intended and to design how it will look; structural engineers to make sure that it will stand up; services engineers to provide water, power, communications and waste disposal; and environmental specialists to consider the impact on the project's surroundings. Then there are the accountants and quantity surveyors to check the cost of it all and ensure a return on investment, and lawyers to set up contracts and make sure that everyone knows exactly what they are responsible for and to argue the case if they do not do what is expected. And a few others.

Out of the design process come drawings, a paper description of exactly what is going to be built. Construction standards define how every part of the construction should be carried out. Tenders are invited, and a contract is signed with a contractor to construct the project. And then, with people, machines and materials, construction takes place.

Few ordinary people become involved. If nothing happens because of the immense inertia to be overcome and costs to be incurred in starting anything, they will probably complain to each other. If commercial interests see an opportunity, they will inevitably try to minimize their costs and maximize profits, resulting in local friction about environmental damage and visual and social implications. Most people will wait to see the project finished, and then complain about where it does not come up to their personal expectations. After all, how on earth could they really understand what was going to be built from the minimal information made readily available to them?

These traditions serve the developers well, but do they maximize the benefits to the community? Do they really identify the best course of action, and enable everyone to play whatever part they wish in the process? In the best cases, yes. But not everywhere. We will consider a few possible trends for the future here as well, as we continue our exploration of the opportunities that new technology can offer.

3 Information basics

Separating information from technology

The last chapter was about 'technology'. This chapter is about 'information'. Why draw the distinction? The media have spent years educating us all to leave that old-fashioned term 'the computer' behind, and to use the wonderful, all-embracing, catch-all term 'information technology' instead.

Understanding the difference is fundamental to understanding where there is likely to be stability in the future and where changes and investment will be unavoidable.

While technology is continually changing and rearranging in the light of new products, technical developments and commercial pressures, information remains relatively constant and secure. Take, for instance, someone's address. This address remains constant as long as that person continues to live in the same place. This address, this piece of information, may then be represented in many different ways, on many different computer systems, but there is still only one constant piece of information.

As technologies change, computers are replaced and new software is implemented, and the representation of this information, the address, may take many different forms. It may be stored on computer disks or on CD-ROM; sometimes the road name and sometimes the town name may appear first in the way it is written or stored; but throughout all this turmoil of technological advances, there is still only one constant piece of information.

Of course, information can change as well: the person involved could move. The information held on all of the computer systems which hold the address then needs to be updated. But this change is in no way caused by anything to do with the technology which stores it.

Information existed before computers were even dreamt of, and would still exist even if computers went out of fashion.

When applying information technology, it is important to think of information first, and what you are trying to do with information; only then should you put the resulting system into the context of the technology currently available to handle it.

What is information?

Let us delve a little deeper into understanding what information is. For instance, what is the difference between data and information? Surely, aren't they the same thing?

Well, data are certainly a component of information. But information encompasses much more than just data. 'Data' is generally understood to mean facts and figures. Anything that can be measured or recorded are data: measurements, values, parameters and descriptions are all things that can be typed on a sheet of paper or fed into a data file held on a computer.

So what else is information then? Essentially everything which isn't technology: concepts, methods, knowledge and all of those things which tie data together and make it useful.

Concepts

What is a concept and why isn't it data? I define a concept as something which can be explained to, and understood by, another human being. Once understood, it can be used to simplify communication dramatically. It may not, however, be absolutely specific: its interpretation and representation can vary between people, and its meaning can change over a period of time, but it is the same concept.

For instance, take the concept of 'a computer'. In this book I am talking about them all the time. What do you understand a computer to be? What image does it conjure up in your mind? Is it an air-conditioned room full of cabinets and flashing lights? Or a workstation on your desk at work? Or a multimedia PC at home with 3D graphics and hi-fi sound? Or a portable computer in your briefcase? They are all the same concept, and the meaning varies depending on the context of the conversation.

Concepts are one of the secrets of efficient communication between different human beings. It used to puzzle me how two people who had never met before, but who both had the same professional training, could assimilate design drawings, identify parameters and agree analysis methods for a building in a few hours, yet it would take days or weeks to convert the same information into data to allow the computer to carry out the analysis. The difference, of course, is that people use concepts to simplify their communications; but for today's computers, despite all of the dramatic advances of technology, almost everything has to be reduced to factual data.

Taking this a little further, it becomes easier to understand why some people do not understand each other. When a person who is fully conversant with all of the technologies mentioned in the last chapter talks to someone who hardly knows any of them, any conversation between them about computers will involve many questions and explanations to establish sufficient common understanding to proceed further. The conversation is, in effect, transferring knowledge about these concepts from the person who understands to the person who doesn't.

Computers, at present, and for the foreseeable future (Figure 3.1), don't understand concepts. This places considerable limitations on the communications that can take place with computers and the potential efficiency of communication. It also means that, in any task, there is conceptual knowledge which is understood by the people involved, but which is information that cannot be represented on the computer.

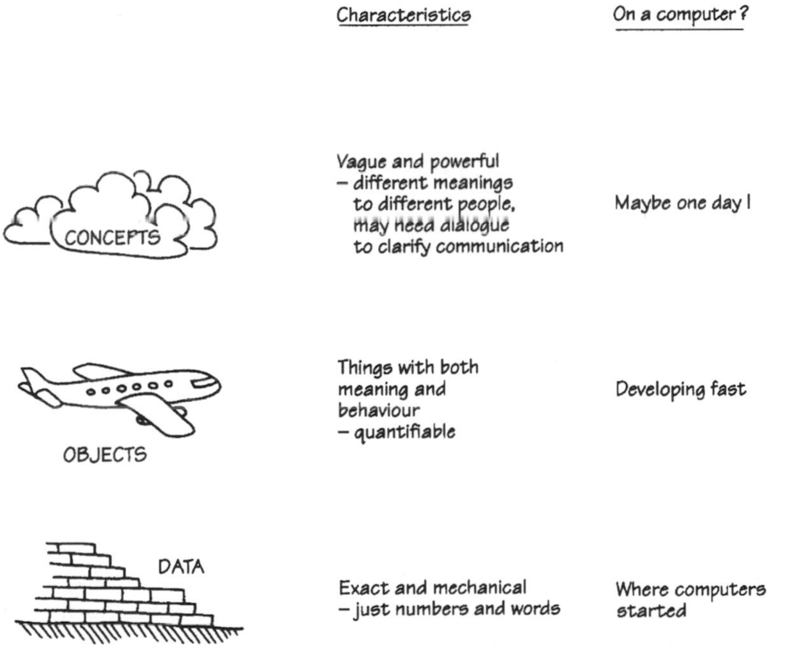

	Characteristics	On a computer?
CONCEPTS	Vague and powerful – different meanings to different people, may need dialogue to clarify communication	Maybe one day !
OBJECTS	Things with both meaning and behaviour – quantifiable	Developing fast
DATA	Exact and mechanical – just numbers and words	Where computers started

Figure 3.1.   Concepts, objects and data.

Objects

This seems a good moment to mention objects. For some years now, the computer press has regularly being talking about 'object-oriented' methods, 'object databases' and other similar terms. Objects have been heralded as another important breakthrough in the development of information technology.

To the purist, an object is a group of data which is associated with something called behaviour. The details really only matter to the computer programmers, but for instance, objects can be made up from collections of other objects, in which case the lower level objects can inherit the behaviour of the objects above them. There are special programming techniques and programming languages designed to work in terms of these objects. Objects can react to their surroundings, as part of predetermined behaviour. For example, when a graphic object is displayed on a computer screen, it might display a different level of detail depending upon how large it is on the screen and hence what may be visible.

For general communication, I prefer the rather more flexible definition of an object as any 'thing' which can be defined by specific parameters. In other words, as long as you can measure it or describe it exactly it can be an object! Any data can be grouped together to form an object. Because an object defined like this is exact and factual, it can also be represented on the computer.

There is a subtle but important difference between an object and a concept. A concept can be approximate, it can be ambiguous, it can be anything which conveys a meaning between two people. An object, by contrast, must be exact and clear, without the potential need for further clarification.

Relational databases

An important advance in organizing and working with large volumes of data on computers was the development of the principles of relational databases (Figure 3.2). The detailed science of relational databases takes considerable understanding, but the basic principles are important.

Most databases consist of tables of some sort, like a list of columns across a page of paper. Then each line of values across the page, of numbers or words, is one unit or record of data in the table. On a modern computer there is little restriction upon how many columns a table can have, or how many lines or records of data; certainly there may be far more than on one sheet of paper.

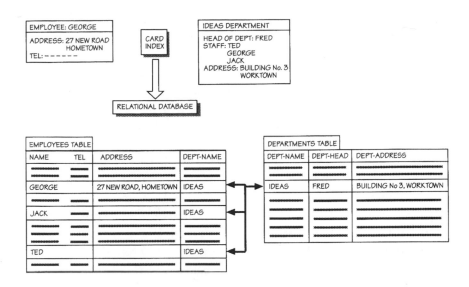

Figure 3.2. The relational database.

In a simple card index in the office, you would put all of the information about one person, one department or one office on one index card in the filing cabinet. Just imagine a database table as a table containing all of the information in one set of index cards.

But what happens when you want to send a letter to all of the employees in a particular department, to be signed by the head of the department? On the manual card index, you have to find the card for the department, look at the list of names on the card, and then look up each individual employee's address on another card index of employees' addresses – rather laborious. The alternative is to put the employees' addresses on the department index, but just think of trying to keep both indexes, and any others containing addresses, up to date!

A relational database works in a different way. The objective is to store each piece of information once and only once, and in the most efficient way.

The analysis might show that there should be two tables, one for the employees and one for the department. But it might also show that the best way to organize information about the department is to put an extra column in the employees table showing which department they belong to. The department table just contains information relevant to the department, for instance the name of the head of the department and the department address.

When you want to know the addresses and names of the employees in the department, you just ask the computer for all of the lines of the employee table with the corresponding department name, ignoring all of the other lines. The computer might put the names and addresses straight onto the letters being prepared by a word processor and add the head of department's name and the department address from the department table.

The details are not too important, and real relational databases can involve very much more complex analysis. But what is important is that the resulting tables and their columns, or the structure of the database, are dependent upon a scientific analysis rather than a particular computer program. When the software changes in the future, data can be transferred into the new database in exactly the same tables. More advanced relational databases can also recognize and retrieve data stored in other databases that were created using different software on a different computer.

Knowledge and rules

Much attention has been applied to the representation of knowledge in computer systems. This was originally part of artificial intelligence research, but soon 'Intelligent Knowledge-Based Systems' became a major research field in its own right, most notably in Japan, Europe and the USA. After a number of years of only limited success, many researchers dropped the word 'Intelligent' from this research territory title, reducing it to 'Knowledge-Based Systems'.

The essence of the way that knowledge-based systems work is to reduce everything to rules. Each rule contains a question. At any point in time, it is possible to put parameters or values into the boxes provided in the question of the rule. In the simplest systems the answer to the question can only be one of two values – either 'true' or 'false'. These parameter values are normally the results of processing other rules, so applying one rule can trigger the evaluation of many other rules in order to determine a result. The computer can then take action as a result of whether it receives a true or a false answer.

For instance, a burglar alarm knowledge-based system might pose the question: 'Is there an intruder in the house?' In order to answer this question it has to evaluate many other questions – are any windows open? Are all the doors closed? Can any movement be detected? Can any sound be detected? There are rules to answer every one of these questions, which in turn interrogate sensors around the house to give these answers. If the result of the original question is that there is an intruder, it sets off the alarm.

Information location and time effects

Getting back to more basic problems, a long time ago systems analysts recognized the potential for errors to occur if the same computer system contains more that one representation of the same information. As soon as there are two separate versions, they both have to be kept up to date, and if they are updated at different times, different parts of the same computer program may give inconsistent results.

This may sound obvious, but it is remarkable how often this problem occurs. Let us take a fictional example of the problem of updating someone's address, mentioned earlier. Most companies have some sort of personnel database, and many have payroll software, pensions software, management systems, and project and departmental databases. In the grand design of the computer systems department, these would all be part of a single integrated system, and somewhere at the heart of the whole system would be a single database table of addresses, accessible to every application. If someone moves house, this single table is updated first thing the next day, and every computer application immediately uses the correct new address.

In practice, the application packages are often acquired piecemeal, one at a time, from different vendors, constrained by budget limits and skilled resources to install and implement the new systems. Since the company's centralized computer resources unit was long ago replaced by distributed departmental computer facilities, the different software applications are probably mounted on several different computers anyway.

So the address is entered on each system independently. When the address changes, every application has to be updated independently. Since this is such an occasional task, and departmental resources are so limited after endless staff cutbacks and efficiency drives, it may be some time before the update takes place on some of the systems involved. Letters may get sent to the wrong address. This is not so critical for one of the firm's own employees one might argue, but it is still a genuine mistake. However, if a customer's address is wrong in a project or accounts database, payments may be delayed, and an image of inefficiency and mistakes may take a long time to overcome.

This example also illustrates another critical problem – time. How long does it take between a piece of information changing and the representation of that piece of information on the computer being updated? It is no good basing next year's sales strategy on the year before last's sales figures. But if the figures are only updated once a year, when the accounts are completed, this might well be the case. It is not just a matter of processing information; it is also a matter of processing the right information at the right time.

Good computer systems must be designed to cope with the old adage 'if it can go wrong, it will go wrong'. Far too many systems are designed for a world rather more perfect than it really is.

Information rivers and tides

It is often useful to think not just of information, but of the flow of information through businesses, through organizations, and through the whole of our society.

We all live in a world of information which is relentlessly flowing around us all of the time. Information technology may have increased the volume of information available, and provided new, much faster, channels through which it can flow, but human beings have been assimilating, analysing and then acting upon the information which surrounds them since prehistoric times.

Implementing information technology solutions could be envisaged as similar to the work of a water supply engineer. Information must be collected, channelled and stored, just like rivers flowing into a reservoir. The size of the dam and the reservoir must be matched to the flows expected. If the dam is too low, it may not hold enough; if the spillway is too small, it may not cope with unexpected flash floods; and if the dam is too high, the reservoir may never fill. A supply must be taken from the reservoir, and it must be purified and tested to ensure that only quality controlled results leave the reservoir. This supply must then flow through an appropriately designed distribution network, right to where it is needed.

Just take a step back, once in a while, and look at the wider picture. Is all of the information being collected useful? Are the right people collecting it? Is it being updated often enough? Is the right information being stored in the right places? Is all of the processing being done really needed? Are all of the right people getting the results that they need? Are outputs being presented in the most useful form? Is everyone happy with the systems? If not, somebody must find out why!

You do not necessarily have to be an expert in technology to apply some common sense in how information and information technology can be used most effectively. Do use the skills of the professional, but don't delegate practical common sense. Back to the student with the pocket calculator: if you don't know how to add up the shopping bill and check the change yourself, you become totally reliant upon the shopkeeper to do these things for you.

Where do people fit in?

So far, a lot has been said about technology, and a lot about information, but very little about people.

In the past, advances in technology were the driving force behind many computer systems developments. People, as the most flexible component of the system, have had to adapt to work with systems in the form that they are provided. In recent years it has been realized that this whole picture must be inverted.

It is people, and their needs, aspirations and limitations, which must be considered first – customers, employees, administrators, managers and directors. And probably in this order too. In the past, the directors' and managers' needs were normally considered first. After all, they are the most important people – they carry the responsibility for the whole business on their shoulders and they have the authority to take command anyway, so why question this?

But this is a very narrow perspective. A fictional example: the manager of the sales department declares that she must have weekly rather than monthly sales returns, so that she can monitor cash flow more accurately. In response, the systems analyst designs a way of collecting it for her. Another data input form is generated and distributed to the relevant staff to fill in, every week. The effect: sales staff had already been reduced to minimum levels to cut costs, so filling in this extra form creates yet another extra burden on their time, which was overstretched to start with. Filling in this form gives no benefit whatsoever to the staff, and it increases their dissatisfaction with their manager. The time spent gathering data and filling in the form actually reduces the time available to talk to customers, potentially resulting in a marginal loss of sales as well. Then the manager complains that because one form is late (the salesman concerned was with a customer clinching a deal) she cannot run the analysis before her weekly review with the director. Oh dear!

The alternative: the sales staff would like to have a better way of keeping track of and progressing their sales right through from the initial enquiry. Many customers would appreciate this too, since it would make it much easier for another salesperson to stand in and progress the order when the regular salesperson isn't available. The sales staff request the manager's assistance. The manager considers the implications. If the sales tracking information was computerized to benefit the sales staff, the sales staff would be able to chase more customers though the time saved and hence they can offer a better service. But there is another benefit too. All of the information needed for the weekly sales review with the director can be collected automatically without any extra effort by using the sales staff's sales tracking data, and it should always be up to date because they depend on these data every day in their work.

A little realism and understanding, and looking from the point of view of the customer and the junior staff member first, might have tangible business benefits.

When the people perspective is right, it is easier to get the information needs and flows right. Finally, sort out the technology. The chances are that the technology will change again fairly quickly, so try to design a people and information system which can outlast several generations of technology.

Information fads and fancies

The last decade has been characterized by endless fads and fancies in information handling, almost all of them salespeople's buzzwords to remind corporate leaders that their computer hardware and software are due for an expensive upgrade: geographic information systems, electronic archives, client–server architectures, distributed databases, data warehousing are a few examples. These may be dazzling and fascinating one year, but are superseded by a new sales line a few years later (Figure 3.3).

They all have their applications, but these are all technology-driven solutions. Just applying technology rarely solves problems successfully. We need to get the people, the business, and the information needs and flows sorted out first. Then we should start thinking about the technology.

It is always interesting to look at the latest technology ideas and talk to the salespeople. Just understanding new concepts may trigger new thoughts and ideas about how to improve the business. But we should try not to get too caught up in the flow of the tide. We have to try and separate the real ideas from the sales messages, and think them through for ourselves.

What makes today different?

So why am I writing this book now? What is different about what is happening today? Why should we be so concerned about the people and information perspectives?

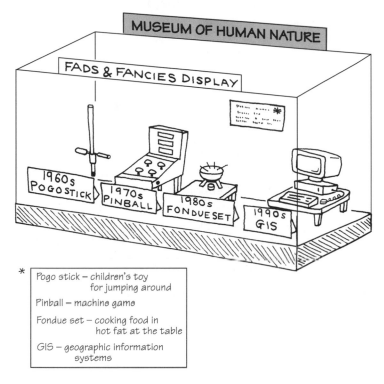

Figure 3.3. Fads and fancies.

A number of changes in the information technology market-place seem to be happening simultaneously, and seem to be coincident with a better understanding of the mistakes of the past and opportunities for the future. There is evidence of a window of opportunity opening ahead of us.

Technology costs are dropping dramatically, removing the barriers which have previously prevented more widespread use of information technology. And this price reduction is not just in one type of technology – it is pretty much across the whole of the board. Almost every aspect of utilizing information technology is steadily getting cheaper.

The components of computer systems have become much more standardized and interchangeable. Natural selection in the competitive market seems to have selected many of its winners. Either a small number of products dominate each part of the market-place, or product specifications and interfaces have become so standardized that the source of manufacture is irrelevant.

Information technology for everybody is becoming a reality. Having a computer at home is becoming almost as essential as having a car or a washing machine. A computer at work now costs little more than the desk it is standing on.

But there are dangers as well. Real technical knowledge is becoming increasingly fragmented in response to the difficulties of staying up to date in so many fields simultaneously. With such a vast range of new technology all becoming available so fast, it is quite natural for the technical specialists involved to concentrate their knowledge in limited areas.

If even the specialists cannot really keep up with it all at once, what hope is there for the general public? A limited level of general understanding could mean that important opportunities are missed, or that when opportunities are seen people do not feel secure enough in their understanding to carry the opportunity through. There is a need to look into the future, to look beyond the complexities of the present day to the possibilities for the future.

Management attitudes are also changing to reinforce this window of opportunity. Conventional command and control hierarchies are breaking down to be replaced by more flexible and customer-responsive teamworking strategies. Managers in many industries have shifted their thinking from departmental structures and administrative systems to businesses driven by customers to create products through efficient processes. Correctly applied, information technology can play a crucial role in providing an adaptive working environment to support new working patterns.

Stakeholders and interested parties

With so much happening so quickly, an intriguing question to ask is: who are the 'stakeholders' in all of these changes? Who are the interested parties? Who stands to gain?

In the past, the stakeholders in any information technology project were usually quite localized. Whether they were the employees of a firm, the directors, or the staff and customers of a bank, it was relatively easy to draw a boundary around the groups of people affected and then to consider their points of view.

These latest changes, though, are so extensive that it is difficult to draw any such boundaries, or to determine many interests that are limited to any finite group. By the time we consider the whole of the domestic personal computer market, and the potential for changing working practices right across many different types of workplace, we begin to see that everyone is involved.

So, if everyone is a stakeholder in these changes, what are the opportunities and threats to the average individual? For home life the main immediate opportunity must surely be entertainment, with perhaps a little education, while for work there will hopefully be a more flexible working environment with greater support for individual needs. The main threat, in most people's minds, must be the effect of the resulting changing patterns of work. Will more people be unemployed as a result? Will it be more difficult to find secure long-term employment?

The only way for individuals to respond to this obvious threat is to increase knowledge and awareness to reduce the fear of the unknown. Just protecting current employment regimes will not work – other countries which embrace the potential for change would soon leave us behind in the international market-place. See the changes early and respond accordingly. Be ready for the future rather than afraid of it.

Information in the community

Returning to the main theme of this chapter, information, let's have another look at our fictional rural market town and the potential for change there. What are all the types of information that may be involved in taking the idea of a development forward towards realization?

First, there are maps of the site, available in 'digital' form for the UK from the Ordnance Survey. These maps are more than just pictures. Every line is coded on the computer to identify what it is – a field boundary, a building, the edge of a road – a rich source of information. With the right software, this electronic map can become the framework upon which to build ideas of what could be done.

We will need to know about the soil at the surface and the geology below the ground in order to understand what it is feasible to build where.

Then we need information about constraints, places where there are limitations on what can be done:

- Sites of Special Scientific Interest (SSSIs), where environmental damage must be avoided.
- Historical and archeological sites.
- Contaminated land, old factories and rubbish dumps.
- Quarries, mine workings, wells and other surprises that it would be best to avoid later.
- Where people are living, to safeguard their rights in respect of privacy, noise and visual impact.
- Vegetation and land use.
- Land ownership.

We also need information to assist in analysing the opportunity:

- The catchment area – who lives where? Census details.
  - ☐ How many potential shoppers? How near?
  - ☐ How many people who might use a leisure centre?
  - ☐ The local workforce: size, distribution, ages and skills.
- Traffic on the roads, and the capacity of the roads as currently designed.
- Documents and regulations.
  - ☐ Design standards.
  - ☐ Legal requirements.
  - ☐ Safety criteria.

All of this information is gradually becoming available in electronic form, making the assimilation and assessment of opportunities much easier and faster. Information will cost money, and we will have to wait to see what levels of cost will be involved. It will be a great pity if the Internet makes communication virtually free while real information becomes too expensive for ordinary people to have access to it. Hopefully the reverse will be true, and any real information about where and how we live will become available to all of us at minimal cost, so that we can all play an active part in defining our future if we wish to.

4 The infoperson's toolkit

Infopeople

At this point, I would like to introduce the concept of the 'information technology-literate person', or 'infoperson' for short. This is just my own shorthand to describe people who understand enough about the technologies and changes taking place in our society that they do not feel excluded or threatened by them. I am not making any hard and fast rules defining exactly what knowledge is required – this is just a concept!

It's a bit like driving a car. When the first motor cars arrived, hardly anyone knew how to drive one, and many people must have been frightened of them and the future effects they might have. In the event, some of their concerns may have been well justified, but today cars are an accepted part of most of our lives. We have learned to respect and utilize cars, and in many countries a large proportion of people have learned to drive cars themselves, as part of their everyday activities. Once a large proportion of people understood cars and what they could do, changes in the ways people lived became inevitable.

This does immediately raise the concern that many people are beginning to think that motor cars are causing extensive environmental problems, and it is unfortunate that they have been so successful. What if information technology might lead to similar unknown problems in the future? But this is giving in to fear of the unknown. It is much better that we learn, predict and develop with the benefit of a broader environmental and social perspective. History has shown that there is little point in trying to halt progress without very well founded reasons. There is certainly no consensus in the world to hold back on all new developments until we have had a few years to consider the possible effects. Quite the reverse! The global economy is applying immense

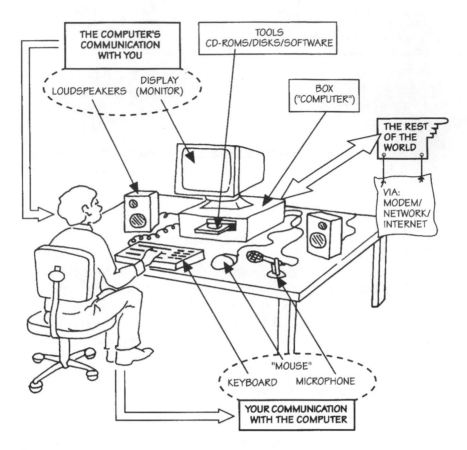

Figure 4.1. The infoperson's toolkit.

pressure throughout the world to implement new technologies without even thinking about the future. Much of the commercial world is too busy surviving until tomorrow to think any further ahead.

Hence it has become critical to extend everyone's knowledge and understanding in the hope of making better and more carefully considered decisions about how to use new technology, everywhere, every day. Because of the diversity and complexity of what is happening, it is impossible to police and control every decision and every situation. What really matters is that good, balanced decisions are being taken by every citizen as part of everything they do, quite naturally. We simply cannot, and must not, rely upon a small number of scientific experts to shape our future. We should all feel part of and in control of the world in which we live. Everyone must gradually learn enough to contribute rather than feel threatened.

Learning and knowledge are the best defence against the unexpected. Here is a little example which was very close to home.

When our son was very young, we lived in a house on many levels with lots of short staircases for a child to fall down. My wife realized that it was impractical to insulate our young son completely from this danger, and so, for his own safety, started teaching him carefully how to turn round and go down stairs backwards from the moment that he could crawl, long before he could walk. He respected the dangers of staircases from a very young age. We soon dispensed with safety gates on the stairs.

Soon after he could walk, we took a holiday in a delightful medieval tower in Italy. To our dismay, climbing up to the bedroom most suitable for our son involved a stone flight of stairs, a conventional flight of stairs, and then a long steep wooden staircase more like a ladder. Tired after the journey, our son showed no concern about this at all, and we put him to bed, with a few words of warning about being careful on the stairs. But then we sat down in the living room on the ground floor, and discussed, with some concern, these staircases, and resolved that we would get up early in the morning before he woke to make sure that he did not slip on the stairs, and then consider changing the sleeping arrangements the next night. To our amazement, at that moment, the door opened, and our son appeared. We had, by mistake, forgotten to take away the cup from his bedtime drink. Without any concern, he quite naturally carried the cup down all of those staircases to return it to us, his early training in staircase safety making this quite straightforward. In the morning, he was very happy with his room with a view.

The moral of this story is that it is impossible to protect against every eventuality – the unexpected will always contrive a situation that wasn't planned for, or corner us into a less than perfect judgement. Human nature involves making a few mistakes. But education and understanding can minimize the risks and increase our resilience against the storms and precipices of the unexpected.

So, the more people there are with a basic understanding of what information technology can and cannot do, and with a wider perspective of how it could, and may, change the ways we work and live, the greater resilience our whole society will have against misconceived or misguided changes.

Skills and understanding

An 'infoperson' needs a toolkit of concepts, knowledge and ideas, much like any craftsperson needs the tools of their trade. A carpenter has saws to cut wood; chisels and planes to shape it; measuring instruments to set sizes and shapes; and many other specialized tools. The carpenter also has tools of knowledge and skill: knowledge of the characteristics of different types of wood and skills carefully practised and learned to direct and utilize the tools in the toolbox to create beautiful, well-proportioned and finely finished artefacts.

I don't think that many of us think about the application of information technology in quite this way – as a craft to be executed with economy, elegance and skill. The results and effects of information technology often seem characterless, poorly proportioned and out of harmony with their surroundings. Once in a while, something grabs the imagination, like a well thought-out computer game, but so often computers seem obstinate and awkward, and to be constraining and restricting the way we work. Yet few of us do anything to change this.

People who write computer software don't set out to make it difficult to use. In fact, with commercial software, they have a vested interest in making it as easy to use as possible, to encourage further business. But the feedback paths seem to be erratic and inconsistent. Relatively few people understand enough to make constructive comments, and since time is money, software producers are reluctant to make changes without a clear and well-presented case for improvement.

The very specialized nature of most computer programming also creates communication barriers, and in the past has fostered protectionism to keep people dependent on these skills to safeguard future employment. However, protectionism rarely works in the long term – it just delays the inevitable and makes it more drastic and more sudden when it happens. If there is a need for it, real skill will always be in demand, and cannot easily be supplanted by inexperienced or inadequate alternatives.

My own days of do-it-yourself activities around my home led me to have great respect for the skilled tradesmen and craftsmen whom I saw while working on construction sites earlier in my career. I remember watching stonemasons at work modifying the facade of a building, and at first I appreciated their skill in producing geometrically perfect surfaces over large areas of new, almost white, Portland Stone, assembling stones cut ready to size and with details already carved before they were delivered to site. Then one day, while checking some existing stonework, the stonemasons found that part of a carving was damaged or missing. With remarkable ease, one of them set to work with his chisels, and carved the missing detail. I hadn't realized the depth or extent of their skills.

However, we do need to be realistic about the extent of skills needed and by whom. The do-it-yourself market in the UK has resulted in simplifications and innovations in the ways in which many items of household furniture can be constructed and assembled. As a result many people with minimal knowledge of carpentry have been able to furnish their own homes at much lower cost and to reasonable standards of finish and quality. The same people have developed new skills in planning and shaping their home environment to suit their own requirements, as a result of this access to a wider range of furniture at lower cost. Somewhere in the furniture supply and fitting business the demand for skilled carpenters must have rebalanced slightly, away from routine work which people could do for themselves towards other work requiring more specialist skills.

A similar change is happening in the world of computers and information technology. No longer do you need a university degree to make productive use of a computer – the average primary schoolchild now often makes regular use of a computer somewhere. But how much do schoolchildren understand about their computers? How much do they need to understand? To assemble do-it-yourself furniture you don't need to know how to use a saw or a plane, and you hardly have to use a tape measure. This is a change brought about by natural market development and commercial pressure. Computers are heading in the same direction. In the future, we may be able to rearrange not just the furniture in our houses, but the whole way that we work and live, how we organize our time, where we have to be and when we have to be there.

The infoperson's toolkit

Consumer pressure to make life easier will undoubtedly eventually eliminate all of the requirements for knowledge that isn't absolutely essential. When I took delivery of my last car, I was intrigued to realise that I had never even asked whether it was front-wheel or rear-wheel drive – an essential piece of knowledge for me a few years before. Nowadays I am more interested in the quality of the radio and whether it has a sun roof. A shift in perception has also made the safety features seem much more important than any of the mechanical details of how the car works.

But early cars required a lot of knowledge and understanding from their owners. There was certainly a need to know what the engine looked like and the basic principles of how the car worked. Older generations of car owner will remember checking the cooling water, the oil, the brake fluid and the battery, and some will even remember greasing various critical moving parts on a regular schedule. And, particularly, the car owner needed to know what to do when the car went wrong. Some people may still remember checking contact breakers, cleaning sparking plugs and checking high-tension leads. Occasionally a fan belt would break and the battery would stop charging and the cooling water would boil. This was nothing to worry an experienced driver, who would know the symptoms and might even be carrying a spare fan belt and the tools to loosen the dynamo bolts and fit it.

It must all have been quite daunting at first, but many ordinary people soon learned the basic knowledge required, became the proud owners of motor cars and started to reap the benefits of the freedom to travel when and where they wanted; the rest is history. Few people look back – most people just get on with it.

One day the knowledge needed to use computers, in whatever future form they take, will be absolutely minimal. For the moment, they are fairly easy to use, but there are still lots of controls to tweak when things don't quite work, and plenty of people with horror stories of things that have gone wrong. But just like the early mass-produced cars, many ordinary people are quite happily using and working with today's computers. The next few sections go through the essential components of the current computer age, trying to pick out the minimum knowledge that an infoperson should know.

Boxes and rodents

Let's start with the humble but ubiquitous personal computer, or PC. The average primary schoolchild can use one, so there cannot be much to it, can there?

At the heart of every PC is what is most easily described as a box – a box full of technicalities which shouldn't really concern us. After all, how many of us really understand how a television works, or even know what one looks like inside? A television is just a box with a switch on it, and so is a PC. PC 'boxes' vary in shape and size, but they are usually either a flat box on top of the desk or a vertical box beside the desk. Both types of box contain the same bits, but the vertical ones can often contain more of them.

Just the box, on its own, cannot do much for us. It's a bit like a car without a steering wheel or any controls or gauges to allow us to drive it. So we need to communicate with the box.

First, it must communicate with us. A computer can actually communicate with us in several different ways, but the main method in use today is through a display screen. This looks much like a television, but in the late-1990s a computer screen can display finer detail than an ordinary television. A conventional television picture is actually quite blurred if you look at it very closely, which is why teletext and other television-based information services use much bolder and clearer lettering than the sophisticated fine graphics of a modern PC. The general use of a television as a PC monitor will not be feasible until the new generation of high-resolution televisions becomes more widely available. As an alternative, a PC screen is quite capable of displaying a very good television picture, but PC monitors are more expensive, of course.

So, let's attach the screen to the box and switch the box on. The box clicks and whirrs and various messages appear on and disappear from the screen. On some PCs the screen flashes a few times. Eventually, like all good employees, it should ask us what we want it to do. This initial flurry of activity, which gets rather tedious the more often one observes it, is really the computer equivalent of waking up, getting dressed, and preparing to do some work. It has to get itself into the right frame of mind, figuratively speaking. Along the way it does a reasonably thorough health check on itself, and if it finds anything wrong it usually gives a message on the screen – like reporting sick and asking you to call the doctor.

Assuming that all is well, you are likely to be presented with one of three basic types of screen to start your 'session' working on the computer: the DOS prompt, a menu screen, or 'windows'.

The first type, the 'DOS prompt' is the good old vintage car of the three. There may be a message or two at the top of the screen, then a symbol or word at the start of the next line and a flashing or blinking 'cursor' just to the right of it. A cursor is just anything which points to a particular position on the screen. This type of interface is the least helpful. That flashing cursor is just teasing you to type something – anything – which the PC may or may not decide to act on, depending on whether you type in something that it recognizes. To the inexperienced user this can be a bit like a game of battleships, as it mockingly rejects everything with a 'Bad command or file name' message (or similar) until one hits upon a perfectly phrased command.

To type commands we need a keyboard – our first method of 'talking' to the box. It has a few more keys than a good old-fashioned typewriter, but fair and square in the middle is the good old 'QWERTY' arrangement of keys, so called because these are the first six keys in sequence at the top left of the alphabetic keys. This arrangement of keys originally designed by Christopher Sholes as long ago as 1873 is now standard throughout the English-speaking world. For those unfamiliar with this gem of knowledge, the keys were originally positioned to minimise the jamming of the keys when typists typed too fast on early typewriters.

Never let a lack of typing skills deter you from using a computer. It is useful to be able to type properly, but far from essential, at least for the casual user.

We now have a keyboard plugged into the computer. It can talk to us and we can talk to it. We give it commands, and if it understands them, it acts upon them. Even with this 'interface' we can do quite sophisticated things, because we can initiate programs which do just about anything: drawing beautiful pictures on the screen or carrying out very complex calculations. A 'DOS command', the line we type, is just the trigger, just like knocking away one vital restraining wedge can initiate the whole complex process of launching a ship from a shipyard.

A memory test – trying to remember the right commands to type – every time one uses the computer is fine for the enthusiast, but even many years ago on the old mainframe computers the more friendly 'menu' interfaces soon evolved. A menu is just a list of options for what the computer can do next, from which you can make a selection by typing a letter or number corresponding to one of them, or by moving some form of cursor up and down through the options before making a selection with the space bar, or some similar technique. It is much like the waiter offering a list of options for the courses of a meal by showing you a more traditional menu, from which you make your selection. There are also question and answer interfaces, and other variations, all of which seek to simplify your choice by presenting you with a limited set of potential actions, from which you make your selection. These were the first so-called 'user-friendly' computer interfaces, because the computer actually tries to help, rather than tantalize, the user.

Skipping various intermediate stepping stones along the way, let us jump straight to the widely acclaimed 'windows' interface, which so many computers now present to us when switched on. Soon after it became possible to draw graphic pictures on the screen, the idea of drawing symbols and objects on the screen and then pointing to them to initiate commands evolved. These 'icons' or 'buttons' can take an infinite variety of forms, but usually consist of a symbol or word indicating what will happen when you 'press' it, sometimes on its own and sometimes in a square or rectangular box drawn to look like a raised button. The purist might well identify a number of different species of button – some start whole programs, while others just initiate actions within a program or move parts of the screen around – but to me the key idea is that you point to the button and press it, and something happens.

To point to it, of course, you need a 'pointing device'. Enter that well-known modern relation of the rodent family, the computer 'mouse' – something else to plug into the box. It's a very simple idea – a small object that you can easily hold in your hand, connected to the computer by a flexible cable. If you look underneath, you find that it contains a small ball inside, mounted so that when you put it down on a flat surface like the desk in front of you and move it around the ball is rotated in the direction in which you move it. Inside the mouse are sensors which can measure this movement in any direction and, through a little electronic magic, a cursor is moved around the screen to match the movements of the mouse on the surface of the desk. The mouse also has two or three buttons, conveniently positioned under your fingers, so that when pointing to an icon on the screen it is possible to initiate two or three different actions, depending on which button of the mouse is pressed. There are other types of pointing device (for instance pressure-sensitive buttons or surfaces), but they are just different means of pointing at things. The computer mouse has been a particularly successful animal – there are many millions of them now in the world.

The windows story then goes a little bit further. A 'window' is just a rectangular part of the screen. This becomes a screen within a screen. This rectangular window can have a life of its own when you point within it to initiate commands. But the same display screen can contain several other rectangles or windows, each of which also has a life of its own, running different programs and initiating different commands. These windows can overlap each other, but you can only press buttons or icons in the one at the front. Any of the windows behind can be brought to the front, usually by clicking on any visible part of the window, and that then becomes the window in which you can issue commands. The other windows continue to run programs while they are in the background; you just have to bring them to the front if you want to look at one or issue a command in it.

There are then endless further developments and features which people have added to increase the possibilities of what you can do with windows-based software. For instance, you might have a bar along the edge of the screen with a label for each of the windows currently in use, and buttons and graphic symbols which change their appearance depending upon the status of some data value used by the software or some aspect of how the computer is operating. But the basic concept of being able to do several things at once, and controlling each of them by pointing at things rather than by typing commands, is just the same.

Before getting overawed by the complexity and sophistication of the latest computers, it is important to understand that everything is about issuing commands and executing actions in response. All you need to know is what action you want to initiate, and then find the right button to press to start it.

Multimedia and hypermedia

The 1990s have seen the explosion of all forms of electronic 'media' associated with computers. When you think about it though, this is quite natural. If a computer has a colour display, why shouldn't it display pictures? If we give it a colour printer, it can print them too. If it can display still pictures, why shouldn't it display moving pictures? If we add loudspeakers, then why shouldn't it play music? Why shouldn't it talk? If we give it a way of looking at (scanning) pages why shouldn't it be able to read? If we give it a microphone, why shouldn't it understand what we say?

Each of these, of course, involves climbing a technical mountain or two, but in principle any of these are possible, and in fact most are now readily available already. Processor speeds, constraining the maximum speed at which reasonably priced computers can work, and the limited size and high cost of a computer's storage capacity were major limitations until relatively recently, but these technical barriers are now evaporating very rapidly. New methods of bulk information transfer, particularly CD-ROMs and the Internet, have also suddenly made it possible to move the large volumes of data needed around very easily, making multimedia a commercial opportunity and thence a reality.

Multimedia just means using a number of different forms of media simultaneously. Just include a CD-ROM drive in the computer box, add some loudspeakers and an associated sound card (an electronic circuit that sends the sound to the loudspeakers) if it doesn't have them already, maybe add extra facilities to display moving video more efficiently, and off you go! Multimedia just means that as well as being able to browse through text documents, complete with pictures, you can also play video or sound clips whenever you want. Multimedia is all about being able to access several types of media simultaneously, media meaning films, video, music, spoken commentaries, picture stills, and anything else which can be used to represent and explore information.

Hypermedia and multimedia are now inextricably linked, and mean just about the same thing, but historically they come from slightly different backgrounds. Hypermedia is a development from hypertext, which was originally all about how you move around information.

In a hypertext document, particular words or phrases are highlighted. Hidden behind each highlighted part of the text is an invisible pointer to another document which explains more about that particular word or phrase.

As you are reading the document, if you see text highlighted (normally by being displayed in a different colour) you can just point to it and it automatically jumps to and displays the associated document. Hypermedia just extends the principle beyond text, to allow you to point to anything, for instance a picture in the text, and to jump to any other form of medium, for instance a short video sequence rather than just another text document. Hence this is now what has already been described as multimedia. The World-Wide Web on the Internet makes extensive use of this idea (there is more about the World-Wide Web in the next chapter).

3D and virtual reality

Mechanical engineers have been creating three-dimensional (3D) representations of complex engineering components for many years, using powerful computer workstations with the ability to assign material properties to these components and then assemble them or apply forces to them, still inside the computer, to see what stresses and strains result. This can save having to manufacture very expensive prototypes to gain only incomplete versions of the same information.

Structural engineers use similar techniques to model buildings and bridges and study their behaviour in high winds, earthquakes and other extreme conditions, in order to improve the safety of the public.

You may have seen the work of some of the more famous architects of our time, who have used computers to create 'virtual' models of buildings so that clients and the public can view them from any angle long before they are constructed, and walk around inside them to see what they will be like to work in or visit.

Film makers can create entire scenes of science fiction movies electronically, where every detail of each scene is modelled electronically, at considerable time and expense, so that the finished scene actually looks very real.

Each of these has in the past required expensive computer hardware and software, together with very skilled specialists to understand how to utilize such sophisticated systems properly. All have represented something of the state of the art of the natural development of basic computer principles, as a natural consequence of taking people with ideas and giving them time and resources.

But now some new ideas are entering the world of three dimensions on the computer, all to do with how the human mind works and how we perceive images on the computer.

First there is the remarkable world of video games. Without the engineering constraint of having to be visually perfect, computer game programmers have used all sorts of ideas to give us dramatic and very effective graphics on ordinary modern PCs. If you look closely at the computer graphics used in these games, you can see all sorts of tricks and illusions that have been used. The most obvious is the use of flat surfaces and rectangular panels to eliminate the mathematical, and hence computational, complications of curved surfaces and irregular boundaries. Unless you look for these things, though, the human eye, and mind, is usually far too busy following the action to notice. The programmers' skill makes these effects work very well.

A slightly different field, which uses very similar techniques, is the world of virtual reality. Whereas the computer game designer can create a new world which is designed to be easy to display, the virtual reality programmer is generally trying to create a virtual representation of anything which might be in the real world, and then allow the viewer to walk around inside it in real time. Using many of the same techniques, the virtual reality designer has to identify which aspects of the scene in view will be studied closely by the viewer and which others are really just there for completeness and hence can be represented in much less detail. Curved surfaces are often included, but usually as a combination of many small rectangular surfaces connected to look like a curve. What looks like a tree in the distance may actually turn out to be a picture of a tree on a flat surface when you, in virtual terms, walk over to it and look at it more closely, but from where you are supposed to stand it probably looks quite real.

Virtual reality systems include many interesting ideas. As well as fixed objects in the virtual world, there can be cars and people moving around and buttons which you can press that result in actions taking place in front of you. You can navigate your way around a simple virtual world on a personal computer with just a conventional mouse by pointing at controls at the edges of the computer screen. In more advanced systems you can attach sensors to your head and hands to measure their movements and mimic them inside the virtual world, and then display the world inside special stereoscopic spectacles, making you feel that you really are inside the virtual world and able to operate controls inside the virtual world with your hands.

This all seems a long way from the basic principles that we were looking at just a few pages ago. But now forget about how the technology works and concentrate on using it. Walking across a virtual world, or exploring multimedia documents, is really just as easy as pressing buttons in a computer window, or selecting the next course of your meal from the restaurant menu.

Video and computer conferencing

The idea of meeting people on a television screen has been around for a long time, but it has always been associated with big business and high expenditure because the data link it needed was, until fairly recently, similar to that needed to take a television broadcast from the studio to the transmitter. Hence video conferencing could save money for busy international executives who normally pay expensive air fares to travel the world to meet, but it was of no practical use to the average business.

The sudden development of video capabilities as an everyday part of multimedia is all set to change this. As video display capabilities become a standard feature of PCs, the advances in communications make it possible to transmit ever more information over less costly communication lines, and as simple video cameras become very cheap, video conferencing could become a much more commonplace event. Just as various advances needed to be made, coupled with user acceptance, for the use of fax machines to become very widespread, video conferencing might become much more common very quickly. In the late-1990s there are already simple PC-based systems which can connect over a telephone line, but the pictures are rather small and jerky as the computer struggles to transmit all of the information it needs to.

Clever techniques used in multimedia recordings, such as only transmitting the parts of a picture that have changed, rather than whole 'frames', can save a lot of communication time, especially when people are sitting down and there is little movement.

The distinction between video conferencing and video telephony can become rather blurred when several people can each sit at their own computers and then connect to each other and see each other on the screens of their PCs. One problem which was once explained to me by someone who had been using such a system is that of managing or chairing a discussion. With much of the usual body language of a meeting hidden outside the areas seen by the video camera, even if a chairperson is appointed, it can be quite difficult to keep order in a lively discussion. However, people rapidly solve practical problems like this themselves without a lot of scientific intervention.

Basic computer conferencing without video pictures is slightly different. It involves several computers being connected together and sharing the same computer screen 'window'. It is really like a discussion meeting around a whiteboard, where everyone might be given a different coloured marker. Anyone can write to this special window, and everybody sees everything written in the window by someone else straight away. Each person probably uses a different colour, so that everyone can see who wrote or drew what. Communicating through the screen may be supplemented by voice communication through a microphone and loudspeakers on each computer, or more simply just by a conference telephone interconnecting everyone through standard telephones so that they can all speak at once and all hear each other. At the other extreme this can be linked to video conferencing as well, when the two technologies supplement each other.

Another interesting anecdote that I have heard is that if a single computer screen is used for both video conferencing and computer 'whiteboard' conferencing, at first everyone likes to see each other, but after a little time the limited area of the computer screen may become more valuable for drawing ideas than for people to see each other. There is also a suggestion that some people are quite self-conscious about appearing unexpectedly on someone else's computer screen, and prefer the slightly indistinct images of the early computer-based systems, which give an impression of you without the other participants being able to tell whether you have combed your hair!

Software

Here we are, almost way up in the clouds of science fiction, and software hasn't even been mentioned yet! Everyone has heard of software, but what on earth is it?

Well, the obvious answer is 'almost everything that isn't hardware', but that may not help a great deal! Computer hardware is all of the physical boxes, circuits, monitors, keyboards, cables, printers and other tangible paraphernalia which are solid and real and which you can actually touch and hold.

Software comes in many different forms and types, but somewhere it includes a very extensive and complicated list of instructions to tell the hardware what to do. At the lowest level, there is usually an operating system, like Windows or good old DOS ('Disk Operating System'), which deals with the basics of allowing a computer to operate, much as the heart and digestion in the human body deal with the basics of being alive.

Then there are computer programs, normally things that you buy to add to the computer to make it do useful things, like word processors, spreadsheets, games, accounts programs, Internet Web browsers, graphic display programs and many others. If you should come across the term 'computer language' it means just what it sounds like. If a computer program can be considered to be the equivalent of a book from the library, the same book might be published in many different languages. The computer must be able to read the right language to use the program, although everything has become highly standardized. These days everything is packaged so that you really hardly need to know anything. A commercial program comes on some sort of disk; you put the disk in the computer and type a command, answer a couple of questions and everything is done for you. Another icon then appears on the screen, and you can run another software package (another computer program).

Networks and communications

A computer network is a means of connecting computers together. Once connected by a network, computers can send each other messages, ask each other questions, read each other's disks, and use each other's printers and other 'peripherals'. A peripheral is simply anything extra connected to a computer, outside the main box.

The idea of networking is simple, but the technicalities of doing it have kept many high-powered brains very busy for many years. Nowadays it works fairly easily. There are usually a few parameters to set somewhere in one of those little 'dialog boxes' – just sub-windows within windows, which you will soon see if you run much software. Your local computer shop will tell you what to do when they sell you the magic 'network card', an extra circuit board to put inside the box which provides an extra plug socket for the network cable.

The complications with networks occur when there is a need to limit who can look at what, and more importantly who can delete what. Establishing an effective security system to define who can do what is rather more complicated, and usually requires some specialist under-standing and expertise. Of course, security needs specialist knowledge anywhere, even just to set up an effective security alarm for a house or an office.

The cabling systems – the nerve fibres of many organizations – can also become very complicated. Thankfully, modern methods of cabling are much more tolerant of broken cables than older systems. In the past, one broken cable could disable many computers until the location of the fault was found. Today this is quite rare. The world of stacking hubs, optical fibre backbones and other technological wonders is another area of specialist technical understanding. But just think of it as being like the telephone system. Few people worry too much about where the telephone cables run or how a telephone exchange works these days – they just get on and use the telephone. Treat computer networks the same way, there to make your life easier.

This is fine as long as we are all in the same building and can run cables wherever we want, but how do we connect computers in different buildings or to our homes? The answer lies in communications.

As the demand for telephones grew at a fantastic pace, the technology used to connect telephones went digital. This technology doesn't go right to the average home – yet. It's on its way (the Integrated Systems Digital Network, or ISDN) but it will take a few years to reach everyone. But once your ordinary telephone line reaches your local exchange the signal it carries is converted from a continuously varying voltage, like the squiggly waves on the instrument screens in science fiction movies, into numbers. Every tiny fraction of a second, the height of the wave is measured and turned into a number. The great thing about numbers is that, with a little mathematics and electronics, you can combine vast quantities of them from lots of different telephone calls together in an organized manner, like a table of numbers, and then shoot them at great speed to another location somewhere else in the world. Unravel the numbers again at the other end and they can be turned back into the original voice on the telephone.

Once converted from sounds to 'digital' numbers, telephone calls can be transmitted by satellite or over optical fibres, in very great numbers and at very great speed – hence the development of an infrastructure of high-speed transmission links all over the world. But, of course, computers, not to mention all the different forms of multimedia, are also 'digital', and ultimately reduce everything to numbers. And these are the signals which are transmitted over computer networks. So the same communications infrastructure developed originally for the telephone network can also be used, with a few more boxes of electronics to tie things together, to link computer networks.

Note, though, that although computer networks inside a building are free to be used as much as you like (once installed), the data links provided by the telecommunications companies between buildings are more expensive to use. Hence, at reasonable levels of expenditure, computers communicate between different buildings rather more slowly than they communicate within the same building.

No description of communications would be complete without mentioning the humble but vital 'modem'. Most ordinary people do not have high-speed digital data links to their homes – they just have an ordinary, conventional, telephone designed to transmit speech, or more generally sounds.

A computer wants to talk in electronic pulses, or numbers, not sounds. A modem converts electronic pulses into sounds, so that the sounds can be transmitted over an ordinary telephone line. At the other end, another modem converts the sounds back into electrical pulses, and onwards to another computer. To do this reliably is actually quite difficult, since the sound quality on many telephone lines is rather poor, with clicks and buzzes and other interference. Modern modems do two things to overcome this. First the speed at which they communicate with each other may vary, depending upon the quality of the telephone line. Secondly they use 'error correction' – mathematical checks to identify when errors have occurred – with the ability to retransmit the data affected.

Communications have made many things possible, not least of which is the Internet, which we will be looking at in the next chapter.

Bandwidth

As more computers are connected together, the speed with which they can communicate with each other becomes important. The 'bandwidth' of communication is a measure of the speed at which data can be transmitted. The greater the bandwidth, the more data that can be transmitted in a given period of time.

The bandwidth required depends upon the nature of the communication. If a computer file is being transmitted from one office to another, does it need to arrive at its destination in seconds, minutes or hours? The greater the bandwidth, the faster it gets there. The immediate or 'real time' transmission of complex graphic designs and good quality live video pictures requires a large bandwidth to keep up with the data transmission rates required.

Note that bandwidths quoted are often maximum bandwidths, which can be quite difficult to achieve in practice. If several computers are connected over the same data link or network, they can each only use a proportion of the bandwidth available; the bandwidth is the total of all communications at a particular moment.

Bandwidth can sometimes be enhanced by a limited amount by using 'compression' techniques to reduce the amount of data which needs to be transmitted. A variety of techniques are available; the basic principle is to analyse the data before transmission to see whether it can be simplified, or compressed, and then expanded again at the other end. For instance, if a document contains the same word many times, this word can be replaced by a shortened code for transmission and then translated back from the code to the original word at the far end.

Processors, storage and working space

We have come all this way through the chapter without discussing the innards of the computer's box. Let's take a brief look inside, so that you can converse intelligently with a computer salesperson.

Each computer has at least one processor. The processor is the equivalent of the engine of a car: the faster the processor (the more powerful the engine), the faster you can go. Whenever you start using a computer with a more powerful processor, you may wonder how on earth you managed with less. But just like cars, more powerful means more money.

Then there is RAM, random access memory. This is rather like a desk at work. The larger your desk is, the more papers you can work on at once and the easier it is to do complex tasks. Look at the software you want to run and see how much memory it recommends.

Computer disks are like filing cabinets – the more you have, the more files you can store. Hard disks can store quite large amounts of data. For information, a 'byte' generally stores one character in a document, a megabyte is about a million of these, and a gigabyte is a thousand million. Generally, software applications will rapidly expand to use as much disk space as you can reasonably afford.

CD-ROMs are CDs containing data. Unlike hard disks, the computer can usually only read the information on them ('ROM' comes from Read Only Memory). They are removable, so you can insert a CD-ROM to provide data to suit whichever program you are running or game you might be playing.

Portability and mobility

Many managers and executives would seem lost without their portable computers. As prices come down, many more people will use them. They really just contain all of the capabilities of their desktop computer relatives repackaged into much smaller and lighter boxes. They run off batteries when away from home, so they will only work for a limited time before the battery needs to be recharged.

In theory, radio connection from a portable computer to a nearby computer network is possible, but in practice this is rather expensive. It is possible to use some types of mobile phone to connect to the telephone system through a modem to enable limited communication while travelling.

Big computers

What about the PC's older brothers – all those mainframes, minicomputers and computer workstations to be found in the more affluent regions of business?

Until the mid-1990s, the personal computer might reasonably have been described as the bicycle of the computer world, in comparison with the corporate workhorse supermini computers (more like cars), and the incredibly powerful real supercomputers (like heavy trucks). But the PC is now at least equivalent to a family hatchback, and it appears that for most purposes that is all that is needed.

There are many cost-effective commercial applications for more powerful computers, with speeds and capabilities far in excess of what a PC is capable of. But whereas a PC used to be thought of as a cut-down version of a larger computer, the balance is switching to where the PC is the norm, and the workstation is a big version of it.

A firm's computer facilities used to be built around some form of big corporate computer, with everything else as satellites feeding to it and from it. Nowadays computer facilities are more like a distributed field of self-sufficient PCs all cooperating to support an organization. There is still a very important place for the central corporate facility, but it is becoming more the central archive and data store, the knowledge base and communications centre of the organization.

Network computers

There is an alternative form of computer installation, which retains the principle of concentrated computer facilities, which may suit some organisations. Where a high-speed network is available, all that is really needed on the desk in many situations is the interface – the display, the keyboard and the mouse. Most of the innards of the computer can actually be located somewhere else, connected by a network cable. This is known as the 'network computer' solution, where much of the inner workings of whole groups of computers are concentrated in one location for easier support and maintenance.

Looking from a different hilltop

Throughout this chapter, I have tried to show that there is no reason at all to be daunted by the capabilities of the wonders of information technology. We have just taken a guided tour of part of an exhibition, stopping to look at some of the more interesting exhibits, and walking past, perhaps not even noticing, many others.

It is an exhibition, not a museum, because we are not just looking at history. We are looking at the knowledge, understanding and opportunities which may shape our future. Like all exhibitions it is selective, not exhaustive and there are many other subjects which could have been included. But there are also many other sources of information. For instance, if you want to buy a computer, buy a computer magazine first to find information on prices and the latest technical details. Books get out of date, and you need to look somewhere where you can reasonably expect to find the latest information.

There are many different ways to look at new technology. Always be prepared to stop for a moment and then climb to the top of a nearby hill and look at what you are trying to understand from a different direction – it may help.

Let's move on to another exhibition hall...

5 Driving the Superhighway

Where is the 'Superhighway'?

As we saw in Chapter 1, while the Information Society is about people and new ways of living, changing people's values, opportunities and constraints, the Information Superhighway is the infrastructure of new electronic communications which will enable this change to take place. The Superhighway is still a concept though; it means different things to different people.

'Super' implies large, grand and fast, like a freeway or motorway in comparison with a rural lane. Hence it seems reasonable only to associate the Superhighway with optical fibres, microwave links and satellite communications, the grander upmarket end of the communications scene. But if we draw our comparison in different ways, for instance comparing sending a letter from one country to another (which takes several days) with an Internet connection over an ordinary telephone (which is able to read a long document that is actually on the far side of the world in 'real' time), even an ordinary telephone line becomes a Superhighway compared with the letter post.

Every salesperson defines the concept of the Superhighway in whatever way is likely to result in the most sales. Because it is a concept, rather than a scientific definition, there is complete freedom to do so. Hence be careful who you believe and what you believe. No one owns or can sell *the* Superhighway; they can only sell access to their own interpretation of it.

The Superhighway is not just about the speed of communication – it is also very much about being able to access new forms of information which were not available before, and about the freedom to access information from any international location whenever you want to.

Speed will come with time, as technology permits and as market forces decide an equitable price for the service offered. Accessibility is easier to provide first at prices that the market-place can afford and will accept.

So, in effect, anyone who wants to, and who has a telephone, can hire an information bicycle from their nearest Internet service provider and explore part of the Superhighway to find out what it looks like. That may be all they need for the moment. Other people, seeing a different part of the Superhighway being constructed near their homes, may pay for access to a cable television network, and find the service developing to provide a seemingly unlimited range of television channels and films on demand whenever they want to watch them, but without access to all of the other information on the Internet.

The more adventurous information cyclist will soon want to have faster access to information and the ability to see films and television channels as well. The thinking film and television channel-hopper is likely to be interested in the opportunity to access a wider range of information with more dynamic interaction. The same optical fibre used for cable television, digital telephone and data lines will progressively give access to the ever more integrated forms of faster and more extensive service that are developing to meet this demand. Larger businesses will be able to access this wider range of services through the high-speed data lines that they have already installed, while smaller businesses are already benefiting from the vast and competitive domestic market for cable television and the Internet bringing prices down for steadily increasing levels of service.

So the Superhighway is on its way to everybody who wants to use it, in some shape or form. Initially, perhaps, it is rather slow and obstinately unresponsive at times, as customer demand far exceeds reasonable levels of speculative development, but, like all things, if there is demand, commercial market forces will provide the impetus to develop the level of service that the market can afford.

What vehicles can you drive?

If the Superhighway is going to be a fusion of the Internet, video and any other new business communication, education or leisure technology that anyone dreams up, whatever sort of electronic vehicle will you need to drive along it, you might ask.

Luckily all of the different technologies to interact with the Super-highway are rapidly converging, so that instead of lots of different communication methods and associated boxes, more integrated forms of 'communication unit' are rapidly evolving.

Both a television and a computer have a full colour display screen. As mentioned in Chapter 4 though, the most common types of these two displays are actually slightly different when inspected closely, but the resolution and quality of both are rapidly merging. Standard televisions were originally designed for group viewing from a distance, with larger screens designed to show approximate moving detail. Computer screens have always been designed to withstand much closer scrutiny, with the average lone computer user much closer to the screen, looking at documents and pictures which are much too detailed for an ordinary television set to reproduce to the same standard. The standards and quality of both types of display are rapidly converging, so that high-definition television displays are of a similar standard to computer displays. Conversion between the different plugs and connectors used for computer displays and television video signals is just a matter of straightforward electronics. More advanced types of display, such as projection display systems working more like slide projectors and flat display screens to hang on the wall, are unlikely to draw much distinction between computer displays and television – they are designed for the multimedia world of the future.

Both television and computer systems have developed hi-fi sound capabilities for more discerning listeners, to match improvements in visual quality. They may use different electronics inside their boxes, but the interface with people is to similar standards of high-quality sound reproduction. It is the consistency of the human interface that really matters here, and it seems natural that the electronics will integrate and merge to achieve economies of production and maintenance.

The computer has a keyboard and a mouse, while the television and the video player have a multiplicity of remote controls. Clearly some rationalization is needed here to get the best of both worlds. We need the simplicity and portability of one integrated remote control, combined with the sophistication and fine control provided by the keyboard and the mouse. Perhaps before this reaches any natural conclusion, new interfacing methods (for instance voice recognition) will become more prominent, or perhaps this is further in the future. As an intermediate step, television 'cards' which can be added to computers can already provide television displays in computer display screen windows as one form of integration.

Then there is all the software, local storage (computer memory and disk space) and everything else involved in providing a working interface or communications terminal, but that is all becoming packaged inside the box, so that it is almost invisible to the user.

So the simple answer is that, to access the Internet, which provides much of the functionality of the Superhighway available today, all you need is a well-specified PC with the right software and some means of connection to the Internet, such as a modem and a telephone line. Looking to the not-so-distant future, a hybrid television-cum-computer in the living room may rapidly become more of a domestic entertainment, education and work centre. With straightforward remote controls which any of the family can operate for basic features, and maybe a keyboard tucked away for more serious use, this can become a normal part of domestic life. As the family all want to do different things at the same time, and prices come down, additional units will probably appear in other rooms around the house. Meanwhile, the office computer will just steadily increase its specification to match.

Electronic mail (e-mail)

One of the first 'interactive' Superhighway services to become part of many ordinary people's lives is electronic mail, or 'e-mail' for short (Figure 5.1). I am using the word interactive in a slightly liberal sense here, to mean anything which involves two-way communication with the Superhighway. Broadcast and satellite television are not interactive – we can only receive programmes, not send any messages back to the transmitting station. Cable television may be just the same, but the cabling provided is generally capable of sending messages back, even if this isn't used. Computer network connections and Internet connections are designed for two-way traffic, and are interactive.

Electronic mail is just another way of sending messages to each other. The concept of sending messages electronically, rather than on paper, has been around for many years in a variety of different forms. Almost as soon as several people had terminals connected to the same computer, the idea of typing a message in at one terminal and the same message appearing on another terminal was put into practice. But systems to interconnect between different computers and between different offices were fraught with problems. Many different independent systems were developed which did not easily communicate with each other, and some of the interfaces used were horrendously complex to understand in the early days.

Today, many ordinary people have their own e-mail address, which they use with hardly any training or new understanding, and the number of people using e-mail is increasing at a quite phenomenal rate.

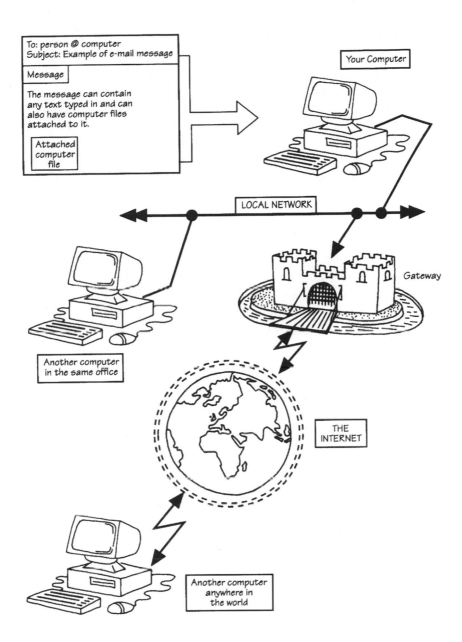

Figure 5.1. Electronic mail.

What has changed? Well, the key changes have been a simplification of basic e-mail knowledge down to the absolute minimum requirement, and international standardization of e-mail addresses on the Internet.

The most basic e-mail message consists of just three things:

1. The one-line e-mail address of someone to send the message to.
2. A title. Strictly, this is optional, but this is so useful for the recipient (to assist in handling, filing and organizing messages) that everyone really should get into the habit of adding a short title to every message.
3. The text of the message. Free-format letters, words and numbers – just type any message that you want to send. Older systems may put on some restrictions, particularly on the maximum size of the message, but modern systems have few limitations.

Optionally, the message can also include one or more computer files as well, as part of or at the end of the text of the message. For technical reasons, most files must be 'encoded' to 'attach' them to the message. The details are not important, but some encoders/decoders have compatibility problems; these are being overcome by international standardization and this should not be a problem in the future. To some people, this ability to attach files is a very important feature. It means that any file – a word-processed document, a spreadsheet, a picture or a computer program, even sounds or video clips – can be attached to the message and sent anywhere in the world. The identical file can be extracted by the recipient at the message's destination, who can then edit, print, or do whatever he or she wishes with it as if it were the original file.

Before going any further, I want to distinguish between two slightly different types of electronic mail system: internal e-mail and external e-mail.

Internal e-mail is mail between different people's computers inside the same business. There is a definite boundary around the system – it may be one office or it may be several offices, but all of the messages stay within the safe and secure confines of the firm's own computer systems. Since this system is independent, it can take any form. There is no need for standardization, but in reality it makes sense to use standard methods and software, compatible with other systems, for instance so that systems can easily be connected when firms merge; unusual and unique systems are going out of fashion.

External e-mail can go anywhere in the world – to any country, to any place, to any person, to anywhere that it is possible to find an electronic connection to. This is what most people mean nowadays when they refer to e-mail, and henceforth when I refer to e-mail I will generally mean this unrestricted, international, standardized form of e-mail.

Nowadays, internal e-mail systems are often connected to the external world of the Internet through a 'gateway'. The gateway allows translation between the two systems, from the limited number of possible addresses in the internal e-mail world to the unlimited possibilities of the external world. This often involves some rearrangement of the address. The gateway should also keep the safe internal world insulated and protected from the harsh outside world, although this often involves a little more than just a straightforward gateway – more about this in Chapter 8.

The Internet currently dominates the international e-mail scene because it provides a straightforward and easy to understand framework for messages. There are other international networks, but all of the open networks connect to the Internet, and most people give any international e-mail address they have in the standard Internet form.

Internet e-mail

The Internet provides a combination of many different services, but essentially it is an unrestricted international network of computers of truly mind-boggling proportions. One of the keys to the success of the Internet is the electronic addresses that uniquely identify every computer and every person on the Internet, however complex the network may get.

An Internet e-mail address consists of two parts: a name and a 'domain' separated by an '@' symbol. Hence an address takes the form 'name@domain'. The domain is the equivalent of a place somewhere in the world. The name is the name of someone to be found at that address.

Just as someone may have an address at a flat, a house, a building, or even a whole organization, a single domain may represent a tiny part of a computer, a whole computer, or even a gateway to the entire internal computer network of a vast organization. A domain name is made up of several words, separated by dots (full stops or periods). There are two basic forms of domain names: by country or international.

Every country connected to the Internet (which is almost every country in the world) has a unique two-letter code. Addresses allocated within a country's local Internet organizations finish with these two letters at the right-hand end of the address (e.g. —@—.–.uk). The next two or three letters from the right, before the next dot, usually distinguish the type of organization, for instance 'co' (e.g. —@—.co.uk) or 'com' for commercial companies, 'gov' for government organizations or 'ac' for academic organizations. The actual letters do vary from country to country, and some countries omit this part of the address.

Then there is an organization name, which must be unique for that country and is usually kept fairly short (e.g. —@infoculture.co.uk). For a small organization this is all that is needed, but organizations with several offices or departments can add further subdivisions to the left of further dots (e.g. —@research.infoculture.co.uk) to achieve addressing unique to the size of 'sub-domain' that they wish to use.

International domains finish in one of several standard three-letter codes (for instance '—.com' for companies or '—.org' for international organizations). The part of the address preceding this has to be registered internationally to ensure that it is unique, and there are certain rules to comply with for a successful registration. Once again, this part of the address can be subdivided into smaller sub-domains by adding further words to the left, separated by dots.

Before the domain name (that is, before the '@' sign), there are individual e-mail user names within the domain. All that really matters is that the names are unique within that particular domain, but each organization will decide its own standardized form. For instance I might be 'stephen.vincent@——' or 'vincent_s@——' or 'stephen@——' or 'sprvincent@——', or any other variation. Usually dots (.) or underscores (_) are used to link words or letters together. There must not be any gaps, and everything in an Internet e-mail address is usually in lower-case characters.

A pure technologist might feel that this is slightly oversimplifying this subject – there are other valid forms of address and extra complexities that are possible. But the success of Internet addresses and their widespread use is to a large extent due to the simplicity of the above concept, with its ability to provide simple, unique, clear addresses for an unlimited number of users throughout the world. You will notice these addresses being used almost anywhere nowadays: on business cards, in adverts and on letterheads.

The Internet

Now let's look closer at the Internet itself. Why is it so successful? Why has it been expanding so fast? What is it anyway?

The first thing to understand is that nobody owns the Internet. It is not controlled or administered by any government or single commercial organization. It is a remarkable, vast, international cooperation of different organizations and commercial companies. It may have had its original roots in the academic and military worlds, but it is now a free-standing, commercially self-sufficient and resilient entity.

The Internet consists of a large number of 'Internet Service Providers' distributed throughout the world. Each service provider has a computer system and telecommunications links to other service providers. The key to the Internet is that all of the service providers have agreed to work to mutually acceptable standards, so they all, in effect, speak the same international computer network language and can all talk to each other. Each service provider then provides local communications links to Internet users, which allow these users to become part of the international network themselves. These local links vary from local dial-up telephone modem links for individual users to dedicated data lines for larger business and academic users. Hence everyone on the Internet at any moment, including local users who have dialled in using a modem and a telephone line, is part of a single vast international computer network.

One of the most remarkable things about the Internet is the way in which people pay to use it. Charging methods vary between countries and competitively between service providers, but in general, charging methods make no attempt to make any correlation between the cost of a communication and the distance it travels.

In places where communications charges are high and services are limited there may be a charge on the volume of information transferred. Wherever Internet services have become well established, the charges soon become related to the time that a user is logged on to the Internet, regardless of where in the world they are communicating with and how much data they are transferring. In really competitive markets, like the UK, some service providers just make one fairly low flat-rate charge to each user each month, regardless of how many hours the connection is used for and without showing any concern for where in the world they are connected to!

This is rather like the electronic equivalent of an airline issuing a cheap season ticket for unlimited travel, and then every other airline in the world honouring the use of the same ticket on any service without any extra charge. At first it doesn't seem to make any commercial sense. But actually it does. Each service provider sets up its computer systems and rents communications data links to other service providers. These links may be to the same or to other countries, wherever the main places that their customers will want to communicate with are. These in turn connect onwards to everywhere else in the world, through further data links and other service providers. Each service provider knows how much this infrastructure costs, and just has to recover it and make a profit from its customers. If a flat rate will cover it and be competitive in the market-place, why do anything more complicated? The cheapest flat rate, of course, is just for low-speed dial-up connections; higher charges apply to high-speed dedicated links. The more customers, the more international data links that need to be rented – this is just demand driving supply.

There are various standard features of this international network. For instance, every user needs access to a local 'domain name server'. This is a computer which can translate between the domain names described above and the numeric 'IP addresses' which the computers actually use to talk to each other. An IP address (Internet Protocol address), which you might occasionally see, just consists of four numbers of up to three digits each, separated by dots, and is unique to a particular domain (e.g. 195.188.174.25). A local domain name server cannot store or stay up to date with all of the Internet domain names in the world. What it does is to remember the domain names most frequently used by its own local Internet users, and whenever it is asked to translate a domain name that it doesn't know, it consults other servers which maintain a more complete list of addresses.

The way in which standards are agreed on the Internet is also quite intriguing. A new standard is published on the Internet for anyone to look at as a 'request for comments' (RFC). If there is general acceptance, it just goes into use after a certain period of time. If someone comes up with valid problems with it, it is superseded by a new RFC. This provides a rather more rapid way of agreeing standards than the more conventional laborious process of international standardization.

Over the years, various services have evolved on the Internet, each for a different purpose and a different group of users. In the mid-1990s, two particular types of service dominated the use of the Internet: electronic mail (for communication) and the World-Wide Web (for access to information). Rapid evolution is taking place in services to provide interactive discussion forums on the Internet, and other new services can appear and gain acceptance very quickly if there is a demand.

In a few areas of the world, only an e-mail service is available, and individual users cannot yet connect, live, to the whole of the Internet. However, the full service is extending all of the time as better communications links become available, even in remoter parts of the world.

The World-Wide Web

The World-Wide Web (often 'WWW' or just 'Web') is a remarkable phenomenon. Its use and acceptance have steadily gathered momentum throughout the world, it is a global phenomenon with no natural boundaries – it just exists everywhere that the Internet reaches, flowing around the world.

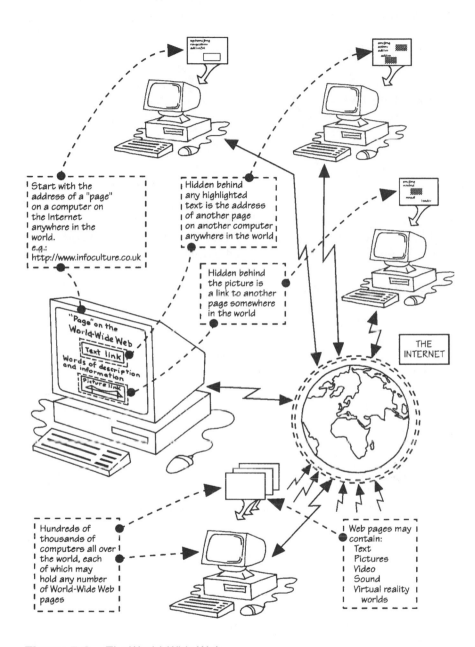

Figure 5.2. The World-Wide Web.

The great secret of the Web is that anyone, without any real technical knowledge, can use it within a few minutes of being put in front of a connection to it. It really is that simple. Quite the opposite of the historical image of computers!

Imagine that you are now sitting in front of a computer screen. Someone has turned the computer on for you, issued a couple of simple commands to find a 'page' of information about your favourite hobby, and in front of you now on the screen is a document on a subject which interests you.

Grab the mouse (or other 'pointing device'), and move up and down the document by pointing to the up and down arrows at the edge of the screen. As you read through the document, you will notice that certain phrases and words are highlighted (in a different colour or underlined). On many systems, as you move the pointer, or cursor, over one of these highlighted areas, it changes to a different symbol, usually a hand with a pointing finger. Choose one of the highlighted phrases that interests you, point to it and press the left button of the mouse (or equivalent pointer). The computer whirrs into action, words blink and flash, and after a few moments, or sometimes a few minutes, a new page appears, the one which that phrase was pointing at (Figure 5.2).

Every page on the Internet uses the same principle. Any phrase or picture (or sometimes just a part of a picture) can point to another page, anywhere on the Internet. Each page can be on any computer, anywhere on the Internet, anywhere in the world. This is the ultimate extension of the principle of hypertext – text containing pointers to other information.

This web of information now stretches over many millions of Web pages, all over the world. Any page is accessible to any Internet user, wherever they are in the world.

The next problem is to find pages of information on other subjects which interest you. Easy – just use one of the many Internet WWW 'search engines'. The software that you are using to view the Internet is a 'Web browser'. On most Web browsers one of the buttons around the edge of the screen is for something like 'search the Internet'. Click on this (i.e. point to it), and a search page appears. Type in a subject and press the button beside it to begin the search. Within a minute or two (sometimes a little longer) a list appears. It may have found just a few pages, or it may have found many thousands and you are just looking at the start of the list. When you look at the list, you will notice that every item starts with or contains a highlighted hypertext title. Look for one that interests you, and click on it. And off you go, 'surfing the net', 'exploring cyberspace', or whatever you care to call this exploration of a seemingly infinite terrain of information. Almost every path that you explore leads to more links and more paths into unknown territory. If you are paying by the hour, and it catches your imagination, watch out for the cost!

The World-Wide Web is not restricted to just text and pictures. It can contain video clips, sounds, music and even whole virtual worlds, if your Web browser has the necessary facilities. You can explore virtual shopping centres, make purchases through interactive Web pages and download free software and upgrades. People are dreaming up new ideas all of the time; to some extent, the only limit is your imagination.

There are many tricks and twists that regular cyberspace surfers will learn, such as keeping the addresses of your favourite pages in a sort of address book; which search engines perform better on what types of search; and even the best times of day when pages in different parts of the world are less busy and the response times to see each page are better. Don't forget that any number of other Internet users could be looking at the same page as you, or connecting over the same data link to a particular part of the world.

You can also, of course, use the Web to look at any one of those addresses you have seen advertised in magazines, newspapers or elsewhere. Every page on the WWW has a unique address. Somewhere around the edge of the Web browser screen there will be a space where the current Web page or 'URL' (uniform resource locator) is shown. You can point to this line, delete what is there and type in something else instead, and hit the 'carriage return' or 'enter' key, and off you go to find that page.

The form of a Web page address is quite straightforward. At the heart of it is a domain name, just like an e-mail address, but often starting with 'www' to indicate that it is a domain (or sub-domain) of Web pages (e.g. www.infoculture.co.uk). This ties the address down to a particular computer, or part of a computer, somewhere in the world. The address of a Web page is prefixed by 'http://' to indicate that it is hypertext and distinguish it from other types of information on the Internet (e.g. http://www.infoculture.co.uk). To the right of this may be a subdirectory and file name to identify a particular computer file or document (e.g. http://www.infoculture.co.uk/webfiles/page1). The so called 'home page' at a particular Web site (the starting page from which other pages branch) often omits this file name completely (e.g. http://www.infoculture.co.uk).

As you will see, when you are surfing the Web or cruising through cyberspace you may have absolutely no idea where in the world the page that you are looking at comes from, especially if it has an international domain address finishing in '—.com' rather than an address including the name of a country. But does it matter? The World-Wide Web eliminates international boundaries and lets you travel wherever you wish, effortlessly, from the comfort of your home or office.

Video and films

Satellite, cable and interactive access to television, videos and films are all part of the range of services that may eventually be widely available through the Superhighway. In the late-1990s, these forms of providing information and entertainment require a 'bandwidth', or speed of data transfer, which is well beyond that available through a domestic connection to the Internet using an ordinary telephone line.

Nevertheless, the form of such services is evolving, through trials and local implementations, to shape the domestic and business information services of the future. The optical fibres used for cable television services are already widely used to provide telephone services as well. Technologically, there is no reason why the same optical fibres should not also provide high-speed links to the Internet. The local Internet service, in turn, would then need to have a fast enough data link to a video service provider, but it is all possible. Exactly how video and Internet services will coexist in the future may take a little time to evolve, but the Superhighway in its fuller sense is really a combination of the two.

A world of information

The extent of the information actually available on the Internet is very difficult to measure, but it has been growing fast. Just like the fax machine, when a critical proportion of the people who could use it, do use it, many others will feel the need to become part of this phenomenon.

But where is the incentive to put information onto the 'net'? Who is actually going to look at it, and what do they use it for? I recommend that anyone should spend a few hours cruising around the Web, looking objectively at what other people have done, before deciding how useful it is going to be.

For clubs, societies, government departments, pressure groups, community groups and many others the benefits are fairly obvious. Taking information which is already freely in the public domain and making it more widely and easily accessible is a straightforward application. The only note of caution that I would sound is to consider objectively whether the people that you would like to look at such Web pages both have access to suitable Web browsing facilities and are likely to want to do so. If not, it might not be worth the effort and expense. Many more people will notice an advert in the right local newspaper than will just happen on the off chance to wonder whether a particular local society has a Web page. Maybe combine the two, creating a Web page and including its address in a newspaper advert, so that anyone with access to the Web can look there for further information.

Web pages for business use need to be considered rather more carefully. If there is technical and reference information which you would like to make widely and publicly available, fine. If you just want to advertise your services, who is the advert aimed at? Are the people that you want to read your advert really scouring the whole world of the Internet in the hope of finding your particular advert? Perhaps they are, but in many cases they are more likely to look for personal recommendations from people they know, or to look in specialist trade magazines, which have a more extensive and comprehensive choice of advertisers.

I find it surprising just what some people are happy to put on the Internet – for instance, every detail of a commercial operation, including staff details, locations, resources, current projects, past projects and future plans. Maybe this all used to be in the company brochure, but in some cases I cannot imagine that it really was. I am sure that attitudes might change in the future, but if I were a client and really wanted to know about a particular organization, I would phone them up and ask them to come and tell me, so that I could ask the questions I really wanted to know the answers to. However, if I were a competitor I would welcome free and unrestricted access to such a wide range of information, to help me assess the strength of the competition. A balance needs to be struck between freely providing information (for instance for the next generation of children researching information for their school projects and future jobs) and commercial common sense.

One rather negative observation that anyone might make after cruising the Web for a few hours is just how good some Web sites are and how boring and uninteresting others are. The international and classless nature of the WWW means that the pages of the most dazzling and imaginative designers may be rubbing shoulders with the most pedestrian and unimaginative pages from other users of the Web in the same Web search. Does it matter? Obviously the more imaginative pages will attract more widespread attention, but other more functional information may be of much greater depth and interest to more discerning readers.

What this does mean, though, is that if you want to attract attention you need to achieve a high standard of presentation. Major international organizations are expected to a certain extent to set the pace because they have the resources and incentive to do so. Getting people's attention on the Web is a very competitive game – you are competing against the whole world and you need to do something to distinguish your particular pages. Luckily, the Web is a wonderfully creative and unrestricted place, where anyone can try out new ideas.

The Web has considerable potential for displaying art, music, video and other media. The only problem is that it is not immediately straightforward to charge admission. The Web is more of an open space for freedom of expression, so it may not provide an easy way of generating income to support the arts. Nevertheless, it provides exposure to a very wide audience, which may in turn generate commissions and income.

Unregulated freedom

Freedom, of course, creates its own problems, and the completely unregulated and uncontrollable nature of the Internet makes it open to abuse by unscrupulous people. It is very difficult indeed to achieve regulation by technical means, because the strength of the Internet is its openness. Every form of communication is open to abuse by determined individuals, and there is no straightforward way of restricting what can be sent through the post or said on the telephone. But of course the Internet is faster, more accessible and more powerful. Just as we rely on our police forces and lawmakers to respond to other changes in our social organization and ways of living, we must rely on them to keep pace in the complex world of technology.

Quality – beware of misinformation!

One aspect of the WWW to be particularly careful of is the variation in the quality of the information which you may find. Since anyone can put anything that they like on the Internet, there is no guarantee at all that the information provided is correct, authoritative or true.

Hence anyone could set up their own page of alternative medical advice, and it could soon be available through all of the main Web search engines. The page might have a fancy looking title, include fictional quotes from supposed authorities on the subject, and actually contain quite misleading and potentially dangerous information. It might not actually be intentionally malicious, just misguided. But to the Internet searcher from the other side of the world, it might come up alongside pages from the top medical schools in the world in the same search results list. There is no quality assurance on the Web. Beware that things are not always what they seem!

Longevity and change

Another aspect of the Internet which longer term users will notice is that it is dynamic, and it is changing all of the time. Just as large numbers of new Web pages and e-mail addresses are being added all of the time, a few are also disappearing. People move to different employment and change their e-mail addresses; and firms are taken over, go out of business, decide to use a different source for their Internet services, or just decide that the benefits are not worth the costs. Academic pages set up by students may be deleted when they finish their course of education or when research projects come to an end.

Sooner or later you go back to look for a certain Web page and find that it has gone. And on the Internet, because you may never have known where it really was in the first place, it can be quite difficult to work out where it has gone. When e-mail is returned as undeliverable, there is not much of a clue to know where to start looking unless you know of a more conventional form of address or a telephone or fax number. Hence, if you really need to stay in touch with someone, it makes sense to know a little more than just an e-mail address.

On the other hand, for some people, an e-mail address may be rather more stable than a conventional address. For people who move location frequently, or who travel overseas, a single e-mail address can provide a consistent and reliable contact point.

Security and fraud

Sending information over the Internet is also rather public, rather like sending a postcard. Although the sheer volumes of information moving around the world make it difficult for anyone to systematically intercept other people's messages for criminal purposes, messages can fall into the wrong hands. Be careful about sending sensitive commercial information or credit card details in an ordinary e-mail message.

Some ordinary Web pages also request credit card details to be typed in for making purchases over the Internet. If the sale is accepted on the basis of this information, and without a signature, anyone else with details of your credit card could make fraudulent purchases by this method. Special secure means of verifying the identity of someone on the Internet are therefore being developed to prevent this happening.

Private highways and toll roads

The Internet has its limitations, particularly where speeds of data transmission and access are constrained by what service providers decide they can afford relative to an unpredictable and continuously varying demand, and also because of the completely unregulated and unprotected nature of the Internet.

Hence there is a market for private, regulated and controlled international communications networks. These are perhaps the private highways and toll roads around and outside the Internet, providing alternative communication routes. They may only provide limited communications services, or they may provide an unrestricted service similar to the Internet but only between specific locations.

Where a business has a clear communication requirement, with known parameters and a definite boundary on its use, a private connection may be more appropriate than the potentially hostile and unpredictable world of the Internet. The main difference is usually cost. The Internet is low cost because you take the rough with the smooth and accept that sometimes it may be slow or unpredictable. If you pay for a more specific service, you expect to get that service.

These private communications services are all really still part of the concept of the Superhighway, because they are all part of the new communications infrastructure of the world.

Turbochargers and jet engines

Fears have been expressed that the Internet just cannot keep up with demand, and will come to a total standstill within a few years, or even a few months. It is easy to understand this point of view in the face of several well-publicized incidents where small parts of the information infrastructure have come to a total standstill in the face of excessive demand and total overload.

In April 1997, even Microsoft had to suspend its e-mail service for 24 hours to implement a rapid upgrade to cope with an excessive peak in activity. Many major Internet service providers have been through some sort of short-term crisis when demand has exceeded supply. But this is just the result of the normal market forces of supply and demand. The technologies already exist to handle much greater amounts of information, but they will not become commonplace until it is economically viable to implement them. All of this upgrading of the Superhighway infrastructure is also hidden, invisibly, behind the electronic doors of the interface with our service providers. We do not really need to know anything about it as long as it works.

In business, we do not stop to question just how the international document courier services which we use every day operate. Presumably, all of the packages travel on normal scheduled airlines, just as part of the normal movement of cargo and luggage. But when we think about it, if demand on one route was to multiply by several orders of magnitude, it might become economic for courier companies to charter the occasional cargo plane to get packages to their destinations on time. There might be a premium to pay, but it is not physically impossible to cope with a dramatic increase in demand.

The Superhighway is much the same. All of the television channels and telephone calls being bounced around the world add up to requiring massive amounts of data transmission bandwidth, and capacity is increasing all of the time. If a data transmission bottleneck appears between two parts of the world, it will be necessary to create a temporary or permanent link to allow data to flow directly between the places concerned, to release the pressure. This is not technologically impossible – it just requires a little insight, initiative and money. If a particular e-mail service provider or Web site becomes totally overloaded, the computer systems at that site need to be upgraded.

There may be temporary setbacks, but the Information Superhighway is here to stay, and it will develop and extend naturally to cope with future demand. If we want a better service, we might have to pay a short-term premium, but commercial pressure will soon even out any inappropriate inequalities to give a consistent service.

A mobile video phone on a magic flying carpet

So the Information Superhighway is going to be rather like having a mobile video phone on a magic flying carpet. You will be able to go, virtually, wherever you want in the world, whenever you want to go. You will be able to communicate with anyone else, and they will be able to communicate with you, wherever you might be, whenever you might wish – all at a price yet to be determined, but hopefully within the reach of most people. In the future, communication on the Superhighway is likely to become as important a part of our everyday lives as the car is today.

The Superhighway to your own living room

Now that we know a little more about what might happen in the future, let us go back to our fictional market town in the countryside and see what has been happening.

While we have been away, there has been a lot of activity! Going back to our living room and looking at the Superhighway address of the community project (Figure 5.3), we find that it has developed from just an idea into a feasible concept. The main electronic page of information provides us with links to all aspects of what is going on.

First, consider the people and organizations. The members of the community most interested in driving the project forward have become very active participants in developing the concept of the project. The local council has recognized that something might really happen, and has joined the team to provide its own knowledge and insight. A key breakthrough is that finance has been found. Through the council's knowledge of possible financing organizations, and its assistance in presenting the concept in a professional manner, a suitable organization has come forward, and with a few preparatory calculations it looks as though the project is financially viable.

As the whole project has gathered momentum, various professional skilled individuals and organizations have come forward to help. Some people live locally and are happy to volunteer a little effort to get things started. Others see the potential to provide services in return for professional fees as the project progresses, and have asked to participate in the preliminary stages with a view to offering their services later. This early involvement of professional skills not only speeds up the process of arriving at a solution, but also allows the members of the community to see these professional skills in action to assist in deciding between any alternative offers of professional help later.

Many of the people concerned have been searching the Superhighway for information to help. Several examples of similar projects have been found (some in other countries), and the communities and commercial interests involved have been consulted by e-mail to find out what problems and successes they have encountered.

Several potential environmental and social problems have been investigated during the search to find the best site for the project. Environmental specialists and lobby groups have been consulted to identify any serious constraints that need to be overcome.

An assessment of demand and potential has been carried out by the financier to justify taking the project further forward and spending money on the next stages of design. The local population has been

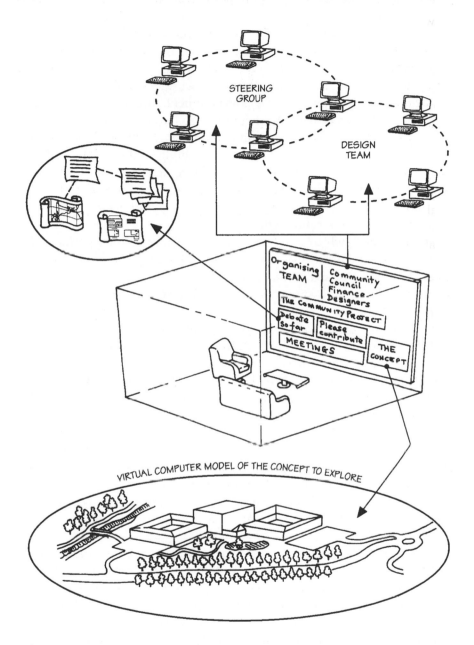

Figure 5.3. The community project in the living room.

analysed from the last census, and alternative employment, leisure and shopping facilities available in the area have all been studied to see just how much demand there is likely to be for the new facility.

All of the details of the investigations and communications to date are now instantly available from the community project page on the Superhighway, so that anyone wishing to understand how decisions are being made or how the new development might affect them can check through exactly what has happened so far at any time.

The next stage is to start appointing the project team – the people who will be paid to make the project happen. Hopefully, although they will be paid by the financier, the community will be actively involved in the selection of the sources of professional services to ensure that they are happy with the way the project will be carried out and the people that they will be communicating with.

The next step, which may even have been carried out speculatively sooner if the skills are available among the organizing team, is to create a virtual computer model of the project. This will be fairly basic at first, containing the ground surface from published maps, coloured boxes to represent the buildings, an approximate representation of the vegetation and the main roads, rivers and other features of the landscape, but it should be enough to get a good idea of what the project will look like. Then anybody with a virtually reality viewer available as part of the Superhighway interface in the living room will be able to look at the project from any direction, see its layout and its relation to the rest of the town, and think about how it will work.

At this stage, changes are fairly easy to make if anyone has better ideas, so now is the time to publicize the work so far and get as many people as possible involved in approving the concept. Anyone with access to the Superhighway can look at the project at home. Anyone else can look at it in the local library or the council offices, or maybe in the local café or some of the local shops. The virtual model makes it very easy to explain what is intended.

Now the design must get under way, filling in all of the details. The design team may be located in several different offices, but they work as an integrated team, communicating with each other all of the time as the design develops. As soon as more design detail is agreed it is added to the virtual model for everyone to see and comment on. Soon the virtual model is much more than just boxes and shapes – anyone can walk inside and view all of the different parts of the project from the inside. What will each room look like? How will the shopping mall be organized? What will the layout of the leisure facilities be? What sort of offices will be available? How will the surrounding land be landscaped? What are the implications for traffic, noise, pollution and parking? Anyone who wants to know just has to look and see.

6 The electronic workplace

The world of future work

For every science fiction dream that comes true, there must be many, many good ideas which just don't actually happen in the real world. There is no magic rule to separate the predictions from the dreams. The future will be determined by an unknown combination of complex factors – market forces, government policies, natural disasters, personal perceptions and many others.

Understanding can lead to complacency. Why take a leap into the darkness of uncertainty of the future when we can survive among the remnants of the past?

It may be wonderful to read grand ideas for the future in the Sunday papers, but for most people it is back to work as usual on Monday morning, wrestling with the realities of today.

It is particularly important to realize that there is no single, easy, universal solution for the future of any business. There are better solutions and worse solutions, but there are also many alternatives.

One of the key themes of the future is diversity. Mankind has moved in fits and starts through different stages of development over the centuries. As values move away from essential conformity towards relatively unconstrained individuality, different people have different aspirations.

Without going too deeply into the philosophy, we simply do not know whether office blocks will one day become the exception rather than the rule, with almost everyone working from home or a community electronic office. Or whether superstores and shopping precincts will be displaced by the richness and diversity of armchair shopping on the Superhighway from home. Or whether travel will become a family and leisure pursuit, to meet friends and participate in sporting events, while business communication shifts to video conferencing in virtual reality rooms. Will manufacturing and agriculture concentrate into giant areas of mass production or disperse into smaller production units closer to local markets? We just don't know.

But any of these would have a dramatic long-term effect on our built environment and our working environment. What buildings will we need in the future? What sort of transport systems? What utilities and support services?

Where will we work, and how will we work? In lots of different places and in lots of different ways, of course, just as in the 1990s. But some people will become much more dependent upon information technology. How many of us could imagine working without a telephone? Go back a few years – how many could imagine working without electricity? Go forward a few years and we will wonder how on earth we worked without continuous access to powerful electronic communications at our fingertips.

Can grand and great things be achieved without access to the wonders of information technology? Just think back before aeroplanes, telephones and electricity. Great cities were constructed around the world many centuries ago. People had water supplies and food transported to their doorsteps, and some people (but admittedly only a few) were able to live in reasonable comfort. Immense irrigation schemes existed in many parts of the world. Great cathedrals were built. Think of the engineers constructing railways across remote parts of Africa, Asia and America, with no telephones and no couriers to solve problems; everything had to be planned many months in advance and transported across the world by ship.

What really changes is not *what* we can achieve if we put our mind to it, but *how* we do things – how we organize ourselves and what we aspire to do. It is unthinkable that we would build another Egyptian pyramid through the efforts of tens of thousands of human labourers. But, although we have the machinery to build a pyramid much faster and more easily now, there is no market for building pyramids today!

Information technology is much the same. Don't just imagine that we will all be doing the same jobs that we do today faster and better in a decade's time. Most of us will be doing *different* things faster and better. Europe and the USA have seen dramatic changes in employment patterns as traditional industries decline and new industries emerge. The changes are not over yet!

Back to information basics

Getting right back down to basics, information is at the heart of almost everything that a firm does – where people are, what they are doing, what materials are needed, what customers have ordered, when things will happen etc.

In the simplest form of business, all of this information is held in someone's head. This is a straightforward information system, able to reconfigure information instantly to suit changing circumstances, to deal with unexpected problems, to see new business opportunities and to guide business strategy.

But the human brain has limited capacity. With any size of business, one person can only assimilate a limited portion of the business and technical information needed at any moment. Hence the obvious move: to put information on paper.

Putting information on paper opens up the possibility of working with greater complexity. Information can be written down and stored to await future reference, freeing human minds to do other things. It can also be used for communication, saving the effort of explaining things to each other through conversation. There is then no real limit to how much information can be handled simultaneously, as long as it can be retrieved for reference efficiently when it is needed. And that is where the problems start.

In a small office, everyone can use the same filing system in the same filing cabinet, readily accessible whenever required. But as the office becomes larger, some form of structure is normally imposed. Tradition-ally, people have been grouped, by the function they perform or the work that they do, into departments, divisions or offices. As people are grouped and classified, so is the information that they need access to. Different people become custodians of different components of the firm's 'information assets'. Unfortunately, requirements to access information tend to be rather complex, and information is not always available where and when it is needed.

Back to human adaptability to solve the problem. Mankind is continuously adapting and improvising to overcome unexpected problems – this is human nature. Just consider how people use the telephone, the fax machine, conversations and meetings. There is often a lot of information-gathering and exchange, filling in the gaps left by an incomplete paper-based information system. There is nothing wrong with this: and there are at least three clear benefits. First, it is usually not worth the effort and cost of systematizing everything – it is cheaper to let human ingenuity provide many minor missing parts of the information system on a day-to-day basis. Second is adaptability: if business circumstances and priorities change, people become used to improvising and will adapt rapidly to revised requirements for access to information. The third benefit is innovation and development. Because unplanned and unexpected conversations and communications are needed all of the time, there are numerous opportunities to develop new ideas and see new approaches to business.

When did we all start using photocopiers so much? Only a couple of decades or so ago. Before that, making a copy required either an expensive and inconvenient copying process or using carbon paper and thinking about it in advance. There was an incentive to circulate papers efficiently between people, rather than just making lots of cheap copies for distribution. It was also obvious which copy – the top copy – was the original.

Nowadays many of us are sinking under a tide of paper, as we are inundated with information – printed brochures, photocopies and copies of word-processed documents. It has just become too easy to distribute information – there is no serious cost penalty to the person distributing it. As working methods change, the need to access different combinations of information has increased, making it increasingly difficult to maintain a standard method of filing and organizing all of this paper.

Even worse, now that we have lots of copies of the same document, distributed all over the place, we have difficulty making sure that all of these copies are kept up to date. When a document changes, we need to know where all of the copies of it are, and then make sure that every one of them, in all of the filing systems in which it is held, is updated immediately. This is a lot of work, prone to errors and mistakes. When you pick up a document, are you absolutely sure that it is up to date? If it is critical to your work, is it your responsibility to check with the originator that it hasn't changed, or is it the originator's responsibility to make sure that you know when the document has been changed? In either case it diverts both people's time to make sure. Wasn't putting information on paper supposed to simplify matters rather than make them more complicated?

Information technology to the rescue?

Will the wonders of the information age solve all of our information handling problems? If we store everything as computer files in digital form, and scan all the documents, pictures and drawings that are not already computer files, in theory we can have access to them whenever we want to. Only one copy of everything is needed, and everyone will have immediate access to the latest copy. Sounds simple!

Well let's see. For the small firm, we replace that central filing cabinet with a single computer. Straightforward so far. Very soon people are queuing up to use that one computer, so we install a network. Everyone now has a computer on their desk, and can access the same central computer with all of the digital files. As long as the central computer is powerful enough and has enough storage space, everyone can see what they want whenever they want to. Many people will still print out the documents that they are interested in though, because they are used to handling information as dozens of sheets of paper spread out on a desk rather than on a single computer screen. This is not a major worry, as long as you keep throwing away the paper on the desk and replacing it with the latest version whenever anything changes, but it is a little wasteful of paper.

Who is authorized to look at which files? And who is allowed to modify which documents – who 'owns' each one? With conventional paper filing cabinets, you can lock some of the drawers and only give the key to certain people. You also have procedures for who does what, and you can sign documents with pen and ink to verify that the right person added a new document or authorized any change.

Enter the network manager. We now need a new skill in the office, someone who can establish authorizations, set up logins and passwords, and turn working methods and processes into a computerized form. But once methods are programmed and established, it takes time and effort to change them, and this can become a constraint upon improvement. Before the computer came along, working method changes could be discussed and agreed between all concerned and then take immediate effect in the office. Now information is more immediately accessible, but changes take time, effort and cost. As the saying goes, in the playground what you gain on the swings you may lose on the roundabouts.

Now extrapolate the problems to organizational level – lots of departments and offices, spread over different towns, regions and countries. How can you keep everyone in step with each other without setting down definitive standards which can then become an impenetrable barrier to change, improvement and business development? How can you organize access and authorization across a diverse and complex modern business?

The early cost benefits of centralizing and controlling information have now been largely superseded by the flexibility and efficiency of interconnected, localized, distributed systems. Centralizing information usually creates an ownership problem anyway. If information storage and update are remote from the people defining the data, it is subjectively difficult for them to retain pride in the quality of the data.

It becomes the computer unit's data, rather than their data, and there is a danger of them feeling like technicians just collecting the data for someone else, rather than being the owners and distributors of important information. As a rule, it makes sense to keep the original copy of any data as close to the people who own it as possible.

Keeping information up to date

This raises the key question: where is the original copy of any particular piece of data? Is it the original paper forms or calculations from which the data was derived, or is the most important definitive copy really the copy on the computer? Which would you believe if they are different? If you have any doubt about the electronic version, then it is no better than another photocopy!

Lack of confidence in electronic information is a serious problem to be overcome when introducing any computerized system. Early computer systems concentrated far too heavily upon the initial conversion problem of translating paper information into computerized digital information, without seriously addressing the problem of keeping the electronic data up to date. Success in keeping information up to date on a computer system is critical to the sustainability of the system and its acceptance by the people who use it. The system users must come to believe that the information on the computer is actually better and more up to date than any equivalent information held on paper.

An interesting case study is the large scale (1:1250 and 1:2500) mapping of the UK by the Ordnance Survey (Figure 6.1). After initially, many years ago, allowing the paper and computerized versions to get out of synchronization for a time, the Ordnance Survey then used new technology not only to overcome this update problem, but then to keep their digital data even more up to date than was previously possible with traditional methods.

At first, the problem of converting the Ordnance Survey's very detailed maps from accurately hand-drawn originals on special film into digital form on a computer occupied many minds. The structure of the data went through various revisions, and the conversion programme to complete the full coverage of the UK stretched over more than a decade, even with considerable resources working full time.

One day, a number of years ago, I realized that the mapping for the area of one my firm's projects had already been digitized, and I immediately thought that we could do the early stages of the design process, which traditionally involved hand drawing on maps, on the computer instead. I was slightly dismayed to discover that, although the

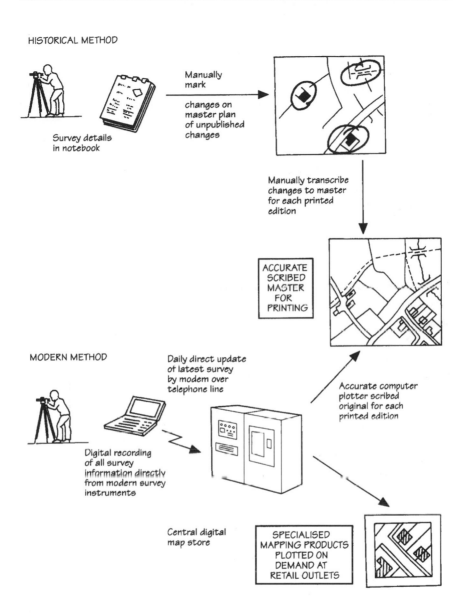

HISTORICAL METHOD

Survey details
in notebook

Manually
mark

changes on
master plan
of unpublished
changes

Manually transcribe
changes to master
for each printed
edition

ACCURATE
SCRIBED
MASTER
FOR
PRINTING

MODERN METHOD

Daily direct update
of latest survey
by modem over
telephone line

Accurate computer
plotter scribed
original for each
printed edition

Digital recording
of all survey
information directly
from modern survey
instruments

Central digital
map store

SPECIALISED
MAPPING PRODUCTS
PLOTTED ON
DEMAND AT
RETAIL OUTLETS

Figure 6.1. Ordnance Survey – keeping maps up to date.

area had been digitized a few years before, the computerized maps were already out of date, and the most recent mapping, essential for civil engineering design, was actually on an unpublished plan which a surveyor had manually updated for future input to the computer.

But this story has a happy ending. New technology in surveying instruments resulted in significant changes in surveying methods. Rather than the traditional surveying method of taking measurements with instruments, making notes in a notebook, and then transcribing this onto a plan at the end of a day's surveying, it became commonplace to record all of the details of a day's surveying directly from the surveying instruments in digital form. The Ordnance Survey saw the opportunity and changed its method of updating. At the end of the day's survey, all of the data is now downloaded from the survey instrument, from anywhere in the country, over a telephone line directly to the central computer mapping database. In one change of working procedure, all of the hand drawing stages were eliminated and the electronic mapping database truly became the definitive and most up-to-date version of the data.

Exactness, approximation and illusion

Computers are 'digital'. This means that they store everything in terms of exact digital numbers, rather than approximate 'analogue' quantities.

To understand this, consider two different ways of delivering a truckload of sand to a construction site. It could be delivered in sacks, each sack filled to exactly the same weight. The delivery is then in terms of an exact number of sacks – it cannot contain any part sacks. It is easy for the supplier loading the truck to measure exactly how much has been sent (by counting the sacks), and for the foreman receiving it to check how much has been delivered (by doing the same). But it does involve extra work filling and emptying the sacks. This is the digital world: everything is exact and clearly defined. The quantity delivered is either exactly right or wrong.

The alternative is just to load a heap of sand onto the back of the truck. The supplier cannot be exactly sure how much has been provided, but it saves the effort of putting the sand into bags. The foreman on the site is also not exactly sure how much he has received, but from experience it looks about right, and there is then no need to empty all those sacks when it is used. This is the approximate analogue world, where nothing is quite so exact – easier to work with, but prone to misunderstandings and inaccuracies and mistakes. The quantity delivered may be roughly right or noticeably wrong, or rather uncertain between the two.

Almost everything done by computers, and all of the latest forms of communications technology are digital. Computers are usually associated with clean, bright, clear new solutions to problems which traditionally come from an approximate, variable and uncertain world. The interfaces to older computer programs were almost clinically precise in the information that they requested and displayed, giving an impression of solid, accurate and dependable results in anything coming from the computer.

Would you be happy working from the approximate scribblings, corrections and sketches made by the site engineer on the 'as-built' drawings of a building – the record of what really happened rather than what was supposed to have happened? Or would you prefer the clear, clean, easy-to-read computer-plotted version, where a junior technician has done his or her best to convert this approximate information into an accurate computerized drawing? All of the evidence of uncertainty has gone from this latter version – it looks accurate, but many approximations and errors may have been made during the conversion. Beware the problems which may be hiding behind the clean-cut facade of the computer.

Clutter on the computer

The apparent clarity of modern computer interfaces can also disguise another problem. At first, with any program, it is easiest to keep all of the documents or files that you create in one place. Just like starting a new job, for the first couple of days, all of the papers that you are working with can be spread out around you on the desk. The limited amount of information can all stay visible all of the time. But soon it becomes necessary to file all of the papers away, and if a filing system doesn't exist it has to be created.

Exactly the same tends to happen with a computer. A new user starts learning how to use it and just puts files created by the software into the default directory. A 'directory' on a computer disk is like a particular filing cabinet. When the number of files in the default directory becomes large, the user creates alternative directories, or subdirectories, and moves files between them. A disk can have any number of directories, any directory can contain any number of subdirectories, subdirectories can have subdirectories of their own, and so on.

The problem is that, just like paper filing systems, there are many different ways of organizing computer filing systems. Directories and files can be organized by date, by project, by computer user, by client, by subject, by department, by office, by country, or by any other logical subdivision. Unfortunately, as working methods and responsibilities change in modern working environments, which filing system to use is by no means obvious. As technology gets ahead of established working practice, the filing system is often set up by the person who happens to be using the computer, rather than as the result of a strategic appraisal of future information retrieval requirements to enhance the business.

It can be even worse than it at first looks. The computer user setting up the filing system is often a relatively junior member of staff, employed for his or her computer skills, with little experience of the full breadth of the business and no involvement in future strategy. At the other extreme, senior managers may have no idea of the potential benefits of properly organized information, thinking that because they cannot program a computer they cannot understand how it organizes information, and are happy to delegate the task without any significant consideration.

Different people may set up different systems and different departments may organize information in different ways. They may each look from a localized short-term perspective, trying to replicate their existing paper systems, without any serious thought about future information access needs by others. In the worst situation they may deliberately try to localize their information in a misguided attempt to protect their own importance. Even when proper systems analysts do get involved, they may only be able to sample opinions from junior staff and middle managers. Unless the strategic senior management get involved, information storage structures will not be planned for the future of the organization, and may well constrain development in the future.

And all this is invisible to the eyes of senior management, hidden from view on computer disks. If corporate headquarters were redecorated and some of the rooms and corridors were painted different, uncoordinated, clashing colours, senior management would notice and do something about it. If papers and files were piled high on everybody's desks and the filing cabinets were empty, senior managers might notice. But if the information critical to a firm's future is distributed in a dispersed and uncoordinated fashion across all sorts of different computers and disks, will senior managers notice? The financial management information system is probably well organised – but what about the lifeblood of a firm: the letters, reports, documents, pictures and drawings upon which the business is actually based.

Without realizing it, it is very easy to leave paper documents behind and to start depending upon computer-based information. When you look for a document, do you look through the shelves for the last printed version, or do you delve around in computer directories trying to remember where you filed the last version? Well, this is one step forward: the definitive version is now on the computer rather than on paper. But unless we are careful, it's one step backwards as well. At least on paper we could see all the time what was on the shelves and in the filing cabinets. We could rearrange documents when we needed to, and see when a document was missing. Without a properly thought out system of organizing information, a computer can become a hidden cupboard cluttered with disorganized and unstructured information, which no-one can see.

The power of indirection

A true information systems professional has the education and experience to avoid many of the pitfalls awaiting the unwary computer system implementor. At an everyday level, it is rather like the difference between servicing your car yourself and getting a properly trained mechanic to do it. You can follow the manual, but the mechanic is trained to use every tool correctly, work rapidly and efficiently and look out for unexpected faults, and has rapid access to the correct spare parts. At a more advanced level, systems analysts are the equivalent of car designers, designing systems to be easy to use, and efficient and straightforward to maintain.

Systems analysts understand the principles behind the information systems that you need, and can offer new perspectives and ideas. One particular principle which was originally very much in the realm of the systems analyst, is now becoming much more of an everyday tool. The principle is that of 'indirection'.

The idea of indirection is really quite simple. It is very similar to forwarding a telephone call from one telephone extension to another.

Any file, document, data, computer or peripheral on the computer system has a real physical location somewhere, and an address at that location. The same physical address can also be reached through any number of points of indirection. Each of these looks like the file (or whatever) that you want to look at, but is actually just a forwarding address that points to where it really is.

For instance, I might be working for a firm where everyone in my office keeps their electronic diary in the same disk directory in our office, so that we can all check with each others' diaries easily to organize meetings. Then, as a result of company restructuring, my duties change and I find that my skills are required by three different offices in the new organizational structure. Where do I keep my diary? There are now three different office diary directories requiring my diary, one in each of the three offices.

The answer is simple: I leave my diary where it is. In the other two offices (assuming that they are interconnected by a computer network) I just place a pointer in the directory where my diary should be, pointing to where the diary actually is. It looks in each office as though my diary is local, but in the other two offices it actually accesses the diary in my original office.

This is indirection in action. Things look to be in one place, but are actually really in another. Several different locations can all point to the same file or item of data.

As people become more mobile, organizations rearrange themselves more often, and different groups and offices want to integrate their activities more closely, this principle offers the means to keep information fixed in one place but then to access it from many different places. Alternatively information can be moved, leaving behind an indirection pointer to its new location.

Let's take a walk back to look at our electronic filing problem again. The problem was whether we structure our information directories and subdirectories by people, by project, by office or by some other criterion. With indirection, we can file it by all of them at once! We store the actual information in a single convenient location. Then we create a set of pointers to this information organized by people, another set of indirection pointers organized by project, a third set organized by office, and so on. Whichever of these you look through, it seems as though the data has been organized just the way you want it!

There is, of course a maintenance problem to keep all of these pointers up to date! But with a little science and understanding, access to information can become a powerful business advantage, rather than a legacy millstone.

The Intranet

An interesting development in office systems is the concept of an 'Intranet'. The principle is very simple: use all of the latest technology designed for the Internet, including World-Wide Web style hypermedia interfaces – but apply it on the internal computer network inside the office, completely isolated from the outside world of the real Internet. Hence the very latest web-browser and multimedia interfaces can be used to develop new corporate information systems and as a 'front end' to existing corporate databases.

The hypertext interface used in Intranet Web documents is itself a form of indirection. Each page of information contains highlighted blocks of text, each of which points to information which might be stored on any computer on the office network.

Going paperless

There has been much speculation and debate about the possibility of operating in completely paperless offices. Will it really one day be possible to put every piece of information that we use in our work into electronic form and to give up using paper altogether? Could we abandon the need to write and sketch using pens and pencils, and just write and draw on computer screens instead? Just think of your average working day: what would be possible electronically and what would not?

There is little doubt that most of us could use much less paper than we do today. Most of our messages, letters and documents could certainly be stored and displayed electronically. In some firms they already are.

But somehow, however hard we may try to do everything on the computer, most of us will still carry a pen in our pocket to note down some bit of information that doesn't fit the established system, or to sketch a diagram to explain something to someone, or just to give a letter that personal touch by actually signing it with a pen. Is there actually a danger of losing those writing and drawing skills that we have spent so many years learning?

Hand-prepared documents convey personal style. Years ago, when many personal curricula vitae (CVs) were handwritten, or at least set out in slightly individual styles, the style conveyed a lot more information than just the words. Pressure to win jobs has led to much more standardized, mechanical, word-processed CVs. This has its benefits and its problems. It is easier to make direct comparisons between candidates for a job when similar information is provided in all CVs, but a more natural candidate who is not so well versed in the intricacies expected of modern CV presentation might not even get to interview. The technology can mask some aspects of human communication.

Another example of the changes brought about by going 'paperless' is illustrated from my own experience of following the implementation of computer-aided drafting (CAD) over the past 20 years. Preparing engineering drawings is a skilled task, and 20 years ago it took many years of experience to learn all of the skills needed to produce a set of ink on tracing paper drawings which showed in precise detail every aspect of the construction of a building or construction project. Important skills included clear writing and stencilling, accurate drawing construction, a thorough understanding of all of the types of notation used on the drawings, and a good three-dimensional appreciation of the objects being drawn.

Early attempts at introducing computer-aided drafting tended to concentrate on reducing the years of learning needed to acquire skills like stencilling. Using a computer and a plotter, a trainee straight from school could produce perfectly stencilled drawings. Where part of a building was repeated over many floors, it became easy to copy details from one drawing to another using the computer. And there was one apparent important advantage: when major changes or revisions occurred, the drawing could be modified and replotted without spending hours scratching or rubbing Indian ink off large areas of tracing paper and then trying to redraw on the inferior surface left behind.

What I began to notice though, after a few years, was that other skills which were not evident at first were also being eroded and lost. Because it is time-consuming and difficult to rub out and redraw extensive areas of a drawing, an experienced senior draftsman would plan the whole drawing process very carefully right from the start, trying to eliminate or minimize changes through experience and consultation with the designers. A good draftsman would also minimize the number of drawings and details, so that there were fewer opportunities for changes. Because the draftsman had spent years learning to think in three dimensions, while also learning how to draw well, he or she would also often see inadequacies in the designs and consult the designers about technical improvements as well. It was in their interest, and part of their professional skill, to find and eliminate any problems sooner rather than later.

For the new generation of computer detailers, things are slightly different. A badly set out drawing or an incorrect detail can easily be modified and replotted later. It doesn't take nearly as long to learn drawing skills, so there is not the same experience to foresee problems. It is easy to copy and create extra drawings, so there is not the same pressure to minimize manual effort.

With understanding, insight and imagination, and especially a good understanding of skill development and education, the benefits of the introduction of new technology usually far outweigh the problems. But very few people ever see the whole picture of what is changing. Always be prepared to think more widely and deeply than the obvious.

A little story about management understanding of using new technology, which I have now heard several times, always worries me. Some people, presented with an e-mail package, delve around inside the software and find the facility to make up address lists and circulate a single message to several people at once. My concern is when I hear a senior manager say how easily he circulates messages to a hundred or more employees at the touch of a button from his own computer and boasts about how much time he saved. But every one of those expensive people then had to take the time to read those messages. It can become too easy to send a message, while the cost of people's time to read it is completely unseen by the sender. The time and effort needed to prepare and send a paper memo may appear wasteful, but it is also a control mechanism which should restrict such circulation to important or relevant information. Again, education and understanding must accompany new technology.

The paperless office

Let us take a leap into the future now. Imagine that we work out how to change our ways of working to eliminate the need for writing, printing and drawing by hand. We have educated the entire workforce to understand what is happening and how to take a positive attitude to the change in order to have the will to make it work. We have changed the culture of our working practices. What does our paperless office look like?

We will, for the most part, need to be indoors, to eliminate the effects of the climate: rain, cold, heat, wind, humidity and so on. Will we all be in neat rows of identical desks, with a computer in front of each of us, like the old typing pools? Unlikely – the typing pools were all about mass production of typed documents, a repetitive mechanical production task, at maximum efficiency. Computers and automation will now take care of most repetitive tasks, so human effort will probably concentrate upon the less predictable and more creative tasks. Hence the working environment must be flexible and adaptable, with people probably doing different tasks on different days.

Just as the office needs an infrastructure of ventilation, heating and light, it now needs an infrastructure for information. Somewhere, mostly hidden from view, information is flowing all around through optical fibres and copper wires. There are reservoirs of information, local and distant, like water tanks and reservoirs in the domestic water supply system. Wherever anyone is working, they need to tap in to this nervous system of information and communicate with it.

There will have to be some sort of interaction interface between the human and the machine: a screen to see pictures. This may be larger than the computer screens of the 1990s, which were constrained by the technology available to manufacture them at a reasonable cost and the speed of processors to drive them. It might be flat or it might be curved; it might be horizontal like the papers on a desk, angled like a drawing board or vertical like a television. It is an information surface. It may even give a three-dimensional view, rather than just a flat surface, one day. The machine may be able to see the worker, through a two- or three-dimensional television camera, to transmit an image to other human workers. There will be a need for two-way communication by sound, both with other workers in video conversations and with the computer through voice recognition and speech synthesis. Will there be a keyboard? There must be a method of interacting through movement of the hands, such as a mouse or a pen-like stylus, or motion detectors on the fingers. Words may be typed at a keyboard, or recognized as they are spoken, rather like dictating to a secretary.

The working unit arranged around one paperless worker must interact effortlessly with many other similar working units. These may be in an area like an open plan office, if distractions of sound and vision are not too great. How much will a workplace be a social place, where you work surrounded by other people and walk around to take coffee breaks and chat to each other? How much will all working interaction between people come through the technology of the computers and cables?

There will surely still be meeting rooms and places for direct face-to-face discussion to solve problems, plan and brainstorm new ideas, and to learn from and educate others. All of these will have access to the same information infrastructure though – whenever information is needed it must be retrieved and displayed wherever the work is taking place, with the ability to add new thoughts and facts.

The computers will be hidden from view. Like the electricity cabling and the air-conditioning plant in an office, the only parts that are really of interest will be the interaction interfaces, the parts of today's computers which you see, hear, talk to and touch. Just as the piping and wiring of our homes and offices has all vanished behind the walls, ceilings and floors that we see, leaving just the switches and taps that we interact with, the technology will vanish into the fabric of our buildings.

Isn't this all rather far-fetched? Nobody really knows. But these are the potential consequences of the changes taking place today. There will be many variations, just as today there are many different makes and models of cars, many different types of house, many different forms of factory. But all cars go from A to B with a fairly standard set of controls, along similar roads. All homes have somewhere to live, somewhere to sleep and somewhere to prepare food. All offices are likely to have extensive access to coordinated and integrated electronic information support systems.

Locational independence

As the information infrastructure becomes more extensive and continuous, joining villages, towns, cities, countries and continents ever more effortlessly, how important will anyone's physical location be? Unless there is a specific reason why you need to meet face to face – to argue, negotiate, mediate, encourage or convince – does it really matter where someone actually is?

If you communicate through the computer, then it makes little difference whether someone is ten metres or a thousand kilometres away. Distance used to mean cost, but that is changing all the time. Just remember the Internet, where today's e-mail messages can travel any distance for the same flat rate cost. In the late-1990s the Internet is straining to cope with demand through an exponentially dramatic increase in its use. But a few years before, the extent and complexity of the Internet were unimaginable to most people. The cost of travel is significant for most businesses, and as travel costs rise and communication costs fall, there must come a point where complex electronic communication for ordinary, everyday work becomes more economic than travel for many aspects of day-to-day tasks.

Travel patterns can also be rearranged to benefit from this new locational independence. If the new office electronic workstation becomes more like a car, with standard controls and similar behaviour at any workstation, it should become possible to walk into any office (of the same company at least), sit down at a desk, issue the right authorizations and continue working from where you left off yesterday, even though you are in a different town, or maybe even a different country. In this scenario, desks or working positions (or whatever they are called), will need to be booked every day in the intended working location, much like booking a hire car or a seat on an aeroplane.

The great benefit of such locational independence is that someone's physical location can be organized as he or she wishes to be present at meetings, presentations, professional discussion groups, weekend family occasions or sporting events in a variety of different places. It can be possible to carry out a normal day's work from one of a number of different working locations.

This same freedom may not, of course apply to factory workers, agricultural workers or others for whom a particular physical location is inextricably connected with their work, but there will be increased freedom of choice for individuals who want such freedom. Even in these areas of work, automation and consistent working methods could provide opportunities for job sharing and mobility of working location, if people want this to happen.

Not everybody necessarily wants to live in an unreal virtual world of technology. There will always be many people who quite sensibly prefer a more solid and consistent world around them each day. Stability and reality will always be particularly important in family environments, with young children learning what is real and what isn't before translating their minds into a changing, moving and unreal world of new technology.

Teleworking

The question then arises: why have an office anyway? Why not just work from home? A remarkable number of people have already seen this logic and have adapted their work to spend a significant proportion of their time working from home (Figure 6.2).

Where work is computer-based and mainly on an individual basis, the transition to working at home with a link to the office via a telephone, or 'teleworking', is quite straightforward. Writing, reviewing, processing – there are all sorts of work which can quite easily be done from home. Many firms have already accepted this as normal practice for parts of their workforce, providing equipment and organizing work accordingly. Other individuals have set up facilities for themselves at home and work freelance or on a contract basis for one or more organizations. The Internet provides cheap, ready access to data communication and transfer facilities from home, if a firm does not prefer a more secure and private form of data link.

There are a variety of motives for wanting to work from home. Being with one's family is high on many people's priorities, especially if they have spent long hours away from their home and family earlier in their career. Some will like to be close to particular social or leisure activities, without a long distance to travel between work and home. It may be that the actual environment of the home, peaceful in the countryside, is more conducive to work than a bustling office in a hectic city. Working from home is a very individual decision, and for many people it will be more suitable at certain periods of their career than at others.

There is a downside to working from home; the lack of business interaction with others. The complexities of the office environment provide many planned and unplanned meetings with different people. These meetings are continually used to gather information, plan career progress, make others aware of what you are doing and to prevent an individual from becoming trapped in too localized or limited a view of the outside world.

Other working environments between the pure office and the dedicated home teleworker scenarios are also evolving, for instance, the telecottage. This is more of a community office resource, near to home. It is quite logical that some resources, which it may not be economical for every individual to provide at home, become economic-

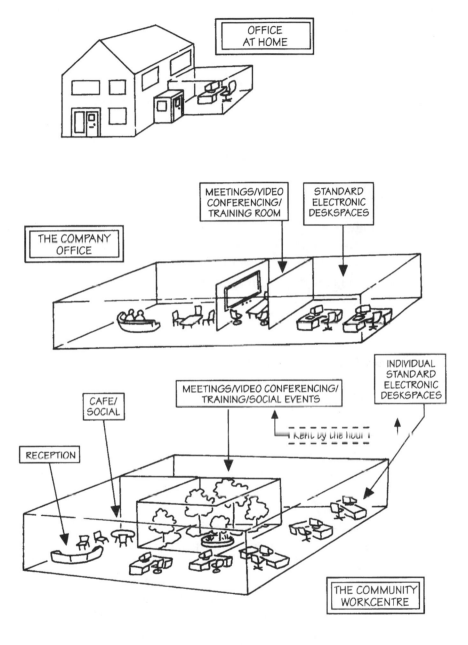

OFFICE
AT HOME

MEETINGS/VIDEO
CONFERENCING/
TRAINING ROOM

STANDARD
ELECTRONIC
DESKSPACES

THE COMPANY
OFFICE

INDIVIDUAL
STANDARD
ELECTRONIC
DESKSPACES

CAFE/
SOCIAL

MEETINGS/VIDEO CONFERENCING/
TRAINING/SOCIAL EVENTS

Rent by the hour

RECEPTION

THE COMMUNITY
WORKCENTRE

Figure 6.2. Possible workspaces of the future.

ally viable when shared among a number of people in a community. Secretarial services, telephone answering, high-speed data links or specialized information communication equipment, used only part time by each individual, can be economically rented from a local centre in the community.

For some people, a telecottage environment can provide an alternative to working from home. Office space with full computer facilities can be rented by the hour or by the day, and market demand will determine the sophistication of the service offered and its cost. The same principle applies whether you live in a small village in the countryside or a street in a large city – if people would like a community working centre close to home it could be provided, and as a commercial business for the person providing it.

This community resource also provides the potential for much more social interaction than just working at home alone. Working colleagues don't have to be working for the same firm – they might just be members of the same community. With meeting rooms in the local centre, some meetings could be held near someone's home, rather than always at head office.

International implications

Locational independence also has other implications. It becomes possible to make use of the skills of someone at the other end of the country or on the other side of the world – someone with specialist skills or contacts who would not normally be available to you if travel and accommodation costs to move around the world were required. With cheap and effective communications, you can employ such specialists for just a few hours, and they in turn can live wherever they wish and market their skills throughout the world.

Alternatively, it becomes possible to distribute a business around the world, to position each process or task in the location where it can be achieved cheapest and best. For instance, you might design a product in Europe, manufacture it on the Asia–Pacific Rim, market it from the USA and provide service backup from Africa – unlikely, but possible. With low-cost communications, the cost barriers preventing smaller firms from considering such strategies are rapidly evaporating. This type of thinking may require a new breed of entrepreneur to limit the risks and see the opportunities, but it is certainly becoming more feasible. Many larger manufacturing businesses have been redistributing their activities around the world for some years, and there is little reason why the same will not occur in almost any industry or profession where someone can separate out components which might be done in a remote location.

Another advantage, or disadvantage, of international working, is the time difference between different parts of the world. If real-time simultaneous discussions are essential, the time difference is a problem. But for others it means that almost 24-hour working is possible, with different shifts of workers working on different continents, moving information between them as the shift changes. This could be much more trouble than it is worth, but for some professions and industries with traditions of short deadlines and high levels of production, this might be a suitable business strategy.

Office space and overheads

Why should any of these dreams come true? There will always be a few innovators and special cases, but what will become normal practice?

The key business driver into the late 1990s is money. Reducing costs and increasing profits are critical health factors for a modern business. Just consider the financial implications of some of the ideas presented above. A major overhead in many businesses is the cost of providing office space. But how much of this office space is well utilized? Someone's office space still costs money if they are out of the office at a meeting – unless you reverse the situation, and they book space when they are in the office. If their working information is all electronic, they can easily work at different desks on different days. This applies equally to all levels of staff, especially senior management staff. When people are working from home, once again they do not need any space at the office that day. It may be possible to reduce the office space needed by half, or even more.

Then again, does a business really need a very expensive office block in the centre of town? A smaller modern unit in an industrial area is just as serviceable for electronic desks, and probably has fewer car-parking problems. Extra, standard, electronic office space could also be rented, short-term, when demand is high, and released when workload is low.

In the UK, British Telecom significantly reduced its requirement for expensive offices in the middle of London by providing more adaptable, bookable, office space at locations around the edge of London and giving staff greater mobility and freedom in their choice of working locations. The larger computer firms have been operating electronic locational independence for many of their staff for years. Now the same opportunity is gradually becoming available to a much wider cross-section of the commercial world.

Office space at the community centre

As the design of the community centre in our fictional market town progresses, the possibility of including office space in the centre is considered more carefully. What sort of office space could be provided and how much is needed?

First of all, are any businesses likely to want permanent office accommodation, which could provide steady income from rents? The site is well located, with good access to main roads, and there is a shortage of such office space locally. Looking at the population details, there is a good cross-section of skills available in the town for any business that decides to set up or move there.

Next, what about flexible office space to rent on a short-term basis? A little consultation in the community reveals that quite a number of people are commuting long distances, while their work is fully electronic and they would prefer to work much closer to home. Flexible office space would also suit the small local businesses likely to rent permanent office space, since they can then very easily expand their offices for short periods during workload peaks.

The real problem is to decide how much of which type of office accommodation is really needed. What will be the requirement for meeting rooms, video conferencing and other facilities? Could meeting rooms have other community uses outside working hours? The design team are now in an intensive phase of consultation and discussion, trying to minimize the risks for the financier while maximizing the opportunities for the community.

7

From processing to integration

Integrating what?

What is integration anyway? A concept, of course, so it means different things to different people!

The general and widespread understanding is that integration means linking separate things together into a cohesive and coherent entity. It is more than just attaching things together – it means creating something new from the different parts.

Thinking a little more deeply, all of the modern talk about integration seems rather ironic. After all, ever since Henry Ford's first production line to produce cars, and with roots that go right back to the start of the industrial revolution, managers of business have been constantly trying to break every aspect of manufacturing and production businesses down into their component, discrete, parts. By separating a business into its components, it then becomes much easier to study, refine, improve and control each of these components in isolation.

Through this methodology, dramatic improvements were achieved in the efficiency of manufacturing many products. These in turn brought down the manufacturing costs of many of the products in our homes, offices and daily lives to levels where everyone can afford them. This was quite a success story through the 1950s and 1960s, why are things different now?

The trouble is that a business divided into rigid components or departments can become both cumbersome to operate and difficult to change. All of the components have to communicate with each other. Procedures are set up where documentation and paperwork must be transferred between different cells of the organization. Each cell can become inward-looking and remote from those around it.

This formalized communication system might make day-to-day operations much easier, and feel secure and predictable for those operating inside it, but it can also create immense inertia against change.

When the world changes, such an organization, which may already be becoming uncompetitive against new competitors with new ideas, may not be able to change fast enough to stay in business. Innovation may be possible at a localized level, but it is at grander levels that real step increases in competitive advantage occur.

Just look at the motor car. Over a few years, nearly all new car designs changed from driving the rear wheels through the back axle to front-wheel drive. The original rear-wheel drive was very logical from a production point of view, keeping the gears and shafts which drive the rear wheels well away from the complexities of the front of the car. The gearbox or the drive train could be enhanced and modified to improve performance and reduce production costs without having to worry about fitting around the requirements of the steering and the engine. A separate design unit could deal with each component. But the market, the public, wanted front-wheel drive, with the associated improvements in road handling.

The engine, the gearbox, the clutch and the steering all had to be *integrated* into an interconnected and interdependent unit. Each had to be designed around the others. If any of these components changes now, it must be done in coordination with associated changes to the others to suit. An even more involved problem is that if every component is being simultaneously improved for the next new model of the car, the designers must all keep each other informed of planned changes; the communication is a two-way interaction.

Computerized constraints upon our imagination

This separation into components and the resulting constraint upon progress may manifest itself in many other ways than just in organizations. Our methods of working and thinking have also been broken into components, just to bring our working activities within human comprehension. In many ways this process of simplifying out complexity has also been transferred into the computer programs that we use in our work every day.

One example that I would immediately draw any engineer's attention to is the simplifications made in structural analysis. When calculations were made by hand, every problem needed to be simplified to limit the extent of the calculations required to determine the right sizes of the columns, beams, floors and walls which make up a building. So beams and columns were reduced to just lines, connected together at points, or nodes. This made the calculation and estimation of the forces in all of the beams and columns in whole buildings quite straightforward, even by hand. When the computer came along more sophisticated methods were developed, but in most cases simplification was still carried out between the real solid shapes of the beams and columns and the computer model, according to prescribed methods.

These computerized method limitations were brought clearly to my attention in the late 1980s, while visiting a local firm of consulting engineers in Uganda in the middle of Africa. After several years of civil war, there had not been any opportunity to invest in new computer technology. The local engineers were therefore still working with the hand analysis methods that I had left behind several years before as computerization took a firm hold in the design office. I had come to install a personal computer complete with contemporary structural design software. I suggested that we should try out the computer software by re-analysing some of the designs currently on their drawing boards.

And there my problems began. The software could only analyse a certain maximum number of beams and columns, or steel members. The first design was for a cantilever roof over a sports stadium. It had more members than the analysis software could handle. We did manage to handle it in two parts, and calculate results. Initially I made a mistake in the mathematical conversion of the real design into the computer, which, although obvious when checked, meant that I had to run this rather artificial two-part analysis a second time. In comparison, the local graphical solution was only limited by the scale it was drawn to and the size of the sheet of paper on the drawing board, and it got the correct answer first time.

Okay, that was a little ambitious. I thought that I might have more success when designing a concrete office block with another standard software package. Oh dear! When I saw the drawing I knew that I was going to have a problem. The software assumed that any building would be formed from a regular rectangular framework of beams and columns, replicated side by side to form a three-dimensional grid. Without such in-built constraints, the local engineers had designed a multi-storey semicircular building. Since they fully understood design methods from first principles, and were not constrained by a predefined computerized calculation format, it was easy for them to set out a design calculation specially tailored to this design situation. The software I had brought assumed that all of the columns were continuous down to the foundations in the ground. Without preconceived constraints like this, the local engineers had arranged to remove one of the columns below ground level to make an easier entrance to drive into the underground car park. We adapted the computer analysis to approximate this situation, but it was rather a contrived solution.

All right: surely road design follows fairly standard methods, and the road alignment software should work? We took out a set of drawings for a road currently under construction and attempted to check the setting out with the computer. The first problem was fundamental. In Europe, accurate existing land surveys make it straightforward to work in terms of Cartesian map grid coordinates, identifying the exact location of any point by using surveying instruments to measure its exact distance east and north of a nearby point, for which the coordinates are already known from previous surveys. This is not so easy in the middle of Africa. We drove for several hours to see were the road started, where we found a peg hammered into the ground where the new road diverged from an existing road. There were no coordinates. The alignment was set out by pegs in the ground and the distances and angles between them, without any need to calculate coordinates. We had to create a coordinate system so that the software could work.

My whole visit to Africa on that occasion was an education in understanding that newer was not necessarily better, and how new technology was constraining our capabilities rather that creating new opportunities. More recent software does not suffer the same restrictions, but every step forward brings unexpected and unforeseen constraints. We must also allow for human ingenuity to solve unexpected problems, rather than always trying to automate out human intervention.

Back to common sense and basics

A few more lessons from the same trip. One day the 'uninterruptible power supply', designed to protect the computer from voltage fluctuations and power cuts, failed. The computer was out of action. If I had broken my pencil while working at the drawing board, I could simply have used another one. But without a computer I could do nothing. Lesson one: dependence. Work out what you are dependent upon and have in place a plan of action of what to do if it does go wrong.

We searched everywhere to find someone who could repair this vital unit. Of course, I did not have a circuit diagram with me. Eventually, we found a couple of electronics technicians who thought they could repair it. After quite a few hours, I became impatient and went to see how they were getting on. I was trying to hurry them up. One of them pointed to a row of metal units on a shelf. Those were the power supplies that they couldn't repair. They were all fancy modern units which required special parts that they could not obtain locally. The unit I had brought for repair was more basic, and they were hopeful that they had the parts that had failed. But some parts they did not have, and one mistake could cause damage that they could not repair. After all, they were working without any circuit diagram or instructions! Lesson two: patience.

Then I became interested in why the repair was taking so long. Their workbench had virtually none of the electronic gadgetry normally found in a repair shop. They showed me what they were doing. They suspected a faulty transistor, and there were quite a number of them on the circuit board. So they were unsoldering each transistor and removing it to test it. They did not have a proper transistor tester, so they used two old test meters, connecting one across the transistor and then applying a small current with the other to see if the transistor responded – right back to the basic principles I learned in my physics lessons at school, but I would never have thought of doing it. Lesson three: human ingenuity. Never underestimate people's ability to solve complex problems by novel techniques. Needless to say, they found several faulty transistors and successfully repaired the unit. The lack of a circuit diagram and the proper test equipment didn't stand in their way.

We may appear to have strayed a little from the subject matter of integration, but integration is actually all about crossing boundaries to understand other people's work and other people's points of view. To develop integrated solutions we must be prepared to cross from conventional, predetermined, predictable solutions into an unknown land of new opportunities.

Integrated electronics

The electronics, communications and computer industries have themselves played an important role in moving forward the application of integrated working. Integration has pervaded every aspect of the electronics industries, from the design and manufacture of electronic components and goods to the organization of the firms working in these industries.

At component level, integration moved through a whole series of stages. Initially, all electronic circuits were assembled from discrete components: transistors, resistors, capacitors, diodes and others. The first stage was to assemble small numbers of transistors into combined circuits to form logic gates and amplifiers. As electronic manufacturing technology improved it allowed more and more transistors to be formed inside each small integrated circuit component, or silicon 'chip'. Increased complexity required very low rates of defects in manufacture – if a chip contained a thousand transistors and just one transistor was faulty the chip was useless.

Gradually, more and more of the functions of electronic circuit boards were integrated inside each chip. The whole of the calculation circuitry for a computer has been assembled into a single 'processor' chip for many years, and these processor chips become faster and more powerful each year. It seems remarkable to think that modern memory chips contain not just thousands but many millions of discrete storage locations where individual binary digits or 'bits' of data can be stored.

In order to achieve this order of complexity of component integration, the whole design process for new chips has had to be integrated itself. The designer, using computer design tools, must be able to send the details of the design directly through to the production facility for electronic assimilation into the manufacturing process. As manufacturing tolerances and methods are pushed to new limits with each new chip, integration between the design and production departments is essential to avoid very expensive mistakes.

In the electronic products industry, anything which can be integrated, and which it makes commercial sense to integrate, either has been or soon will be integrated. If it makes sense to integrate an Internet terminal with cable television and hi-fi stereo, someone is busy organizing it. Every integration problem requires innovative thinking to carry it through.

Automating the present or preparing for the future?

As we look further into the opportunities for integration in other business sectors, we must first carefully consider exactly what we are integrating or automating. It is always much easier to look backwards than to look forwards, and it can be very difficult to separate the essential from the irrelevant, in the long term.

For instance, a business might be managed and controlled through a comprehensive management information and accounting system. Such a system would naturally reflect the basic structure of the business, and would seem to be an appropriate backbone or core around which to design future integration. This would enable the integration of existing departments, and their information and communications, with the minimum of expensive changes and associated disruption.

But is this really going to be the structure of the future? With new working methods and production technologies, will all of these departments still be needed? Will new groups or teams need to be created in the future to respond to new technical challenges, and where will they fit in? Remember the dangers of dogmatic compartmentalization discussed near the start of this chapter, constraining progress through failing to see new opportunities.

There is a serious danger of integrating, and automating, current systems without making suitable provisions for the future. In almost every walk of our current lives there are computer systems which are in some way constraining progress. These 'legacy' systems were designed to improve specific working methods without taking proper account of the ways in which the world and technology are changing.

In the next few sections I shall outline some of the pressures for changes in business practice.

Process thinking

First of all, the power of processes. In senior management circles 'business process re-engineering' has been a contemporary buzz-phrase for some time. As a business analysis and improvement technique, it has moved from initial obvious applications in manufacturing processes to trial applications in all sorts of different business sectors and government departments.

Most businesses are organized in terms of functions or departments: Design, Sales, Production, Distribution, Accounting, Personnel – it all seems quite logical. These departments must all then have systems to communicate with each other and work together. The result – administration and bureaucracy.

This administrative framework alone can cost a lot of money to operate, before any work is done or any product is sold to pay for it. The organization can become the centre of all attention, while production, sales and profits struggle the whole time to keep up with providing the money needed to keep the organization alive.

Process thinking (Figure 7.1) involves turning this whole way of thinking on its head – another concept. Instead of working forwards from the organizational structure, work backwards from the end products – the reasons why the organization exists. In process thinking, it is essential to leave behind any preconceived ideas about how an organization should work, and to start with a clean sheet of paper.

This is quite a jump in the imagination in most cases, but it can lead to some very interesting conclusions. For instance, draw a bubble on the right-hand side of a page with the name of a product in it – let's say a leisure centre. Draw a long line leading into the bubble from the left. Now draw arrows feeding into this of things that will need to happen

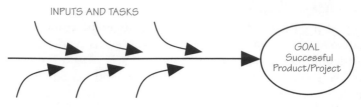

INPUTS AND TASKS

GOAL
Successful
Product/Project

* Ignore conventional departments/skill boundaries
* Eliminate unnecessary administration
* Delegate responsibility to support rapid action

Figure 7.1.   Process thinking.

first, finishing with maintenance planning and staffing and going back through construction, public acceptance, statutory approval, environmental balance, practical form for the intended purpose, functional integrity, appropriate location etc. Arrows can come from above and below the line.

To re-engineer the process, it is now necessary to reconsider how best to achieve each of these sub-processes. Think in terms of skills and people, rather than organizations and departments. Which teams of balanced skills are needed where? Rather than having a firm of architects to decide how it looks, a firm of structural engineers to make sure it stands up, and a firm of mechanical engineers to provide ventilation and services, with all the attendant formal exchanges of drawings and communications, contracts and administration, why not just put the three skilled people actually doing the work in the same room and let them get on with solving the problem?

But, I hear many experienced campaigners muttering, if you do that, who is responsible for what? Which firm gets taken to court when something goes wrong? Surely formal procedures are essential in a professional environment. They are the cornerstone of ensuring proper accountability for everything done on behalf of the client.

Take a step back and think about it. If someone successfully cut out all of the expenses involved in ensuring that contractual responsibility is properly allocated, the cost of administering and organizing formal departments, and most of all the cost of endless reworking and revisions by everyone as a result of poor and delayed formal communications, they might be able to do the job much more cheaply! With proper teamwork, where everyone loses and nobody gains if anything goes wrong, they might even make fewer mistakes!

120

This is a little far-fetched, many will say. But this is exactly what has happened in many industries, and is gradually working its way across others. Dramatic cost reductions in forward-thinking firms have left people who thought it couldn't happen without any customers.

Business process re-engineering exercises frequently identify extensive areas of unnecessary administration and wasted effort. As you go through a working day, think to yourself about every piece of paper you create, every computer form that you fill in, every meeting that you have, every person that you talk to. How did that activity directly (not indirectly) contribute to a product that a customer is paying for? If it didn't, could the business still operate without it? Is the right person doing every activity? Should someone more junior, or more senior, or with different skills be doing a particular job? Don't fool yourself – other firms may be more ruthless or less inhibited in deciding what they can do without.

And this is not about reducing quality either. The right teams and the right timing may significantly improve the opportunities to improve quality.

Then there are the opportunities for dramatic reductions in time, and associated savings. If decisions can be made directly by a team, without passing paper up, down, across and through appropriate channels of responsibility between different firms, decisions can be taken now, not next week or next month.

But you have to have the confidence to leave behind the straitjacket of established structures, and be prepared to swim in an ocean of change. And everybody has to gain this same confidence to make it work, not just the senior managers. Everybody, right down to the junior staff, has to care about everyone else and contribute positively to every situation. No mean educational challenge in many established organizations. Worryingly easy for small new firms, carefully selecting their staff to match a suitable mix of personal values.

Process re-engineering necessarily has to involve a deep and extensive re-think, often of a whole commercial sector rather than just within one firm. The result is usually a dramatic reduction in self-perpetuating administration through innovative thinking, and much faster and more flexible response to customer requirements.

An interesting example of re-engineering in action is the relationship between manufacturers and their parts suppliers. Some time ago, it became an economic necessity for some manufacturing industries, like the car industry, to subcontract the manufacture of many components to specialist firms rather than attempting to maintain the in-house capacity to make the same components.

This has generally been through a tendering process, on the assumption that tendering should produce the lowest price. But does it? Effort and expense are wasted all over the place! Suppliers waste effort putting together unsuccessful bids. Every new subcontract requires administration and paperwork. The main manufacturer has to maintain a considerable stock of components in case of disputes and delays, with associated advance payments and storage costs.

The alternative is to enter long-term agreements with specific suppliers. There are examples of suppliers directly linked to the main manufacturer's computerized production schedule. The supplier can plan parts production well in advance, invest in the best machinery with confidence in a long run of work, and with a very good working relationship may even deliver the parts on the day they are needed direct to the production line, saving double handling and storage costs. Everybody wins because unnecessary costs have been eliminated and uncertainty has been reduced. It is possible both to reduce selling prices and for everyone to make more profits if an appropriate commercial balance can be agreed and maintained. But everyone has to see the benefits in working for the common good rather than grabbing whatever they can get, if they in turn want to reap the benefits.

Among all of the process improvements in this example, a well designed computer system can simultaneously remove a lot of paperwork and administration. By providing a common work scheduling system for the manufacturer and the supplier, the computer system can ensure that the two companies don't need to ask each other for information – they both have the same common information at their fingertips.

Total quality management – self regulation and enhancement

Quality control, or quality assurance, has been a hot topic for decades. Different perceptions of quality by customers appear to have been a deciding factor in shifting patterns of purchasing and supply around the world.

If we first look back many decades, to the age of the individual craftsman, quality was always a matter of experience and customer choice. If a particular craftsman wanted to sell his services, he did so on the basis of work he had done in the past, and customers decided whether they wanted to pay the price for the longer hours it would take to produce articles with finer and more elaborate craftsmanship. The craftsman was responsible for quality; he learnt it over a number of years, and applied it as a natural and everyday part of his daily work.

The industrial revolution changed all that. The objective of a business became to use less-skilled staff to operate machines to produce much more of every article, and faster. Then, as manufacturing finally moved from mechanized mass production to assembly lines, individual workers became more and more remote from the end product of the process. Each worker concentrated on just one small part of the manufacturing process, doing progressively less skilled and more monotonous tasks. A mistake could be made by any worker, at any stage of the assembly line, but as less-skilled workers changed employment more often and just worked their hours, all sorts of defects crept in to the finished products. The car industry was a particular example, where customers really started looking for cars which would not go wrong through manufacturing defects.

Enter quality control. Checking and testing became more systematic, developing techniques designed to detect any possible defect and to prevent faulty products reaching the customer. Quality assurance procedures were written down and international standards of quality assurance were defined, and it became desirable to achieve accreditation of a firm's quality assurance system to the defined standard. To customers this became some form of guarantee that everything which could be done to ensure acceptable levels of quality in the finished product had been done.

But in many cases this became a preventative and costly measure rather than an improvement in manufacturing quality. The danger is that it catches the faulty products and sends them back for re-work or rectification, but it does not necessarily improve the manufacturing process in the first place. Re-working and correcting mistakes both cost money. The quality checking system itself involves a lot of people and paper to make it work – all additional business costs. So all of these additional costs have to be built into the price of the finished product. And then the quality assurance system itself can become a serious brake on improvement, since any change in the manufacturing process may require an expensive re-drafting of procedures and potential re-training of quality control staff.

Total Quality Management (TQM – Figure 7.2) has been billed as the potential saviour of such firms, as it provides a whole new approach to achieving quality.

The principle is really quite simple: make the individual workers fully responsible for the quality of what they do.

How could it be so simple? It is really just a change of management attitude. Instead of just telling people to get on with their work, then checking their work and rejecting and sending back anything which is

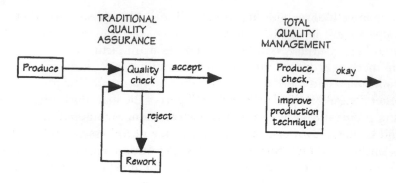

Figure 7.2. Total Quality Management (TQM).

not up to standard, the individual, or a group of people in a team, carry out a stage in a manufacturing process, and then *the same person (or people) check the quality of it.* Well, how on earth could you possibly trust people to check their own work? After all, people are naturally lazy aren't they? They will overlook the defects when it suits them. Or will they?

The first consequence is the need for training. Rather than just training quality control staff to look for defects, every worker must now be trained to be thoroughly critical of their own work and to actually understand what customers are looking for and expect. The workforce has to become more skilled. They have to develop a real attitude of pride in their own work. They become valuable employees, rather than just hired hands who can be laid off at a few days' notice. It all sounds rather expensive.

Look at the other side though. First, there is the cost saving of eliminating most of the quality control department. A few random quality checks may still be needed, but more for reassurance of the high standards being achieved than as a detailed search operation to make sure that rogue products cannot reach the market. Next come productivity improvements. Workers learn how defects occur, and can study their working methods to find ways of eliminating the defects at source by improving the ways that they work. Less time is wasted making faulty products which are thrown away or which need to be re-worked, and all efforts are directed to getting things right the first time, and producing more in the same time.

Then the real opportunities start to appear. If workers are trained and educated to understand more about what they are doing and why they are doing it, they can start to look for actual improvements in production techniques. Rather than relying on the limited resources of the research and development department (which is, in any case, remote from the work itself) to come up with ideas for improvements, mobilize the entire workforce to look continuously for ways of improving what they do – quite a change of attitude! Everybody is working to improve quality: total quality management.

Breaking down boundaries

A key theme throughout much of this chapter is breaking down barriers: organizational barriers, administrative responsibilities and technical responsibilities. Question everything. Perception barriers are some of the most difficult to break down. Everyone lives within their own beliefs and ideals, and when these are questioned the natural reaction is defensive.

Changes also inevitably make people feel insecure. Who will still have a job in the new configuration of the business? Will skills that have taken years to learn still be needed? The answers may not be reassuring. But failure to be realistic may make things much worse. Seeing the changes early gives the maximum opportunity to adjust to a new situation.

Boundaries and taboos about what can be discussed must also be broken down. Many people imagine that their value to a business lies only in their technical skills. In adapting to new working cultures, attitudes and perceptions may be at least as valuable. Accepting that changes have to occur, and working hard to achieve them to everyone's benefit, makes someone much more valuable than the most skilled person who will not accept change. In the past, highly skilled people felt secure in the belief that they could not easily be replaced. In today's business world such people are a high risk, to be contained and minimized. What happens when a key player falls ill, or decides to take another job? The most valuable person is the one that uses their skill to enhance the business, but minimizes dependence upon him- or herself by developing and training others to take their place if the need arises.

Question every line drawn between people, between skills and between responsibilities. Reconsider every box in the organization chart – why does that box exist? Could it be drawn around a different group of people? Do certain people actually sit in several different boxes at once, when you consider what they really do? Have the courage to think about it before someone else does!

Empowerment and teamworking

'Empowerment' is a buzzword of the nineties. It seems to be some sort of magic which can solve all sorts of problems. Rather like Total Quality Management, if it is such a simple idea why doesn't every business

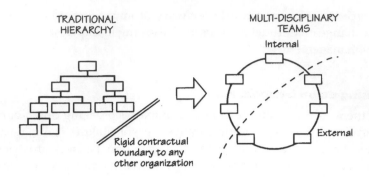

Figure 7.3. Changing organizational structures.

indulge in it? In fact, empowerment is very similar to Total Quality Management. In effect, it means giving junior staff more authority to solve problems and make improvements at source rather than always having to redirect everything to higher authority.

Have you ever been surprised when a junior member of staff in a shop agrees a refund, exchanges an item or offers a discount, without calling the manager first? It was all done with confidence and authority, but you expected to have to wait five minutes while the manager was located, then go through your explanation and wait again while the manager checked your receipt and considered the request. How could a junior member of staff be given such authority?

The answer is simple: it is good business. And more and more businesses are realizing why: you feel good about the store, will probably tell your friends, and will probably come back again to make further purchases. The manager's time is expensive. Is it really worth involving the manager and diverting him or her from other activities? But the real trick is that the young assistant usually makes a good decision – the same decision that the manager would probably have made. The assistant has not just been given authority, he or she has also been trained and educated to apply good judgement, within a reasonable understanding of the parameters involved in making the decision. The assistant has been 'empowered' to understand what he or she is doing and to take the decision on behalf of the manager. There may, of course, be a few mistakes. But the improved customer relations and savings in management time probably far outweigh the cost of a few minor mistakes. The assistant knows the boundaries of refund values within which he or she is expected to operate. These are designed to limit the risks, but the customer doesn't need to realize that. And if a mistake is made, it is a mistake in training and preparation rather than the fault of the assistant.

Take the same principle and apply it to any business. How often are junior staff waiting for decisions by senior staff? Is there any way that junior members of staff could be trained and educated to make good decisions themselves without having to wait? Would the savings in management time outweigh the apparent loss in authority? Could the business operate with fewer expensive managers and more empowered staff?

Staff at all levels below senior management can be empowered; the principle is not restricted to junior staff, it just means pushing authority further down the chain of command, but at the same time linking it to the learning and understanding needed to make good decisions.

As we chip away at the pillars of the conventional hierarchy of management command within a business, let us return to ideas of teamworking again. Empowered individuals do not need to refer upwards all the time to do their work. So when they are working in a team they can speak with authority within the bounds of their area of skill. The whole concept of a hierarchy within the team starts to break down. Who is senior and who is junior? Who has the authority to do what? Does it really matter anyway, as long as good decisions are made?

My brother pointed out to me many years ago that the manager of a team does not need to be the most senior member of the group. In high-tech projects, it is quite normal to have very senior and experienced experts who place themselves under the control of a junior project manager to get the job done.

Teamworking can become the ultimate flat, flexible working structure, assembling the skills needed to carry out a particular task or project, and working to achieve everything by consensus, or at least through majority decisions with no objections, rather than through the authority of any one individual. Teams may be within one firm, or may extend across many firms.

Coaching rather than commanding

The whole question of what a manager's job should consist of now starts to become a subject for discussion. If junior staff are empowered to make their own decisions, what do we need so many managers for?

The whole tradition of management by commanding and controlling people starts to be undermined by giving everyone so much authority. But is this not a natural consequence of the modern working world? No longer can a single, dominant mind stay informed and ahead of every aspect of a modern business. There is really no alternative but to use the intelligence and knowledge of everyone in the organization to stay ahead of the competition.

Good ideas could come from anywhere. An improved manufacturing process from the shop floor. An idea for a product improvement from a customer. An agreement on industry standardization from a meeting with a competitor. A new product idea from a junior office worker. Every idea must be filtered, tested and considered without wading through a long administrative process. Unworkable ideas should be eliminated quickly; good ideas must reach people who can use them rapidly.

Senior management has the task of creating the environment, the working culture and the strategic framework within which this can happen. No longer can senior managers afford to be the commanders directing the troops, issuing instructions with unquestionable authority. They must become coaches and trainers, preparing people for situations and supporting them in action.

When a football team is playing, and the striker has the football in front of the goal, he does not stop and ask the manager whether he should kick the ball, or consult the coach about the best way to kick it; he just gets on with scoring the goal. In fact, faltering for even a moment will probably lose the opportunity as defenders run to intervene. But scoring that goal is a result of the shared values and determination of the whole team, developed by the manager, and of the technical skill of every player, developed by the coach. There is no time for decision making and lines of authority – just the application of training, skill and experience to achieve an objective. Modern businesses have to operate with the same efficiency and confidence.

Integration through depth of understanding

Perhaps we might seem to have strayed from understanding how to apply information technology. But we are now right in the core of trying to understand business cultures. There is little point in setting up computer systems for a business until we have a proper understanding of a particular business's operating methods, information flows and responsibility structures. Many existing systems may not be quite as stable as they seem if we look objectively into our crystal ball to try to predict the future.

Integration is not just a matter of stitching together information and communications through computer systems. It involves getting right to the heart of the business culture and its values and objectives, and then designing systems that really do address the likely problems of the future.

Real integration is not a superficial subject to be tackled by an external expert with a lot of technical understanding but little knowledge of the business; it is a fundamental plank of business strategy which must be designed, planned and managed into reality by the firm's most senior executives. They are the only people who fully understand all aspects of the business and where they want it to go, and they are the only people with sufficient depth of understanding to make sure that it really works.

I am not suggesting that senior executives need to become systems analysts or programmers. But they must be happy working in terms of the principles outlined above, deciding which to apply and which to reject in developing the culture that the technology will support. The senior executives must also become the bridge between the technology specialists implementing any solution and the workers who will use it. It is no good standing aloof and delegating the critical decision making to committees of junior staff. The coach must be there on the touchline, watching every game, assessing the quality of the skills being applied, giving confidence to the people who need it, adding skills and knowledge when they are lacking, and identifying and correcting poor judgement and superficial solutions. Just as in a game of football, everybody becomes an amateur coach when they are watching the game. When rearranging and integrating business functions, senior management must be the professional coaches, keeping everything on a steady course in the face of many well-intentioned but less well-informed suggestions coming from all directions.

Flexible support for whole businesses

Once we really know what we are doing and why we are doing it, it becomes more straightforward to develop appropriate support for the business through the application of information technology. Technology must *support* and not control what a business can do. In the late-1990s many businesses are only just recovering from the constraints of so called 'legacy systems' – systems which seemed a good idea at the time, but which ultimately constrain a business from developing or adapting to new conditions. The problem may be out-of-date hardware or software systems, where continued lease payments have prevented reinvestment, or dependence upon accounting, management, operating or customer support software which just cannot adapt to new business structures.

A firm's information infrastructure can become as much, if not more, a part of the foundations and structure of the business as the buildings from which the firm operates. If it doesn't perform the job needed, it cannot just be replaced overnight – changing information systems is a major task. Just as you cannot replace a column at the ground floor of a building without extensive propping and temporary construction to hold up the building without it while it is replaced, you cannot just remove a critical information system and replace it. The accounting system is vital to a business. Senior management must know the financial operating position at all times. The tax inspector will expect regular comprehensive tax returns regardless, and is not interested in internal matters like introducing better systems.

Flexible thinking is needed. Don't just mechanize the obvious: look for and understand what is behind what is visible. An interesting view to apply is that there are two extremes of systems which work acceptably. At one extreme there are difficult to use and obstinate systems which are very successful because of the enthusiasm and tolerance of their users. At the other extreme are brilliantly designed systems which work success-fully despite uncooperative and intolerant users. Just think of some of the systems that you use and try to classify them on this basis. There are of course two other classes – bad systems with intolerant users which don't work, and the ultimate business support success: brilliant systems with enthusiastic users. The latter is relatively rare.

Legalities and impediments

A number of constraints upon what is possible have been conveniently ignored so far – legal constraints for a start. In many instances, paper records need to be maintained for contractual reasons, to record what has happened for future reference. It is worth considering, in line with earlier concepts, exactly how much information really is worth keeping for legal reasons. Is it being kept as evidence for prosecution of claims, or in defence against mistakes? Whichever is the case, in a true mutual trust teamwork environment there is little point in wasting too much money going to court – all the legal costs are ultimately lost profits somewhere in the system. Hence detailed records, just in case they are needed to settle courtroom arguments, may be a waste of money. However, this certainly isn't the general case yet, so some records are needed and the system must include the most efficient method of maintaining a minimum set of records.

Then there is the need to comply with national and local statutes and laws. Employment regulations may restrict working hours or working conditions to the detriment of new systems and business efficiency. Environmental regulations, safety regulations and tax requirements all have impacts upon what can be achieved, and considerable ingenuity may be needed to implement the most cost-effective solution. Most regulations are carefully designed to protect the rights and living and working conditions of individuals, but sometimes they are not as adaptable as the world of business would like.

There may also be strong social barriers and perceptions constraining what people are prepared to do. If the terms and conditions of a job are undesirable, and there is a choice of work, the best employees will take alternative work. Worse, staff may take the training opportunities offered to learn new skills and then move to another job which is closer to their preferred ideal. Staff turnover and skill depletion are very real problems, which the system designer can easily ignore. Going back to senior management and culture, the workplace must become a desirable place to be. The alternative is to deskill the operation and lose all the benefits of applying the minds of the whole workforce to solve problems and develop new solutions.

Then there is organized resistance. The traditional management view of trade unions has tended to assume that they will always try to protect existing positions and prevent changes. A disturbing history of management versus union confrontations has generally resulted in lose-lose results: whether the management gives in and pays more, or antagonizes the workforce by strongarm tactics to get them back to work, the result tends to be the same – the industry withers away because too much effort is being wasted in conflict. Struggling industries need to stop looking inwards and fighting each other, and look outwards, applying every mind available on *both* sides to stay ahead of the competition. The world is changing, though; the trade union movement is all about people and jobs, and common sense can easily prevail. Some of the most remarkable achievements in business reorganization have been achieved through involving trade unions right from the start. Instead of setting up battle lines and training for a fight, walking the battlefield together first may just come up with even better combined ideas than either would have thought of on their own.

Distributed (integrated) responsibility

We are beginning to cross old ground again, but just think about the responsibility structures in a fully integrated working environment. As barriers are removed, as people's job descriptions become more fluid, and the old ideas of rigid hierarchies of command evaporate. The need for so many managers is reduced, and we arrive at much 'flatter' structures: one senior member of staff with many team members working directly below. There is no longer such a rigid structure of who gives orders to whom.

Management 'fan out' becomes much greater – there are many more people below a manager at a particular level, and as a result fewer levels are needed in whatever is left of the hierarchy.

What about distributed working? We have just worked our way through a whole chapter without mentioning geographical independence, national and international, or smaller working units distributed across the landscape. But wait: information technology makes locational independence possible, regardless of the organizational form. When we speak to someone on the telephone it is irrelevant (apart from the cost of the call!) whether he or she is in the next room or on another continent. Many aspects of business communication do not require people to be physically in the same building.

As mentioned already, there are no perfect solutions, just better solutions and worse solutions. Better solutions require a mixture of ideas – organizational and technical, information technology and working culture, an appropriate *infoculture*.

A speculative case study: the construction industry

It is always easiest to generate examples from one's own experience, and my background is in civil engineering, the construction industry. What would happen if these ideas were applied, without constraint, hypothetically, in the construction industry?

This ties in with the fictional example that we have been developing throughout the book. This is the process through which the project would travel from just an idea into a functioning, economically viable, socially acceptable, and environmentally compatible reality.

First let us look at the traditional organization of the construction industry. Figure 7.4 depicts a simplified, perhaps rather personal, view of how the industry operates.

Inspiration and opportunity come together to create a concept. The construction industry is then hired to turn this concept into reality. Established professions divide up the cake, decide who is responsible for what, how established methods and standards will be applied, and set up the contracts and constraints upon what information will be exchanged with whom, how and when. Experience is applied, intellectual input is assimilated, decisions are made, and a comprehensive design specification is prepared. This tends to be a production process, minimizing effort in every component to minimize costs to the party concerned, with little incentive to do anything outside fixed contractual compartments of activity.

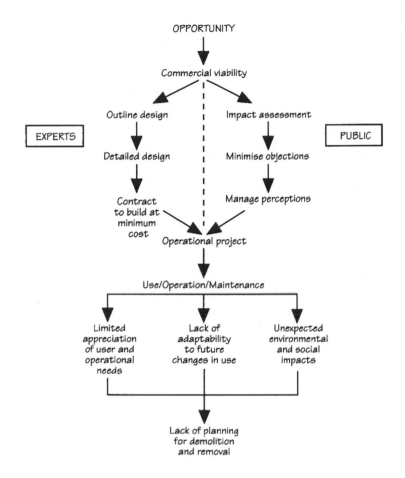

Figure 7.4. The traditional project life-cycle.

Throughout these early stages, the experts are generally busy trying to get on with the design without too much interference from the public at large. Time costs money. Impacts must be assessed, objections must be minimized, and perceptions must be managed to avoid any major hold-ups, but the active input of the public and future users of the project is very difficult to engage through traditional means. Most members of the public are too busy to attend meetings, or even to visit offices to look at drawings, and they don't feel that they can have much effect upon what will be built anyway. In some cases there will be an active lobby group against the project, probably on environmental grounds, in which case any attempt at consultation becomes more of a confrontation than an opportunity to refine and improve the project.

A contractor is appointed to turn the specification into reality. This contractor then enters a series of subcontracts with specialist firms to distribute the contractual liability and to minimize and limit the cost of construction. All effort is concentrated on reaching the important stage of handover, when the client, who has paid for all of this work, becomes the owner of the project, and the contractor can walk away from it and start another project.

Now we move into the project use phase, when it must be used, operated and maintained. Limitations become apparent when real users actually start to use it. Perhaps the doorways are too small, or the lighting is inadequate, or the offices and working areas are designed for last year's, not next year's technology. Inefficiencies arise in operation and maintenance under practical working conditions. Social and environmental impacts may become apparent: perhaps the main entrance is on the wrong side for the bus service, or excess heat is wasted into the atmosphere while the school next door has to buy expensive fuel for heating. During the design, everyone applied the best practice and knowledge available, but there was no real opportunity to mobilize all of the ideas and advice of the whole community, who will have to live with the results for at least a few decades. Where public consultation does take place during design it has traditionally tended to be to make sure that the public knows that the experts have made the right decisions. By that stage the design tends to be too far advanced to consider alternative ideas seriously.

Finally, when the project is no longer needed, demolition is an expense which creates waste. Ever since handover, the project users and operators have been making the best of the legacy of the design and construction process.

This is perhaps a slightly extreme view. Everybody is really working to avoid problems, but the system has many inherent weaknesses. How could we achieve a 'better' solution?

Jump forward a decade or two, to the science fiction world of Figure 7.5.

A practical need for a project links up with inspiration to generate an idea (back to Chapter 1). The boundaries between traditional professions have been broken down – all of the same expertise is available, but in new flexible organizational forms configured to form efficient cross-disciplinary teams, with distributed authority working to achieve a common aim rather than to avoid risk and responsibility.

These teams will communicate with each other through new forms of presentation and interaction – probably three-dimensional models built out of semi-intelligent objects. Look at the model in a virtual reality

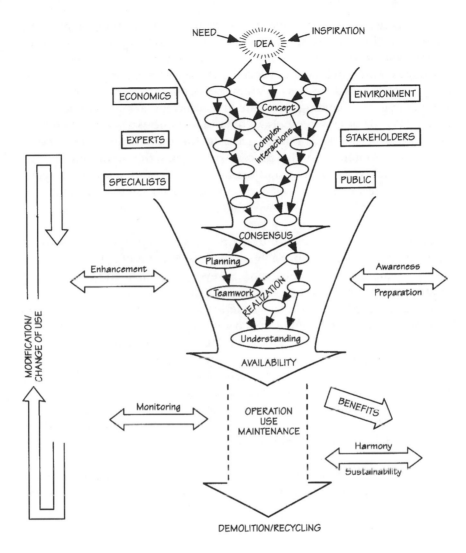

Figure 7.5. The communication-rich project environment of the future

viewer and see the visual impact or the size and shape of working space. Put the model in a virtual wind tunnel, and measure the stresses and strains caused by the worst storms in the winter. Fill the model with virtual people, and consider how social interaction and business interaction will occur, and how people will evacuate or respond in an emergency. A total environmental balance of the model checks what natural resources need to go in and what waste products come out.

The model must start from a conceptual version and progressively develop in detail as design progresses. The existence of such a model creates new opportunities for interaction. New professions and skills can investigate environmental and social effects from the early stages of the design. New predictive simulation services can try operating and maintaining the building, simulate the effect of a major flood or an earthquake, or do anything else which public and private interests may demand to be checked. Public access to the model can involve every potential stakeholder in the process right from the start. Community groups, schools, public transport operators, retail store owners – anyone with an interest can start considering the likely effects from early on. Of course, they in turn must allow public access to any plans and ideas of their own!

Then the project moves through a process of realization. This may be by a single contractor, or possibly an integrated team of subcontractors – the main change is that they can test every aspect of the construction method on the model before carrying it out in practice.

The project then becomes available for use, with concurrent operation and maintenance and monitoring of whether it performs as expected. The objective of the whole process has been to achieve sustainable harmony with people, air, earth, business, finance and government. There may be stages of modification, before reaching a final stage of termination which has been planned carefully in advance to maximize recycling and minimize waste disposal problems.

Stakeholders and interested parties have been freely involved throughout the process, with a motto of 'if it can be improved, let's improve it'.

The reality may be different – time will tell – but this example is intended to illustrate just how much could change if people want it to.

8

Depending upon machines

Trust and independence

It's time to take off the rose-coloured spectacles and come back down to earth again. There must be a serious downside to letting computers organize too much of our lives, so let us try to quantify and identify the risks and problems of becoming dependent upon the wonder machines.

People trust computers with their businesses like they trust their cars with their lives. But whereas there is a well-developed safety culture in the automobile industry, where any new development is carefully monitored and tested before it is allowed into widespread use, computers are still at the stage where a bigger engine (processor) and go-faster stripes (graphical user inteface, or GUI) tend to be much more important decision-making parameters than whether the system is intrinsically impermeable to malicious attack (such as computer viruses) and can recover automatically within moments from any type of computer hardware failure (such as a hard disk crash).

When you select new employees or working colleagues, you can interview them first and study their past performance records to establish their knowledge, attitude and experience. You spend time forming a picture of what you believe are their values, and as a result you make judgements about how much you trust them, and what you trust them with. Would you give them the key to the front door of the office to work out of hours? Would you give them the key to your filing cabinet so that they can access papers they need, whenever they need to? Would you give them the key to the safe, so that they can draw their own petty cash when they incur expenses in carrying out their job? Probably not, until you know them quite well and develop some trust in their integrity.

What about the computer? It is not feasible to interview a computer! What proof do you have of the integrity of the hardware or the software that is operating on it? How do you know that the processor does not have a fault which creates systematic mathematical errors in all calculations? Or that the disk does not lose the odd digit of a number once in a while when storing files away? Or that it does not have an unknown virus which mischievously or maliciously modifies data once in a while?

In the early days of using computers, back in the 1960s, people were very cautious about the effects that they might have. Any new application was carefully tested, just to make sure that it worked as intended. My own experience of the 1970s was that the introduction of computers was considered sufficiently critical to a business that many senior executives took a personal interest in understanding the consequences of these expensive investments; hence a high-level strategic and risk view was automatically being applied by the very nature of the people involved. However, as information technology has become more of a specialized area of understanding it has been delegated to specialists who may not have a full appreciation of all aspects of the business. All of the departments and compartments which exist in many traditionally organized industries inherently prevent anyone except the most senior members of staff having a full understanding of how the business works.

What can go wrong? Expect the unexpected!

There is no infallible list of what could go wrong, there will always be new problems that no-one had previously thought of. A good example is the effect of bomb scares or 'security alerts'. The sudden and unexpected evacuation of entire business areas can create a whole series of problems for providing the integrity of computer systems. For instance, a business might have two fully operational computer centres in different buildings, designed so that any level of catostrophic failure in one location can immediately be compensated for by spare capacity in the other location. But what happens when bomb threats cause the simultaneous evacuation of both facilities? It might be essential to have a mobile external control system, which can monitor and control the critical functions of the facility through a mobile phone data link, for example, during such a scenario.

It seems an inevitable fact of life that whatever you plan for, something else will happen to shake your confidence. Just imagine an operating system bug (or planned fault!) which brings every PC in the world to a standstill on a certain day. What on earth would we do? It would be rather like waking up in the morning and finding that an unexpected and unthought of atmospheric change had stopped every motor car engine working.

I have seen localized examples of this in the computer world. I can remember hearing that one commercial software package would not work one morning. Upon investigation it turned out that every version of the same program everywhere in the world had stopped. I never did find out whether it was actually a bug or a malicious act. Every computer running that software had to turn the date back a day in order to run. Goodness only knows what this did to the integrity of filing systems, as new files with yesterday's date suddenly started appearing to be older than the last files created the day before! If anyone had applied a 'purge' utility, which automatically deletes older files by date and time and keeps newer ones, it could have left rather unexpected results. The current 'system' date and time (which should be the real date and time) affects every piece of software running and every file created.

If you get a chance, plan what you would do in the case of a total failure, before it happens, and hope that it never will. Just the exercise of studying the consequences is likely to identify refinements and improvements to normal working practices which will help to minimize some of the risks.

If it can go wrong, it will go wrong!

Anyone who has worked with computers for a few years will probably have plenty of horror stories to relate. Here is an example.

A few years ago, all larger computers were cosseted in the luxury of an air-conditioned computer room. Carefully controlled temperature and humidity were needed to get the optimum performance and minimize maintenance, and it was essential to minimize the amount of dust and dirt which could get anywhere near the delicate magnetic surfaces inside the disk drives.

Computer rooms have lights, and one day it became necessary to replace the flourescent light bulbs in the computer room. You can guess what happened. After replacing countless flourescent strip lights in other parts of the building, it had to be one of the ones in the computer room which the young lad doing the job dropped. And not in just any location – it was the one right over the top of the computer disk cabinets. Lots of dust and broken glass in the computer room! Remarkably, the computer did not suffer any immediate damage – it kept on working. But almost inevitably, despite careful clean-up operations, one of the disks failed within a few hours as dust found its way in somewhere.

Another factor which it is easy to forget is the people factor. I remember an occasion when the computer manager was away for a couple of weeks on annual leave. Careful forward planning of leave meant comprehensive coverage of all of the skills needed to run the system was still available. Then the system manager was unexpectedly ill. And then one of the main disks failed, followed by an unintentional mishap while trying to rearrange disk space to compensate which caused the contents of another disk to vanish! Things were not looking very good at this point.

First there was the time to repair the damaged disk. Always look carefully at the call-out time and repair time in a computer maintenance contract. The time that matters is not how long it takes someone to arrive on site, but how long it takes them, from the call-out, to identify the fault, obtain the necessary spare parts, fit and test the parts and return the system to full operation. That does not necessarily make the system usable again – in the case of a disk failure, someone then has to put all of the data back onto the disk.

This particular system had a full backup procedure in place, and backup copies of files had been taken early that morning. But it was an 'incremental' backup system. Copying all of the disks onto computer tape every day would have taken too long, so each disk was only copied in full every few days, and in between only the new files created each day were 'backed up'. It was the worst point in the backup cycle, of course. The disks had to be recreated from the last 'full backup' several days before, and then each day's incremental backup was applied to gradually bring each disk back up to date. There were a few other problems as well, all of which were dealt with along the way, but it was still two days before the system was fully operational again, despite long working hours.

What impressed me most was that despite the apparent lack of the right senior staff to take control and solve the problems, all of the problems were solved. Never underestimate the important component of people in any system. This story dates back a few years now. Today, how long could your business survive without any key component of its computer systems before serious economic damage to the business started to occur?

As well as the unexpected, unmeasurable and unplannable problems, there are plenty of routine and mundane risks which it is quite possible to quantify and minimize.

Environment

Before looking at the computer equipment itself, what about the environment that it sits in? Most older offices were not designed for computer equipment, and compromises are often evident. Even modern office designs may not correctly predict the needs of future equipment. The most obvious problem is the lack of provision for all of the cables and connections required. Are enough power sockets provided where they are needed? How is each computer connected to the network, to printers, and to anything else? All too often, there is a bird's nest of intertwined cables and extension leads behind the computer. Even where proper ducting and connections are provided, how do you turn the power supply on and off? There is often a whole series of mains switches: one on the computer, one on the monitor, one on the printer, and others on the other peripherals, all of which need to be turned on and off every day, which is rather tedious.

Structured cabling systems go some way to overcoming cabling problems by providing a regular grid of computer or telephone connection points throughout an office. These in turn connect to a distribution panel, so that individual sockets in the floor can be connected to particular telephones or computer network hubs.

More subtle are the lighting conditions, background noise, and seating position and ergonomics of each computer workstation. Safety and health regulations are progressively raising standards in many countries, but it is still important to consider properly how a human being interacts with the computer. If the screen is badly affected by reflected light, or the computer is in noisy or distracting surroundings, or badly positioned for the user sitting in front of it, vital mental effort is diverted to overcoming those problems rather than concentrating upon the job in hand. In bad situations, the computer user may suffer from headaches or other problems.

Sometimes forgotten, especially in well-established offices, is the heat that computers generate. Although energy requirements are steadily reducing, the air-conditioning systems in older buildings were designed for the comfort of people rather than people plus computers. Computers generate significant amounts of heat, and a computer on every desk can generate more heat than the air-conditioning can compensate for. If the air-conditioning cannot cope, offices become hot and unpleasant, but it can be very expensive to improve existing air-conditioning systems.

Hardware faults

Any mechanical or electronic component in a computer or communications system could fail at any moment. Considering that standard computer processors may switch pulses of electricity hundreds of millions of times *per second* (hundreds of 'megahertz'), it seems remarkable that modern computers actually work reliably at all! To go faultlessly through an almost unimaginable number of calculations for one second is difficult enough to comprehend, let alone continuing to do so day in, day out, for years. Just to put this into proportion, the average modern desktop PC goes through more calculation cycles in one minute than a human heart beats in an average lifetime!

Every time that you hear quiet whirring or clicking noises coming from inside the disk drive of a computer, a tiny recording and writing 'head' is being moved precisely over the magnetic surface of the disk to very fine tolerances. Through a combination of the disk rotating at high speed and the disk head moving in precise steps between the edge and nearer to the centre of the disk surface, it can find or write data 'bits' anywhere on the surface of the disk in tiny fractions of a second. The slightest mechanical error, or any damage to the disk surface can make the whole disk unreadable.

Although it is unlikely, through faulty manufacture any wire in any of the cables attached to any computer could break. Any one of the hundreds of electrical connections where components and chips are fixed to the circuit board might be faulty. Any of the components or chips might itself have a minor manufacturing flaw which only becomes apparent when it fails. Considering the complexity involved, it is surprising that such faults are very rare. In fact, modern components and circuits are actually manufactured and tested to very high standards. If they were not, consumer confidence to use computers would be much lower. Quality makes sense, dramatically reducing the need for expensive warranty repair and supporting staff and facilities.

The inherent reliability of modern computers does tend to build a false sense of complacency. In years gone by, people working with computers expected them to go wrong and were used to dealing with the consequences. Nowadays many more people are using computers and there is much less familiarity with what to do when they go wrong.

There is, yet again, quite a good parallel with the motor car. Years ago, people travelling by car expected to have punctures, broken fan belts and other failures fairly often, and planned their travel accordingly. Nowadays, we do not expect our cars to go wrong, and do not waste time planning for failures. In many countries there is also a well-developed infrastructure of breakdown services and motoring organizations to swing into action to sort out the situation when things do go wrong.

Although the same sort of services for computer systems may be well developed in larger organizations, smaller firms are generally left to their own devices to sort things out. With a car, a motoring organization recognizes the car user's principal need with a 'get you to your destination' or 'get your vehicle home' service. With computers, the basic service or warranty is more aligned to repairing the component that went wrong, without attempting to sort out the consequences for you. There are no 'get the documents to the people who need them' or 'divert your communications to another office' services.

The motoring market tends to show the maturity of averaging the risks across the whole market as well. In the UK there are a limited number of well-organized motoring organizations. Each of these covers the whole country, regardless of the make or age of the car. The car manufacturers usually offer one of these standard national services with new cars rather than attempting to provide their own. With computers you are still much more dependent upon who manufactured which part and where you bought which component from. Risks are still often assessed on individual components rather than averaging across industry sectors. Economies of scale tend to get obscured by the need to administer and apportion the blame for any failure to the right party.

Software errors

Now let us move out into the swampy quagmire of software reliability! At least with computer hardware it is usually relatively clear whether a piece of equipment works or does not. There are specified actions which should result in reactions, indicators which can be checked, voltages which can be measured, and standard decision-making processes for deciding what needs to be replaced or repaired, most of the time.

Perhaps an analyst can divide software errors into many specific types of failure. However, to computer users, unable to complete their work, the actual reason why it does not work is rather less important. When standing on a railway station waiting for a train that is several hours late, the actual reason that the train is late is of little more than passing interest. It doesn't really matter whether the engine has a fault and a standby wasn't available, or the sophisticated new signalling system has a fault, or the driver was sick. The fact is that the whole system of

143

providing the service is unreliable. But the consequence is that the more often it happens, the more it will strengthen the passenger's resolve to find an alternative means of transport in the future.

It is, perhaps, fairly easy to divide computer software problems into three rough classes: 'show stoppers', inefficiencies and irritants.

A show stopper is a problem which means that there is no way that the work can be carried out by the method originally intended, and serious consequences are almost inevitable.

Inefficiencies lead to significant extra costs and extra time, stretching and testing the narrow financial margins of the modern business world.

Irritants are just inconvenient, but they can reduce morale and job satisfaction.

Show stoppers are frequently the consequence of technical misunderstandings between the computer programmer or analyst and the computer user. People are adaptable and flexible; computers tend to be obstinate and inflexible. How many times have you filled in an application form for something to find that there isn't enough space for the address the way that you normally write it, or for the full name of your organization, or to write an alternative phone number, or what hours it is best to contact you? Perhaps you have been lucky and have never seen the problem. On a paper form you find a practical solution. You write a note on the form for the benefit of the person reading it. But when the completed form is entered onto the computer, your written note is lost. The computer programmer believed that 20 characters would be enough for the name of any company, or that nobody would have a telephone number more than nine digits long. Or perhaps there was some other simplification which suited the programmer, who had no understanding of the consequences.

In many cases, such errors make the software completely unusable. Some fundamental misunderstanding or mistake makes it impossible to use the software in a normal production situation. It may not be the data input form. Perhaps the printouts were designed for the old wide-format line printer paper, whereas all printers, photocopiers, fax machines and business activities now use the standard A4 format. Or the system relies on copying data onto floppy disks, when realistic file sizes are larger than can fit on a single disk. There are plenty of ways to make such mistakes.

When mistakes are made, time is often wasted 'searching for the guilty'. Who made the mistake? Who got it wrong? The analyst or programmer wrote down in the specification exactly how it was going to work, and the user approved it. But the user employed the analyst as a professional who should have given advice to avoid such problems occurring. Meanwhile, the business is losing money, and everyone is unhappy.

The actual reason for the failure is rarely vested in one person. If the analyst made a mistake, perhaps the manager was trying to save money by employing someone without enough experience. Perhaps the analyst did not realize that a particular word had a different meaning in a different professional circle than they normally work in. Civil engineers talk about road networks and water distribution networks, while communications experts talk about computer networks; but in normal conversation they all just abbreviate to 'networks' and assume that the person that they are talking to has a common conceptual understanding. When a practical person says that a stock code is six characters long, they mean that all the codes that they normally deal with are six characters long. When computer programmers say six characters long, they mean exactly six.

Inefficiencies take many forms. One of the most common is unnecessary re-entry of the same data. Either lots of different computer forms or computer programs all need exactly the same data entered again and again, or data printed out from one computer program has to be typed into another. For instance, every time that you write your address on any sort of paper form, someone probably has to type it into a computer somewhere. Every retyping introduces the opportunity for typing errors. It also costs someone's time and needs a computer terminal to type it on, which is costing money to someone. This is a fairly trivial example. Inefficiencies can be much more serious, such as when whole databases of information need to be retyped because of incompatibilities between computer systems.

Legacy software

One of the problems created by rapid technological development is the 'legacy' of everything that has gone before. As mentioned before, existing systems cannot just be replaced overnight – that would be rather like trying to replace the engine of a car while it is still being driven along the road!

Many organizations have well established 'legacy software' at the centre of their critical business systems, which must sooner or later be replaced. Because of its importance to the business, such software is often kept inside a cocoon of interfaces and procedures to protect it from changes which might cause errors and problems.

Software vendors and consultants will always have all sorts of wonderful solutions to 'protect past investment'. But always look at what is being preserved. There is no point in putting a jet engine into a Mini motor car, or trying to fit a Rolls-Royce engine into an old Morris Minor. Why preserve a system which works in terms of numeric codes that no-one can remember when modern software can easily select meaningful words from a menu which 'pops up' somewhere on the screen? Does the system make assumptions about the organization (such as the number of departments, regions, locations of offices or names of management posts) that no longer apply? Are those regular tabular printouts considered so critical to daily work really in the best form for efficient working, when graphs, pie charts and histograms are so easily available now?

Communications and time

The speed of modern communication creates its own problems. Things can go wrong and errors can multiply very fast. The delays inherent in older methods of working were also a form of moderation which helped to allow serious errors to be detected before they propagated too far. A single error in important data can now be copied to thousands of computers all over the world in a few moments if suitable controls are not in place.

On the other hand, delays in communication may cause problems. Systems may come to rely upon always having up-to-date information, leading to serious problems when critical communications do not occur on time.

One problem which has become to a large extent a thing of the past is communication errors, thanks to modern data communication standards. In the 1970s, communications over telephone lines through modems were fraught with problems because of data errors. To send data over an ordinary telephone line, electronic numbers or pulses need to be converted into sounds by a modem, and back to numbers or pulses at the other end of the telephone line. Unfortunately any clicks, hiss or other noise on the telephone line was added to the sound, producing different numbers at the far end. This was a serious problem with using modems for many years.

However, modern standards have successfully eliminated this problem through 'error correction'. All data transmitted by modern modems includes extra data to check whether it arrives okay. To illustrate the principle, imagine sending someone a list of numbers. Just to make sure that they are received correctly, ask the person receiving them to add them up while you do the same. Then ask if the result is an even number or an odd number. If the other person's total is even and yours is odd, you know that there is an error, and you send the list again. Modern error correction uses sophisticated techniques of this type to check that data is received correctly.

Which is the latest version?

Another problem, created by the ease with which information can be printed out on demand, is that of multiple versions of printed output. When you have two versions or more of the same printout on your desk, how do you know which is the latest?

It becomes important to make sure that the printout includes a clear date and time or version number on it somewhere to avoid any confusion. A discipline of removing or destroying older versions of documents is also required. Of course, one solution is to go electronic, so that you always read the data directly from the computer; then you know that it is up to date.

Impregnability or encryption?

Every business has information regarded as confidential, and sooner or later a lot of this information will be entered onto a computer, where it becomes vulnerable to unseen prying eyes. Who has access to the building, and hence the computer at night? The security guard? The cleaners? They might have friends with an interest or a grudge, or student age children looking for a computer security challenge just for fun. Who has access during the day? Does everyone log off the computer at lunchtime and coffee breaks, or are terminals left logged in to sensitive systems for anyone walking by to investigate? Are there any unseen network or modem connections to the outside world, to other offices where security may be more relaxed or even to the Internet?

It is very difficult to eliminate all of the methods that a determined individual might use to gain access to your data. Someone really determined might just break in and steal the whole computer, in order to decipher the security protection at leisure afterwards. Every data transfer is a risk – whether over a network link, via a modem over a telephone line, or just as a disk in a courier package. There is always a chance that information might fall into the wrong hands.

This is a major subject, where professional help is likely to be needed if it is of critical importance. There are many books on the subject and sources of information. I would just draw attention to two different basic approaches to security to consider when deciding upon a solution, which I would term impregnability and encryption.

The first approach is just to try to ensure that no unauthorized people can ever gain access to information that they should not see. This might be through physically locked doors and cabinets, or through sophisticated systems of passwords and working procedures. The weakness of this system is that someone might find a way in. Just like stealing jewellery from a castle, someone might dig a tunnel under the moat, past the guards and into the strongroom. This parallel can be used to illustrate a few of the ways to minimize the risk. Build a castle on rock, and tunnelling is more difficult. Try not to let anyone know where the strongroom is, so that they do not know where to go. Put some extra security around the strongroom itself; don't put it on the ground floor, but put it behind more locked doors upstairs. Alternatively, lateral thinking might suggest suspending the strongroom in the middle of the courtyard, where it is constantly in everyone's view, rather than hiding it in an obscure corner where it might not be checked for days.

The alternative to impregnability is encryption. This means converting all of the important data into a coded form where it is useless to anyone who does not know how to decode it. This seems very attractive, since it saves all of the expense and inconvenience inherent in the impregnability solution. Information can be made freely available, transmitted openly between people by any means available; it is just useless to anyone who is not supposed to be able to read it. However, this approach has its Achilles' heel. If someone does manage to work out how to decode the information, most likely by stealing the details of the encryption from somewhere, they immediately have access to all of the information. There are also situations where encryption is not allowed; for instance, some countries have made it illegal to send encrypted files in electronic mail messages over the Internet.

Ultimately, a balance must be struck between risk and convenience. In general, the more secure a system is, the less convenient, more expensive and less efficient it is for its users. For most organizations, different levels of security will be needed for different information, and a combination of techniques will be needed depending upon who needs access and where they need access.

Random attacks – viruses

There are thousands of computer viruses out 'in the field', mostly on personal computers. Every time a disk or a computer file is transferred between two computers there is a risk of transferring a virus. Many are relatively harmless, but some can do serious damage to a computer system and the data stored on it.

Essentially, anything which is 'executed' on a computer might contain a virus. That means any computer program, a command procedure of instructions to run a program, or a 'macro' sequence of instructions embedded in a word-processor document or spreadsheet or any other data file which includes automated procedures.

A virus propagates itself by inserting extra instructions into programs or files which are already legitimately supposed to be on the computer. When the program runs, it executes the extra code, which takes actions that are not intended by the user. One action will be for the virus to copy itself and 'infect' any other suitable files that it can find access to, on the computer's hard disk, on a floppy disk, or over a network. At some stage, the virus will make its presence known to the computer user. This may just be by putting a message on the display or by changing the display, or it might be far more serious, deleting or damaging files on the computer.

Unfortunately, new viruses are appearing all of the time. Although efficient and effective virus-checking programs are readily available, which can detect all of the viruses that are known to exist, there is always the possibility of a new virus which eludes the investigations of the virus-checking program.

Always virus check someone else's files, even from your friends and colleagues, before using them on your computer. Do not accept the results of someone else's virus checker; there is no such thing as a means of guaranteeing that a disk does not contain a virus. Your friend may have virus-checked a disk, but the virus checker might be six months old and miss the latest viruses. Every time you load a new program onto your computer you risk transferring a virus; make sure that you minimize the risk and that the risk is worth taking. Do not forget that free software and software downloaded from the Internet are obvious targets for someone intending to propagate a new virus. A virus may not make itself apparent straight away, so the fact that someone else is already using the same software without any problems does not guarantee that it is virus-free. Some viruses only manifest themselves on certain dates, such as Friday 13th of a month or particular anniversaries or birthdays.

Targeted attacks – hackers

Computers have generated their own specialist group of criminals, the so-called 'hackers'. They specialize in gaining access to systems that they are not intended to. This electronic trespassing into other people's private data may sometimes be benign, but it can also form part of premeditated serious crime. Breaking into someone's computer system just for fun is rather like breaking into a bank vault just to prove that it can be done. It takes time, effort and planning, and it is difficult to believe that there is no deeper purpose in any such incident!

Responsibility for life-threatening mistakes

It is important to understand that a computer cannot actually take responsibility. Only people can ultimately be responsible for actions resulting from the use of a computer. When something goes wrong it is no good 'blaming the computer'. Someone, somewhere, decided to use a computer, and someone accepted the results that it gave.

This is particularly important where people's lives are entrusted to the results obtained from computers, for instance in structural engineering. Computers can execute many complex calculations to assist in deciding the optimum sizes of all of the beams and columns in a building, but ultimately the professional engineer responsible for the design must confirm that these sizes are correct and safe through experience and independent cross-checks. There is always the possibility that some of the data was typed incorrectly in the input to the computer analysis, or that an unusual design goes beyond the intended capabilities of the software.

It is a complete fallacy to imagine that the firm supplying the computer software can take responsibility for the structural integrity of the buildings designed with it. The engineer has always been responsible in the past and it is the engineer who must remain responsible in the future. Unfortunately, it is far too easy for an inexperienced junior engineer to feed information into a computer program and receive a printout of results in return without understanding the calculations that have occurred between.

The development of the specialist software industry in structural engineering illustrates how a misunderstanding of responsibility could occur and that it must be avoided. In the early days of computers, in the 1970s, major engineering firms purchased their own computers and wrote their own software for engineering design calculations. Everyone was very cautious of new technology, and computer software was thoroughly tested and checked by very experienced engineers before going into general use. As computer software became more sophisticated and diverse, natural economies of scale led to the establishment of specialist computer software firms who could sell their software to a number of firms and therefore invest in more development and better long-term support than individual engineering firms could afford to do themselves.

However, the firms buying the software were now relying on the accuracy and reliability of software over which they had little direct control. It became necessary to introduce a quality checking system to make sure that the software was working correctly and accurately, as it was intended to, and to recheck the software every time a new version was provided in case errors had unintentionally been introduced. Obviously, the software firm would do everything in its power to prevent any errors occurring in the calculation (otherwise it would not be successful in selling its software), but it would have no control over how the software would be used.

In this situation it is unrealistic to try to offset the risk contractually. It is no good saying that if the building falls down it is the fault of the software vendor and hence take the software vendor to court. Even if the court agreed, the small software firm involved would be unlikely to have the financial resources to pay compensation for the damage; it would just go out of business. It is the engineer who has the training and expertise to make sure that the results are reasonable.

At this point, I would comment that the likelihood of a computer error working its way through into construction is thankfully very small, thanks to all of the experienced people involved in any construction activity. First there is the design engineer, who should spot any serious error through experience. Another professional engineer should also check the calculations, just to make sure. Then a draughtsman turns the calculations into drawings. Most draughtsmen have drawn many similar drawings before, and although they may not know the details of all of the calculations, they will notice anything unusual and point it out to the designer.

Then the drawing goes to site, for the contractor to build. The contractor's engineer will look at the drawing to decide the best way of building it, and as another experienced engineer he or she is likely to notice any serious discrepancy from normally accepted sizes and shapes. Then the foreman in charge of the gang actually doing the construction will notice whether the design is significantly different from normal practice for that type of construction. And finally there should be a supervising engineer, checking the construction on behalf of the client, who is looking out for any problems.

All in all, this is quite a resilient system as a result of all of the human experience involved. Of course, if, in the future, the whole process of construction becomes completely automated and 'deskilled', there is a greater possibility that computer-generated errors might slip through the system.

What affects who?

Returning to the main substance of this chapter, our dependence upon computerized machines, it is of the utmost importance to identify who might be affected by any failure, error or malicious attack, and then consider how to minimize the risk.

Which is more important: the computer system itself, or the data stored on it? How long can the business survive without what? This needs to be thought through, as an exercise at every level, from losing one computer through a disk failure, through losing all of the computers in one office as a result of a computer theft, to suddenly losing all of the computer networks in an organization through an unknown virus.

Just losing one computer might prevent delivery of a vital tender document, ultimately resulting in the loss of millions of pounds worth of work. Alternatively, manual systems of working may have been so carefully planned that the organization can survive for several days without major parts of the computer system.

Values and consequences

Before deciding how much to spend on measures to minimize the risks, consider the financial and business consequences that might be incurred in the event of a failure or loss. Concentrate effort where it can have most effect. Consider which risks it may be more cost-efficient to insure against than eliminate.

When taking professional advice and paying for professional services, make sure that you fully understand the scope of the service offered and try to identify any gaps or loopholes yourself. Computers may be very logical and exact, but computer security and dependence are a continually evolving and developing subject area, where you need to keep your eyes open and listen to what is in the news or affecting other firms. No textbook will ever be complete – there will always be new wrinkles, errors and tricks as every new technological development unfolds.

Minimizing risks

There are well-established methods of minimizing most of the well-known risks, which professional information systems engineers or computer specialists are well aware of. This is an area where it makes sense to utilize existing knowledge and skills.

Data on computer systems is usually very valuable, and requires efficient backup procedures to ensure that it cannot be lost. Don't forget the necessity of maintaining comprehensive 'off-site' backups, in case of a total loss of the computer system itself or the entire building containing the system. A complete backup of all important data and the software to use the data should be transferred regularly to another office or location from which it can be retrieved easily if it should ever be needed. Don't forget that if this backup contains confidential data it should be kept secure and somewhere where any attempt to access it or tamper with it would be noticed rapidly.

Be careful about introducing specialized 'one-off' pieces of equipment. It may be prudent to standardize on certain types of equipment and then to have several of the same available in the organization, so that an alternative can be used if one should fail.

Make sure that staff are properly trained and prepared for failures and problems which are likely to occur. The actions taken immediately after any unexpected incident may significantly influence how long it takes to recover to full operation.

Recovering from disasters

Recovery from almost any disaster is usually possible, but it is a matter of time, effort, expense and technical skill. For organizations that are critically dependent upon their computer systems, it may be necessary to maintain a duplicate central computer centre in case of a major failure, ready to swing into action at a moment's notice. Mobile computer centres have been offered by some specialist disaster recovery firms, which can be moved to any location, connected up and put into full operation within a few hours of any disaster. It may be necessary to reconfigure major communication networks as part of recovery procedures. Some data-linking communication services can offer considerable flexibility in rearranging communication links at short notice.

As an alternative to a centralized strategy, some organizations may find it easier to implement a distributed system strategy, where each office or department is almost self-sufficient in its own right, and the loss of one part of the system will not seriously affect systems at other locations. This is a very resilient approach, but it does require considerable technical understanding, and may still be vulnerable to attacks from software viruses.

Malicious attacks – moats, gateways and firewalls

A final word about some of the terminology invading our conversations. When two computer systems are connected, whether it is in the same office or across the world via the Internet, a 'gateway' is often introduced. This gateway has two purposes. First, there may be technical differences between the two systems so that they could not otherwise talk directly to each other. In this case the gateway provides the necessary translation, for instance between different formats of electronic mail address. Secondly, the gateway defines what is visible when one system looks at the other. Through the gateway, one system can see particular computers and disk drives of the other system. There may be much more there that cannot be seen.

But a gateway does not in itself provide any security. It provides free passage from one side to the other – if a disk is visible through the gateway, it can be interrogated, and it may even be possible to modify it from the other side of the gateway without restriction. The only protection that a gateway can give is by making things invisible.

Hence a gateway to the Internet is a major risk. By giving all of the users of an office computer system the ability to look at the whole of the World-Wide Web on the Internet, a gateway may also allow anyone anywhere on the Internet to look at any of the office computers if they wished to. To guard against this, the science of 'firewalls' has been developed. A firewall stands in front of the gateway, and guards exactly what is allowed to pass through. It looks at, and checks the credentials and authorization of, everything passing through the gateway. The idea is to provide free and transparent passage to bona fide communications, but to block all other communications. An effective firewall is an important component of any major organization's connection to the Internet. Like any software, firewalls are subject to the ingenuity of computer hackers to find a way through them, but it is the firewall vendor's business to make them as impregnable as possible.

The only complete security is to isolate the system from the outside world – build a moat around it, close the gateway and pull up the drawbridge. One compromise is to let only electronic mail pass between the system and the outside world. This is far easier to control, rather like lowering the drawbridge every so often to let the postman deliver and collect the post. But don't forget that e-mail messages themselves can contain files, and any file transfer can unwittingly transfer a virus.

Disasters which could happen!

Back to our fictitious community project of the future. Let us look briefly at a few scenarios which could have caused major problems:

1. Total loss of the computer containing all of the plans and correspondence for the project. Nobody bothered to keep a paper copy of anything – why should they?
2. A malicious rumour that there is a new computer virus which affects any computer taking part in discussions of this project curtails the debate, and everyone has to resort to using telephones and attending meetings, slowing progress to a crawl.
3. There is a major error in the software used to carry out the environmental or economic analysis for the project, which makes it appear that the project is not viable.
4. The e-mail address and project discussion address given out in newspaper articles at the start of the project are wrong, and most people who might have become involved never manage to make contact.

9 Educating people

The key to the future

Throughout this book I have repeatedly tried to highlight the crucial importance of the most important ingredient of any system – people.

Machines cannot progress. Even so-called intelligent machines just apply predefined rules to achieve a given goal. They can only solve the problems envisaged by the people who programmed them, working within a world of limited boundaries and parameters.

Human beings may be fallible. They can make mistakes. They work in more approximate terms of perception and understanding than the clinical digital precision of computers. But human beings can also instantaneously assimilate new situations, formulate solutions never tried before, and apply them immediately to commercial, social or environmental advantage.

The human factor is the key to success, both in commercial terms and for the benefit of society. The better educated and trained that people are, the better the results for everyone.

The difference between people and machines

People learn over a period of time, gradually acquiring, refining and applying new skills. It takes many years to learn the skills to do a job well, and great care must be taken when making changes which replace human skills with computerized machine skills.

In a production line environment, with closely defined working procedures and little opportunity for applying individual skills and knowledge, the human operator has all but been replaced by robots and machines in many manufacturing workplaces already anyway. But when mechanizing or automating any process it is vitally important to look beyond the obvious, and to see what else is being replaced. The human element often introduces many cross checks and enhancements which are not evident at first sight.

One important difference between a human being and a computer, is that human knowledge and perception are not constrained by fixed limits. New ideas can come from anywhere – from a television programme, from a chat with a friend working in another industry, from formal training courses, from group discussions, or from anywhere else. If allowed to do so, the human mind can then convert an idea into reality, through practical understanding and experience. If properly handled, new technology can then become a tool to support such new ideas, rather than a constraint upon progress.

The challenge is to create a working environment where there is an attitude of continual improvement of both skills and methods, where it is considered a positive career step to promote new ideas rather than just accept what exists already.

Deskill or reskill?

Skilled people cost money. There is therefore a natural management tendency to reduce the skills needed in the workplace, to replace costly skilled people with cheaper less skilled workers operating automated computers or machines – to 'deskill' any operation.

But is it really possible to deskill a business today and still develop new business for the future? Take a close look at those skills that are being dispensed with before making too many changes. As well as the obvious skills to carry out their immediate tasks, staff learn many other things while they are working for an organization. It takes many years to build up working relationships with the staff in other offices. Knowledge of customers and countries, the history of past projects, and all sorts of knowledge which was not originally part of the job may have been learned. Older staff tend to have a very well developed sense of responsibility and confidence, which it is more difficult to find in junior, less skilled, staff. Every business needs people that can be relied upon.

Existing staff may like the idea of a change in their job anyway. Or they might prefer to work at home to save overhead costs, or be happy to work part time to transfer their skills to a new generation, if support is also offered while starting another career. It may be worthwhile to 'reskill' existing staff into new jobs, with different responsibilities, rather than just deskilling and dispensing with staff. Once experience has gone it is very difficult to replace. A computer can be switched off in an instant, or reprogrammed in a few minutes. Reliable human experience takes many years of learning and considerable expense to replace.

Innovation to success

With the movement towards a technology-rich, information-dependent Information Society, we are in the middle of a period of rapid and complex changes. No longer can one senior executive control, plan and organize every aspect of a modern business. Every part of the business is being affected by changes. The commercial environment is ever more competitive, ever more global, ever more dependent upon the information and communication technologies ('ICTs').

Business success needs innovation. Environmental sustainability needs new levels of understanding. Everybody needs to know more, understand more, and apply new skills. The successful enterprise of the future will not need to waste time watching what competitors do. By the time the results of the analysis are assimilated, it will be too late to compete. The successful business of the future will lead through understanding and internal innovation. Confidence must come through knowledge. If everyone is waiting to receive orders, time will be wasted and the initiative will be lost. Senior executives must become the coaches and team leaders, coaxing new levels of achievement out of their staff, rewarding success, and extending extra training and access to vital information to prevent the repetition of any failures.

Everyone must know where they stand – what they are responsible for, where they are authorized to take the initiative, and how to progress changes when ideas go beyond their immediate authority. This is not anarchy. It is effective teamworking, where everyone is encouraged to develop their full potential; where everyone knows and understands their position and responsibilities within the working structure; and where overlaps between responsibilities are seen as positive opportunities to brainstorm and develop ideas with several minds, rather than incursions upon each other's territory.

The training value perception barrier

Over the past few decades, as the importance of training in the development of 'human resources' has been properly recognized, training has become a major commercial industry. Unfortunately though, as the true commercial cost of training has become more evident, this has also become an impediment to the changes and development which need to occur.

To the accountant, training has become an overhead cost. But not just any overhead cost. Because the rewards from training are not necessarily immediate, it is easy to rationalize a policy of postponing training until more money is available. Other overheads cannot be postponed. If the interest on loans is not paid, the firm will go out of business. If the rent on the office isn't paid, there will be nowhere to work. The furniture, the computers and the company cars are all necessities of life without which it seems a firm cannot operate. As the recession took hold around the world in the early 1990s, training became an easy target for cutting immediate expenditure and improving cash flow.

But the successful firms coming out of the recession were not necessarily making better profits again by charging more money. They have successfully cut down their fixed costs of office space, moved their production to lower cost areas of the same country or to another part of the world, drastically cut their senior management bureaucracy by pushing responsibility downwards, improved teamworking and given staff more freedom to improve the ways in which they work. For such changes to occur, training and learning must be at the top of the agenda, not an optional extra to be deferred for a few years.

There are few areas of modern commercial activity where major changes are not taking place as a result of the rapid development and introduction of new technologies. The key to successful change lies in people. Leadership must come from the top of any organization, but implementation takes place at every level. If the people involved have not been properly prepared through training and education, they will be fearful of where the changes may lead, and will resist change.

People are the key to the future, and appropriate education can make people an asset rather than a burden. If job losses are an essential component of a change, perhaps the staff involved may have some good ideas about the most painless way to achieve it. Rather than perpetuate a confrontational 'us and them' situation, managers must make sacrifices as well, and try to meet in the middle for serious debate. Unfortunately, if training has been neglected for many years, and staff have intentionally not been kept informed of the developing situation within which their future is framed, this may be very difficult to achieve.

Learning as an individual responsibility

As the whole framework of employment gradually changes, so must attitudes to training and education. No longer is employment with a major firm upon leaving school or university a guarantee of a job for life. No longer do children always follow in their parents' footsteps, learning the same skills and working their way gradually up the organizational hierarchy of management towards retirement. In the UK, for instance, many of the major employers of a few decades ago have shrunk to a tiny fraction of their former size. The coal industry, shipbuilding and many areas of traditional manufacturing have all changed dramatically in response to international competition and changing market needs.

Many people will come to expect several major changes of direction, and hence skill and education requirements, during their working lives. No longer is a working life about a single linear career; it is likely to consist of several shorter careers in different types of job, linked by changes of direction to adapt to changing circumstances. The flexibility of the modern information age may make some of these changes a personal decision rather than something enforced by an employer; a young person might prefer to live in a major town, then move to the countryside and work at home while bringing up a young family. As the family grows up, new challenges in a different country might be high on the agenda.

In many industries, training has become viewed as the employer's responsibility. Because training courses are expensive, it seems unreasonable even to consider that employees will pay for training themselves. And the time spent training must come out of normal productive working hours. So the employees place themselves under the complete control of their employer, totally reliant upon their employer to develop their future career – like sheep. Unfortunately, sheep have a useful lifetime, during which they should be well fed and well cared for. But there is an optimum time to send them to the slaughterhouse, determined by business economics. A business may not intend to treat its employees the same way, but the ravages and storms of the modern commercial world may force it to. When a firm cannot survive financially, costs must be cut immediately and staff must go. If individuals are totally dependent upon the firm for all forward thinking and career planning, they will find themselves out in the wilderness when this happens.

In the past, some firms have taken an attitude of making their employees very dependent upon the firm for their future, in order to reduce employees' mobility to apply for other jobs. But hardly any organization can really guarantee future employment many years ahead, and the more forward-thinking and creative people are likely to resent any attempt to limit their opportunities and to take opportunities outside regardless. This naturally leaves the less adaptable, less creative, more dependent staff behind, who are much less able to cope with changes and turn them to the advantage of the business when opportunities occur.

161

So, in the Information Society of the future, it seems logical that training, learning and career development must become much more of an individual responsibility. As employment becomes more volatile, with more flexible employment arrangements, remuneration will be closely tied to skills and experience. If individuals want particular types of job and work responsibilities, it is their personal responsibility to make sure that they find the right training and experience first. Of course, in most situations, it will also be in the employer's interest to contribute to such training, since employment terms are likely to be for several years at a time. Alternatively, employers might remove training costs from their overheads and add it to salaries paid to their staff. This then places the onus upon the staff to decide whether to take the money in the short term as extra pay, or to invest in training for a better-paid future in the long term.

Learning from each other

Pushing the responsibility for training back onto the individual appears at first to be just another way of cutting overheads and indirectly cutting pay. On the other hand, training has become expensive and formalized, and the extent of training really needed is well beyond the financial means of many commercial organizations. Individuals will be far more cautious about the money spent on hotels, training centres and travel expenses.

There will always be a market for professionally organized and well designed commercial training courses. But in order to make the transition into an information technology rich culture, and reap the benefits of the change rather than suffer the consequences, far more extensive and much less expensive opportunities for training are needed.

We need to look more closely at what we learn and how we learn it as part of our everyday lives. We all learn something new every week. We read the newspapers, watch television, talk to friends and colleagues, attend meetings, go to concerts and plays, surf the Internet or delve into multimedia 'edutainment'. We are bombarded with information which we each, individually, assimilate and sift, retaining some of it and discarding the rest.

Most of the changes happening in our working practices as a result of the shift towards the Information Society must first be understood in conceptual terms before they can be converted into practical benefits. We must first understand the concept of making the computer, rather than a paper file, the definitive place to store information, before we get into the technicalities of how we use the computer to do it. We must understand the concept that if all of the information that we use in our daily work is electronic, we could actually log on to a computer terminal in a different town or even a different country on different days and carry on working as normal. We need to understand the principles of using electronic mail and the basic facilities offered by hypertext and the World-Wide Web on the Internet.

The first step in understanding many of these things is to recognize the need to learn. The next step is to realize that we may not need to go on an expensive training course to understand the basics. Find another way of learning. If one person has managed to understand the basic principles, why not explain them to someone else? A little introductory knowledge can soon be reinforced through reading or other learning methods if you want to know more. Learning can be as formal or informal as you like. You hear the details of the weekend's sports successes and failures in conversation over coffee. You learn about international politics and natural disasters on the television news. Everyone must also be constantly learning about the skills needed in the Information Society. When you discover something of interest, does your working environment encourage you to hold an informal seminar at lunchtime to tell your colleagues? Is there high-level support for stopping to explain new ideas to your colleagues at the coffee machine, or does senior management frown upon this as diverting staff from the vital work of today's deadlines? When you visit another office, does the manager there automatically organize an informal gathering over lunchtime sandwiches for the local staff to hear about what is new in your area of the firm, and let you know what they have been doing?

Knowledge and information must be allowed to flow freely within an organization. Lack of knowledge leads to mistakes. Trying to hold back the flow of information is like building a dam to hold back a flood, with associated expense and effort. If the information is allowed to flow, it will just flow past those who are not interested, without diverting their time and effort, but it will also naturally reach those who need it most.

One of the first skills which everyone must learn, though, is to apply learning time and activities effectively. There is a critical balance to be struck between broadening knowledge and wasting precious working time. Management cannot hope to control and direct the flow of information completely. If the flow of potentially useful information is intentionally constrained for fear of diverting precious working time, the limited internal communication and learning opportunities which do occur will be spent discussing sporting events, new cars, and other topics which will not have such an important impact upon the business. Just as with the telephone, where everyone must learn not to waste the firm's money on personal international calls and to minimize the length of long-distance trunk calls, everyone must learn to manage and organize their personal learning and teaching opportunities to benefit both the firm and the individual without diverting excessive time or resources from other activities.

It is also important to develop a good sense of understanding what is basic knowledge that everyone should know, and what is specialist expertise which requires reference to an expert or to technical reference literature.

Teaching and informing skills also become important to everybody. Anyone in the organization should be able to write an article, give a talk or lead a discussion. These are no longer just senior management skills. If junior employees have good ideas about how to utilize new technology in the firm, they should be able to explain those ideas to their colleagues in lunch hour seminars, and participate in discussions with their colleagues and managers to decide rapidly whether the idea should be taken any further and who is the right person to champion the cause and present the case. Everyone should understand how to participate in a constructive discussion, with full knowledge of the value of everyone else's time and the need to complete the session by a specified time with a clear list of further actions to be taken.

New technologies to develop training opportunities

Just as the need for much more training to be delivered at much lower cost has become apparent, new technologies to deliver knowledge efficiently are becoming available at a practical cost through advances in information technology.

Multimedia has initially been directed at supplementing conventional children's education through multimedia encyclopaedias and interactive exploration environments, mainly on mass-produced CD-ROMs, played on an ordinary domestic PC. But the cost of the technology needed to prepare multimedia material is reducing dramatically.

High-quality digital still and video cameras are available in the high street. With an image stabilizer to reduce the camera shake of an inexperienced operator, and fully automatic focus and compensation for lighting conditions, almost anyone can take usable video footage. Computer processing power has increased, the cost of disk storage has decreased, international standards have been established in video compression, and the cost of multimedia authoring software has come within the reach of even a small business. The special CD-ROM drive needed to write a one-off CD-ROM disk is now little more expensive than a laser printer. Almost anyone could make a specialized training multimedia CD-ROM if they wanted to.

Technology is one thing; skills are another! Good training material requires skills and experience which are well outside the background of most employees of the 1990s. But the techniques are becoming well developed and can be taught and explained to anyone who is interested to learn. When I was young, my school used to make a film each year. A small number of the more senior pupils learned to operate a portable movie camera, and filmed every major event that the school participated in during the year, then edited it together to show to the parents at a suitable evening event. Other pupils produced plays and organized debates and concerts. Our workplaces have to become similarly diverse and rich environments, where employees with an interest actively develop secondary skills in communication and education to help their colleagues present and convey important information to others through new technologies. Cost is evaporating as a barrier; skill, understanding and imagination are now the principal obstacles.

Other technologies are also rapidly coming to the fore, just as access to education must dramatically increase if we are to enjoy an understanding of our new society rather than fear the unknown. Suddenly there is the potential for vast numbers of television channels through satellite and cable television. As costs come down, dedicated television channels could soon exist for particular professions or industries. Individual firms can already rent satellite transmissions by the hour to broadcast regular messages to every office or retail outlet in a country or a region. Several professions in the UK already have a video cassette television 'channel', which distributes several half-hour current affairs and educational programmes every month to regular subscribers. The principles of distributed television learning pioneered by the open universities in several countries can now be extended from purely academic education and developed right across all other areas of human activity.

Another important opportunity is for distributed interactive presentation and debate through video conferencing. Setting up a video conferencing session used to involve scheduling the use of expensive high-speed data communication lines, and could only be carried out between specially equipped video conferencing rooms at fixed locations. The latest video signal compression technology allows video conferencing to take place today over much more widely available digital ISDN telephone lines. Standardization of video conferencing will also allow individuals to participate using a cheap video camera connected to an ordinary PC.

165

It is becoming feasible to hold a lunchtime seminar in several offices simultaneously, or to hold a professional meeting in one location with participants asking questions from locations hundreds of miles away.

Will the office of the future include an 'education corner' – a television-cum-video-conferencing-cum-multimedia facility, where employees gather at lunchtime or at the end of the working day to learn? Certain days might have a general industry sector update by television broadcast, another day might be devoted to particular skills courses presented via multimedia, another might be for an open discussion of new ideas, and yet another might be given over to a talk by an employee who has just returned from completing a new project. In the evening there might be a learned society meeting linking several different countries to debate an important issue of the day.

The power of debate

Debate and discussion have an important role to play in formulating solutions. In contrast, most industries have a tradition of strong leadership, of decisive high level actions taking companies into new territories of business with associated success and profits.

However, many parts of the world are now suffering some of the debris of such single-minded actions. Unconstrained industrial development has created a world littered with environmental disasters and hazards. Attempts to extrapolate from past successes have left whole industries decimated in the face of global competition, as small numbers of powerful industrial leaders try to comprehend and stay ahead of the entire intellectual capacity of the rest of the world.

There seems to be a difference between the strong decisive leadership needed in the industrial world, the similar unquestioning confidence of the trained professional in any field, and the academic openness to debate when resolving any problem. This has been illustrated to me through a whole series of different international meetings, conferences and committees. The cultural diversity evident between the different European nations is a rich source of ideas and different viewpoints.

In the commercial or professional world, people are employed for their experience and their expertise. They are expected to get things right, and always to put forward a clear solution which they can confidently defend when questioned. Because they aim to get things right first time, they are not in the practice of changing their views, and will normally staunchly defend their position rather than show any weakness or room for manoeuvre. They have spent years of training to acquire such confidence.

At the other extreme, a pure academic is working at the limits of understanding, and will happily put forward an incomplete and unconfirmed solution for debate, to test its validity among his or her peers. The ensuing debate will either strengthen the case and fill in the gaps, or expose serious flaws for further investigation. This is how new knowledge and understanding develop. There is no penalty for making a mistake, and finding problems early through debate can save a lot of wasted effort. There is no stigma attached to withdrawing an idea – some will succeed, some will not, and that is the nature of research.

Modern business can no longer sit at the decisive extreme of strong leadership without enhancement through debate. No longer can the chief executive aim to understand every opportunity and limitation of the new information technologies or of human perception. Neither can the director in charge of information technology actually know all of the parameters and effects. The young graduate who has just completed a final-year project testing the latest technology developments from Japan or the USA might have a valid contribution to make. Or the chief accountant might have heard from counterparts in other companies of technical problems or delivery delays which could affect the proposed solution.

The mechanisms through which contributions can be made will vary from one organization to another. Care must be taken that debate and confirmation do not slow down decision-making processes and cause a commercial disadvantage. The effective use of tools like electronic mail to efficiently target and consult busy people while they are travelling or during breaks between meetings must play a role in this. But margins and deadlines are too tight to make unnecessary mistakes, and if the knowledge to refine a decision exists within an organization, it must be utilized.

Changes and more changes

Continuous change has been a feature of human civilization for centuries, gathering momentum over the past few decades. The movement from the Industrial Society to the Information Society is not a sudden step change, but part of a complex process of changes which will continue.

Hence this education process is not just a single, one-off re-education to learn to use a computer. In another three years' time, the computers will be completely different again. The change is really a change to where education and training become an essential and continuous part of everyone's working life, rather than just an optional extra when money permits.

Lifelong learning

The tradition of education has been as a preparation for a working life, a formative stage that we all go through on our way to becoming adults. We go to primary school, then to secondary school. Some people continue through more advanced exams to university. Then the paths normally diverge. There seems to be a general attitude that at that point, for a working person, education is complete. The rest of a person's life is to be devoted to working, not education. The alternative path is a career of research, extending the frontiers of human knowledge in research establishments.

This attitude has to change. Learning has to become a continuous, lifelong activity. There is no point at which learning ends, at which education is complete. In the future, many people are likely to go through several different careers in their lifetime, as industries change, as their family circumstances change, and as they look for new challenges. While in one job, many people will start learning for the next. Within the same job, learning will be essential to make career progress.

Even conventional education may become more distributed through an individual's lifetime. Why does a degree have to be taken immediately after schooling? With flexible learning techniques a degree can be taken at any time that suits an individual. As soon as one degree course is finished, why not start planning another in a few years time, as part of a strategy towards the next phase of a career?

Nearly all of the discussion above has revolved around working activities. Leisure time has been steadily increasing for several decades in many countries, leading to greater diversity of non-working activities. Once again, development of any activity involves some form of learning, and all of the new technologies and learning opportunities will also enhance leisure opportunities. The boundary between what is work and what is leisure may gradually become less clear, as part of leisure time is devoted to education for future working opportunities, and communications reduce the need for business travel creating more free time.

The core knowledge of the future

It is interesting to conjecture what the core knowledge from basic education that everyone will need in the future will be. If everybody is continuously extending their knowledge, there is a possibility of divergence between the knowledge of different people as they specialize more and more in different areas. There are already many different groups of knowledge held by different people, making some communication easier and some more difficult. For instance, people who understand the technicalities of how computers work tend to communicate at a different level from people who do not.

The basic education of the future must set down a framework of basic knowledge which will allow everyone to communicate with each other. This must encompass far more than just language – it must also include concepts and attitudes that will stay with people throughout their lives.

An important element of basic education, or core knowledge of the future, must clearly be a positive attitude to lifelong learning. Everyone must expect to learn as part of their everyday lives. Learning must become as much a necessity of life as eating and breathing for people who want to look positively towards the future. Learning opportunities will be available everywhere, but understanding how to use these opportunities wisely will become an important skill for future citizens of the Information Society.

Another group of concepts which must be learned earlier rather than later is an understanding of potential career structures and opportunities. No longer will there just be a search for a first job with an expectation that it will be a job for life. More assistance will be needed to get on the first rung of the ladder, with a plan for how to climb up further, or transfer to another ladder if that first job does not prove a success. A basic understanding of management methods and teamworking skills will also be a distinct advantage right from the start, to understand what is expected of an individual and why.

A learning culture

This whole chapter has been devoted to describing the 'learning culture' which it will be essential to develop within the Information Society. This learning culture is a combination of a general positive attitude by everyone towards wanting to learn, supported by government and business strategies and policies designed to create learning opportunities wherever possible.

Training does not have to be expensive. If people want to learn, they will find a way of learning. The basic tools of learning are cheap and simple: just holding a meeting and discussing a subject is the first stage towards extending knowledge. With a widespread positive attitude towards training, the new technologies of the information age offer many ways to support and extend this learning culture.

169

Learning in the community

Back in our fictional market town community, let us look at how the learning culture of the future has enhanced the community centre project, and made it much easier for everyone involved to understand what is going on and how best they can contribute. The project design is now complete and construction is well advanced, and we can look at how different people's ideas have been integrated through the power of debate and understanding.

The leisure centre is at the heart of the development, and there has been considerable debate and discussion about what leisure facilities should be provided and what provision should be made for the future. What sporting facilities are needed? Is a swimming pool required? If so, should it be a training pool for swimming clubs and the local schools, where competitions and galas can be held, or is it a family fun pool with slides and a wave machine? Or have ingenious people, through research and experience of similar centres elsewhere, anywhere in the world, found a way of combining both types of swimming pool for everyone's benefit?

A major retail store has signed a contract to take a significant part of the retail area, greatly improving the financial viability of the whole scheme. However, shopkeepers in town were very concerned that this would take business away from them completely. A whole series of electronic debates and discussions with executives of the retail store, and a few face-to-face meetings, have arrived at a range of solutions that nearly everyone will accept. Some shops in town have decided to move to the community centre or open an extra small branch there. Also, some local corner shops have decided to become agents for the major store, with an electronic link through which their regular shoppers can order anything from the major store, and either pick it up at the corner shop or arrange for home delivery.

There will be a direct, convenient and pleasant footpath from the new community centre right to the middle of the town. There will also be a frequent local minibus service, diverted on request to any household, connecting the community centre to the centre of town and all other parts of the town. Although the centre is on the edge of town, it is intended to become part of the whole community. There will be a café and a garden with a lake around the new centre (Figure 9.1).

Building the centre has also generated the opportunity to build a short bypass around the centre of town, along the main route used by heavy goods vehicles. This will be screened from view and the noise reduced by earth mounds and trees. Although business travel may have significantly reduced in the new information culture, goods will still need to be distributed everywhere using heavy trucks.

As the new leisure centre was designed, the lack of a properly equipped local theatre was highlighted by the local amateur dramatic society. It was soon realized that the same theatre could be electronically equipped for many other purposes as well, such as relaying discussion meetings, talks, concerts, and major theatre productions from other locations.

With everyone's increased consciousness of the need for education and learning, it was also realized that there was an opportunity for a properly equipped education centre to supplement other educational

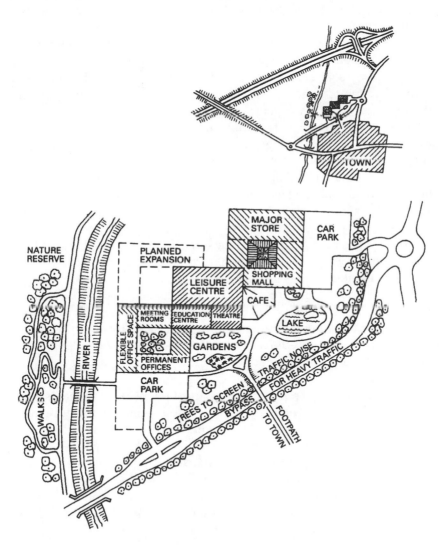

Figure 9.1. The community centre.

facilities in the town. This will be able to provide direct links to various universities and colleges of further education, making most of the facilities of major education institutes available locally. The education centre will be supplemented by the theatre for lectures and by the meeting rooms of the office centre for workshops and video conferencing tutorials.

The office space will be a combination of fixed permanent offices and flexible office space and meeting rooms which can be rented by the hour. Demand was slightly uncertain, so provision has been made for a significant expansion of the office facilities if demand is greater than initially expected.

Transport and traffic requirements generated by and modified by the new development have been carefully analysed, modelled and designed. Infrastructure requirements to provide water, power and information technology, and to remove waste water and rubbish, have been carefully integrated into the infrastructure of the town.

There was much debate about the environmental effects of the development, and many people were consulted along the way. The present site was carefully fitted in between a variety of constraints. All of the local plant and animal life was studied in some detail to minimize the effects upon natural habitats. Energy requirements have been minimized through the application of international best practice. The project has been thoughtfully blended into the surrounding landscape, and the opportunity has been taken to create some footpaths for short walks in the adjacent countryside, and a nature reserve at the edge of the development site.

The whole development is the result of extensive teamwork by many members of the community and a whole range of experts and specialists. Some people, who depend upon selling their skills for their livelihood, have been paid for their efforts, while others, with local or wider interests at heart, have freely contributed their input without expecting any direct financial return.

Now that construction is in progress, most people know what is going to happen and when it will happen. They know when there will be traffic diversions and delays and they know when there may be noise and mud on the roads. But many of them also know the people involved. If they see a water pipe leaking on the site, or an excavation left open that a child might fall into, or see some minor improvement which seems to have been overlooked as the scheme takes shape, they know who to contact to do something about it. After all, it is their community and their centre, and they will be living with it for many years, so they want the best.

10 Where the money goes

The only thing that you can guarantee...

I have been working with computers for more than twenty years. For several years I managed the provision of computer facilities for over a dozen offices of varying sizes, and checked every detail of expenditure on the computer systems and the staff needed to support them. There is only one thing that you can definitely guarantee about computers: they will cost money!

Cost−benefit disillusionment

The world is full of horror stories about cost overruns and computer systems failing to live up to expectations. In the 1980s, computers were going to be the wonder machines to streamline businesses and lead the way into a bright new world. Did it ever actually happen? If not, what went wrong?

The implementation of new ideas always requires money. The availability of money drives new ideas forward, and the lack of money controls and constrains progress. This is the reality at the end of the concepts. We can talk ideas forever, but nothing will actually happen until someone finds some money to do something.

An established business can find money through one of two routes. Either money must be borrowed, to be paid back in the future through improved profits or reduced operating costs, or it must be generated from the sale of assets or through not making other planned current expenditure. In either case, a strong financial case is essential to justify the expenditure.

Hence the need for a cost−benefit analysis. Introducing new computer systems must result in a benefit, and it must be possible to quantify this benefit in pure financial terms. Compare the financial benefit with the cost of implementing the new system, and if the benefit exceeds the cost then it must be a good idea. On this basis many major computer systems projects were initiated, but unfortunately many of them did not live up to expectations (Figure 10.1). Why not?

Every project has its own particular unique combination of factors, but common causes of failure and the resulting cost–benefit disillusionment are:

1. Failing to consult future system users properly before starting.
2. Underestimating hardware costs.
3. Overestimating the useful lifetime of computer hardware.
4. Failing to quantify operational staff training costs.
5. Failing to allow properly for long-term system management and operation costs.

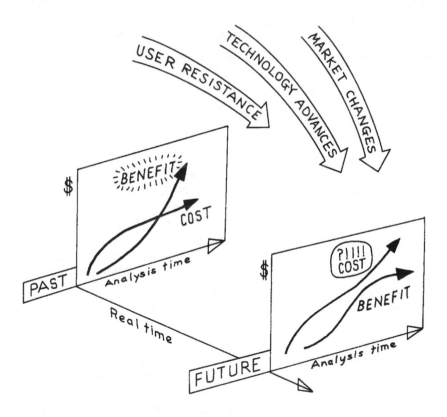

Figure 10.1. Cost–benefit disillusionment.

6. Software development cost overruns.
7. Software development time overruns.
8. Failing to provide appropriate user training.
9. Failure to gain proper support from all levels of management.
10. User resistance to new ideas.
11. Overestimating future sales or revenue.
12. Failure to predict technology changes.

Costs rarely reduce, and often increase. Benefits tend to be very sensitive to critical factors like the date at which a new system becomes operational. If money has been borrowed on the expectation of future benefits when the system starts operating, the equation changes very rapidly. Borrowing for longer costs more money. If the benefits don't start on time, it takes much longer to generate the money needed to pay back the loan. Benefits soon become losses.

Once a project is started, a commitment to almost all of the cost rapidly becomes inevitable. Equipment is purchased, staff are employed or contracts are let – the cost side of the equation is pretty much guaranteed to happen right from the very start. Benefits are much less tangible and far more difficult to ensure. Any of the factors listed above (and there are many other possibilities) could delay or prevent the benefits happening. This is a high-risk situation, with a good chance of something going wrong.

Failures are always far more memorable than successes! A few expensive failures, and senior management will soon become very sceptical about the use and benefits of information technology, and it is easy to see why.

The cost-benefit approach is also dangerous because it becomes more important to prove benefits than to be realistic about losses. Costs are offset under other budgets to improve the figures, and there is little incentive to try to assess the full extent of the damage to assist in future investment planning.

The person responsible for the project is identified as having failed. Not the senior management who should have know better, and who delegated the detail because they didn't understand it. The manager behind the project is now the firm's most experienced technology manager – he or she knows what went wrong and why. But because of the failure, someone else will be selected next time, and we go right around the same loop again. Money drives, money controls, money destroys.

Long-term strategies and dramatic step changes

Enter the information technology strategy, the IT strategy, the framework within which to plan and monitor the future. With a strategy you know where you are going and how you intend to get there. It should have high-level approval, so senior management will have taken full responsibility for the development and use of information technology within an organization and given authorization to implement it.

The main problem with IT strategies is that they can become out of date rather fast as technology develops. The senior approval of revisions then becomes an obstacle to progress. A strategy must be versed in the right terms, at a fundamental level. It must say just enough, but not too much, so that it can remain valid.

For instance, it is sensible to define it in terms of the level of service to be provided rather than the specification of the equipment to be used. Hence the strategy might be to 'provide a computer on every desk, of an appropriate specification to run a suitable integrated office package which will be installed on it', without getting into the details of makes, versions and models which are likely to vary as the market changes. Then it is necessary to include details of the central services to be provided for data storage, archiving and backup ('data warehousing'), corporate management support systems, corporate information support systems (such as an 'Intranet'), specialist dedicated software systems, printing and publishing facilities, communications and conferencing links internally within the firm and outside to the world at large, and the operations and support service needed to keep it all running and sort out any problems.

In every case the strategy should try to define a practical level of service while trying to leave some freedom to implement the service in the most cost-effective manner within the prevailing situation and market-place at the time.

One interesting phenomenon when comparing the implementation of systems in small and large organizations is the inertia effect of existing systems. I have been intrigued to watch on several occasions how a small firm with only a few computers can take a snap decision to re-equip with the latest equipment to take advantage of new technology or special price offers, while a large firm with dozens, hundreds or thousands of pieces of equipment must replace and update equipment in an organized manner over a period of months or years. This inertia, slowing down change in the larger organization, is as much a result of the limited capacity of an efficiently staffed support service to reconfigure and replace equipment in an orderly manner as it is of the constraints of costs and cash flow.

But an IT strategy is all but useless in isolation. It must be an integral part, and a supporting component, of an integrated business strategy. It is no good deciding that every desk in an organization should have a computer of a certain performance with certain software without first deciding how many desks are needed in the future and where they are going to be located. Will the number of staff decrease or increase? Will some staff be working from home, with different equipment require-ments? Will certain staff be mobile, booking desks in different offices on different days? How many staff will need portable computers?

It is also no good just deciding a total budget for the computer equipment alongside the entertainment budget for clients and the budget for office stationery. The first decision must be what business you are going to be in, followed by how you will carry out that business; then the decisions about how much computer technology will be required and how dependent upon computers you wish to be should become much clearer. Somehow, in the past it seemed easy to understand that a draughtsman working with pen and ink had to have a drawing board to work on – it was part of the cost of employing a draughtsman. It would have been completely unreasonable to expect the draughtsman to work efficiently on an ordinary desk. Similarly, if someone is employed to do a job which needs a certain level of computing power, the computer must be provided or the business will suffer.

Time-scales for change are also an important element of business strategy. I once chaired a meeting with a number of presentations from different firms about their approaches to investment and development of computer facilities. One speaker described a very positive and carefully planned strategy to completely update an organization's computer systems. The benefits were clear, and it seemed that a dramatic step forward had been taken. Another speaker described a process of evolution, developing new capabilities as older equipment was progres-sively replaced. At first sight, these were completely different strategies. But on closer inspection, both involved a systematic change from a centralized system to a distributed system of PC networks. Although for the step change a single decision to proceed was taken at a specific moment, I was surprised to find that the logistics of replacing equipment and training staff meant that both strategies implemented the main elements of the change over similar time periods of two years or more. Strategies may not be as different as they first appear.

Investment patterns

In the early days of centralized computer rooms, and continuing through the era of the first supermini computers, investment was fairly straightforward. These were large investments, and if they couldn't be bought with cash they were generally leased. The leasing system in the UK is quite straightforward. The leasing company buys the equipment on your behalf, and then leases it back to you, effectively renting it at a monthly or quarterly cost which includes an appropriate amount for providing this financing service. The lease is for a fixed period, after which the original investment has been repaid with interest, and thereafter the equipment continues to be leased for a small nominal fee until it is eventually disposed of.

In the early 1980s, a supermini computer might have been provided on a five-year lease. Its useful service life might have extended to eight or even ten years, so it was a good investment. By the end of the 1980s, high-power computer workstations were in vogue, and because of their high cost it seemed obvious to lease them as well, like the computers in the computer room before them. But then something changed. Powerful PCs rapidly came to the fore, vying with the workstations for business, and winning in many areas because of the lower cost of the PC and the greater variety of standard software which would run on them. If the workstations were purchased on five-year leases, they were superseded by new PCs before the original leases were completed, requiring the payment of new leases for the PCs at the same time! Not a healthy scenario, as the UK economy went through a rather depressed period in the early 1990s.

The useful lifetime of modern computer equipment is becoming so short that it is doubtful whether leasing is a good idea at all now. The productive life of a PC before it is completely superseded by new models may be as short as two years. However, businesses must invest to survive, and if cashflow is tight leasing may be the only option. If equipment is bought on a three-year lease, every attempt must be made to keep the equipment in productive use for at least three years. With PCs, one way of achieving this is to buy high-specification equipment, and then to plan for its use to change over a period of time, downgrading it to a general use system when even higher speed PCs are purchased the following year. There may even be a third stage in the working life of the PC for routine work requiring less processing capacity.

When investment money was very short, I remember applying a rigorous principle of deciding whether any new equipment bought on a three-year lease would still be in use in three years' time. If this seemed unlikely a different solution had to be found, perhaps buying new equipment as an upgrade for another office, so that the equipment displaced in the process could fulfil the short-term need.

Some investment strategies take a dramatic upgrade approach of re-equipping a large portion of an organization with new computers at the same time. This allows a bargain to be struck on the supply of so much equipment in one go, improves morale and makes that vital change to making more widespread use of computer technology much easier to realize.

However, extensive one-off investments may also be storing up problems for the future. If all of the equipment is purchased at one time, it will also all need to be replaced at once in a few years' time. There will be a dramatic short-term peak in support staffing requirement, and disruption and confusion at the time of the change. If the equipment is all replaced in three years' time, just before it is replaced it will all be three years out of date, giving a serious business disadvantage until the change takes place. Far too many cost–benefit analyses assume that the benefits achieved in the first year will be repeated in the second and third years after any change. But the evolution of technology is continuous at the moment. The business advantage of re-equipping this year will be eroded next year against competitors who re-equip then. And eroded more the year after.

At first sight it seems a good idea to re-equip every part of the business at the same time. Everyone then has compatible systems, giving integration and communication advantages right across the organization. But before very long this immediate advantage can become a millstone, locking the whole business into a historical time warp as the rest of the world moves on. Upgrading components of the system becomes an essential requirement to keep pace, but every expense upgrading old equipment to keep pace reduces the investment available for new equipment in the future.

How many people redecorate every room in their house at the same time? Or replace all the carpets at once? Maybe some people do, if they can afford to, but when money is limited people replace and improve one step at a time, gradually spending money on their homes and improving living standards as resources permit.

Steady reinvestment, apart from giving a more even spending profile, reduces the chances of dramatic investment mistakes, provides steady employment and development of support staff, and allows achievable training programmes for staff. Technology 'refresh' starts to become an accepted part of everyday life. A firm's resources can be concentrated on developing its core business and doing it well, rather than being diverted into struggling to cope with sudden changes.

As an indication, if computer equipment is seen to have a useful life of approximately three years, then one third of all of the firm's equipment will need to be replaced each year. That can mean a lot of equipment! And during a three-year life, items like PCs may be moved to several different locations, keeping the most powerful PCs in the locations needing the greatest performance for the benefit of the business.

As this replacement occurs, there must obviously be clear guidelines as to the service that anyone can expect. Senior staff must not automatically have the right to the most modern or most powerful computers – everyone must have the equipment that is most appropriate to do their job. The most powerful computers will probably be needed in the graphics or computer drafting department, or for routine calculation and analysis carried out by junior staff.

Real costs

Let us explore how much computer equipment really costs a little more closely. This calculation will change rapidly, so you will need to put in some figures from your own business and from recent advertisements if you want to see some actual numbers.

First, consider the cost of a reasonably powerful PC. Put it on a desk. Put a seat at the desk, and some shelves beside it. Take the cost of the PC and compare it with the cost of the desk, the chair and the shelves. Now work out the costs of renting the office space that the desk sits on, heating, lighting, taxes etc. Then look at the salary of the person sitting at the desk, plus associated employment costs.

To do this calculation correctly, two further important refinements are needed. First look closely at the lifetime of each component, and convert it to an annual cost. The furniture will inevitably last much longer than the computer.

Second, consider all of the other less visible costs which must be allocated to this working location: central computer facilities, support services and communication costs; management and central administration costs for the firm; and training costs. Depending upon the type of firm, there is probably some element of marketing cost. There are also stationery, secretarial support and other costs. They all add up – see Figure 10.2.

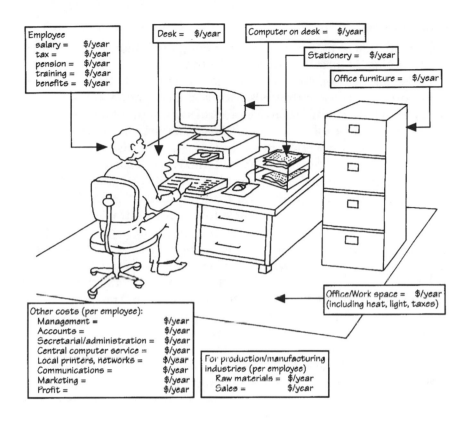

Employee
salary = $/year
tax = $/year
pension = $/year
training = $/year
benefits = $/year

Desk = $/year

Computer on desk = $/year

Stationery = $/year

Office furniture = $/year

Office/Work space = $/year
(including heat, light, taxes)

Other costs (per employee):
Management = $/year
Accounts = $/year
Secretarial/administration = $/year
Central computer service = $/year
Local printers, networks = $/year
Communications = $/year
Marketing = $/year
Profit = $/year

For production/manufacturing
industries (per employee)
Raw materials = $/year
Sales = $/year

Figure 10.2. Putting costs into proportion.

Now look closely at the proportion of all of this cost taken up by the provision of computer facilities. In most cases, it is not all that large a proportion. Then consider carefully which elements of all of these costs are most important and put them all into an order of priority. Does a fancy modern desk actually produce more work? Does all of the work really need to be done in the office or could some of it be done from home? Does the employee actually spend three-quarters of the time visiting clients, so that he or she only needs a desk and a fixed computer part-time anyway? Will a more powerful computer allow the employee to be more productive? Could the office be in a low-cost out-of-town industrial unit rather than in an expensive town centre office block?

In the information age, it is essential to break down conventional boundaries and to take a holistic view. The result of the analysis will be different for every business, and will also change continuously with time.

Real benefits

In the early days of computers, everyone was looking for financial benefits to justify their investments. The trouble is that it is easy to slip into believing that benefits exist when in reality they do not.

For instance, in the early 1980s I worked for a period in the field of computer-aided drafting. There was a lot of sales hype about the benefits of this new technology. Computer-aided drafting meant that it was possible to dispense with drawing boards and ink pens and produce perfect engineering drawings all of the time. When it came to looking at cost savings, just consider a large multi-storey office building. Instead of preparing a separate hand drawing for every part of every floor from scratch, the computer made it possible to take an electronic copy of the previous floor, make whatever minor changes were needed, and then plot the new drawing with very little effort. The advantages seem obvious. But in actuality, draughtsmen had for many years been able to take an old-fashioned dyeline copy of the original drawing, then rub out the parts that needed to be changed and re-draw them. The quality of the drawing might not have been quite as good, but the client was not actually paying any extra for an improvement.

A number of firms tried to prove that computer-aided drafting was more cost-effective through pilot trials. They purchased one computer workstation, and prepared similar drawings under controlled conditions by hand and by computer. Some people were convinced and some were not. The results were very dependent upon the type of drawing and the experience and training of the draughtspeople involved. The results were also very sensitive to how the computer costs were calculated, especially how many years the equipment would continue to be used for, and also what allowance was made for central equipment, management and support staff. At the time, computer workstations and plotting facilities were quite expensive.

In my mind, at the time, I never saw conclusive economic proof of the general case for a move to computer-based drafting, yet it rapidly became commonplace and the norm in many organizations. The calculation of benefits was really too complex to prove one way or the other very clearly. In the early days, greatest success seemed to be where there was commitment to change the way of working and then getting on with the change without wasting a lot of time on analysis. If the investment is made, there is no way of undoing it, so there is little point in looking backwards. When it comes to making new technology work, it is far more dependent upon the attitude and motivation of the people involved than upon scientific analysis. There will probably be problems, and initiative and commitment will be needed to overcome them.

This commitment of everyone to make it work is a sort of invisible economy of scale. If there is one workstation in the corner, sitting under the time and productivity analysis microscope, vying for recognition with conventional workers in the room next door, there is too much scope for personal rivalry and wasted internal competitive effort. Strong leadership may be needed to initiate the necessary consensus and commitment needed. Benefits will result from people and their attitudes.

As long ago as 1532, Machiavelli wrote a very pertinent paragraph, which can be roughly translated as:

There is nothing more difficult to take in hand, more perilous to conduct, or more uncertain in its success, than to take the lead in the introduction of a new order of things, because the innovator has for enemies all of those who have done well under the old conditions, and luke-warm defenders in those who may do well under the new.

Human nature hasn't changed a great deal. Today I am amazed to find experienced staff well into their careers who feel that they cannot touch a new piece of computer software until they have had a complete training course, while a teenage schoolchild will have no hesitation in trying to use a new program with virtually no knowledge about it at all if it allows them to do their homework faster. These are opposite extremes, and the optimum is somewhere in the middle. Just think of a young driver learning to drive a car for the first time. Some professional tuition is a good idea to develop good road sense and understand the correct techniques. But it is very expensive only to learn driving from a professional instructor. A lot of practice is needed, which can be provided much more economically under the passive guidance of another ordinary driver rather than through formal instruction. This is an economy of scale again. If lots of people are learning to use a new computer program, they can assist each other rather than needing continual individual supervision from an expert.

The purohasc prioc mcntality

One of the greatest problems in understanding how much computer facilities really cost is the financial simplifications with which everyone is bombarded every day in advertisements. Newspaper and magazine advertisements constantly remind us just how little a single PC appears to cost in relation to other business costs. This can become a source of significant misunderstanding between computer managers and computer users.

The computer user sees a cheap computer advertised with a comprehensive package of software included. Why can her office not buy one now? They are so cheap that everyone should be able to have one. It seems so simple and so obvious.

The computer manager, responsible for overall investment and long-term costs sees it completely differently. The computer may be so cheap because new, more efficient and easier to support technology will be available in a couple of months. Another different model of computer is an extra headache for support staff already coping with a great range of different types of equipment. The disk or its interface might be slower than the next generation of software will need. The screen graphics might be based on technology which is rapidly being superseded. The computer needs to be networked for support and backup at extra cost. The free software is probably different from the standard packages in use in other parts of the office or may be a different version. The warranty may be much shorter than from other suppliers, requiring extra maintenance contracts or support staff. All in all, sudden changes of purchasing policy tend to create all sorts of extra complications.

There are two sides to this though. The special purchase of different low-cost equipment might fulfil a short-term business need, giving a business advantage, so it should not be rejected without proper objective consideration. If the alternative equipment is not a good investment, it is important to explain why to the computer user. Next time, a special purchase might be a good idea, and if the person making the suggestion understands more it will help to filter wasted effort and concentrate on real opportunities.

There is no perfect or right answer, and modern business does need to use everybody's ideas to succeed. The more that everyone understands, the more efficient the process of arriving at decisions.

As an example of a decision process, when I was responsible for recommending PC investments a few years ago, I kept to major brand names which were advertising built-in upgradability for the future, rather than choosing cheaper models. As it turned out, with natural commercial selection, some computer manufacturers were more success-ful than others, and through takeovers and amalgamations of different firms much of that upgradability never really happened. The decision was perfectly logical, but the market did not behave exactly as expected. Whatever promises computer manufacturers may make about the future, they are completely dependent upon the commercial success of their businesses. Always make sure that investment decisions add up based upon what exists today, with anticipated future development viewed as an added bonus rather than part of the basic equation.

Data costs

One of the costs which is completely dependent upon the situation in which computers are being used is the cost of acquiring and maintaining the data that the system uses.

Before getting too carried away with calculating 'data capture' costs though, do sit down and think about the overall system and the information flows. Is the capture of information on the computer a special one-off event, viewed as an expensive and difficult exercise, or is it a fundamental change happening in the way that work is done, so that information flows into the computer as a natural part of the system?

If the computer is running in parallel with a paper-based system, where everything is recorded and filed on paper first and then transcribed onto the computer system, there is clearly a lot of extra work. Could information be entered directly onto the computer system at the point of collection, using a portable or handheld computer? If a paper copy is needed for checking or other purposes it can then be printed automatically.

Is a major exercise really needed to copy all existing data onto the new system at once, or could the introduction of the new system be phased over a period of time, so that most data is naturally added to the system during an annual cycle of work? Perhaps new data could be entered on the computer, but printed out and handled on paper for a few months to remain compatible with existing paper files, while staff are trained to use the new system. Obviously this depends upon the application.

Many computer systems need vast amounts of data, and data acquisition and handling can become the major cost involved in implementing the system. A particular example is a 'geographic information system' (GIS), which integrates maps and plans with extensive information held in databases about the sizes, shapes, owners and other characteristics of anything shown on the maps. A GIS might include details of all of the buildings in a city, or the ownership of all of the land in a region of a country. At a conference I recently attended about GIS, Jack Dangermond, a well-known figure in the GIS community, pointed out that the computers are almost free in comparison with the data and other costs.

Purchase, lease or rent?

Information technology often seems to offer wonderful business benefits, but at quite a considerable price. Conventional business wisdom is to assess the benefits, quantify the costs, and borrow money to buy the new technology sooner rather than later to see the benefits now.

In the UK, as in some other countries, much computer equipment is leased (as mentioned earlier in this chapter). This method of payment means that the organization using the equipment does not actually own it, which has tax advantages.

Whether equipment is leased or purchased with a bank loan or any other form of borrowing or financing, it is effectively purchased against the expectation of finding the money to pay for it in the future. When times are good, it is all too easy to think that the financing costs seem small in comparison with the benefits. But any of these arrangements is a fixed cost, like a mortgage on a house, and will not go away when times are not so good.

Beware of ending up in a situation where revenue decreases and where margins are so tight that cost savings are essential. Nobody is interested in buying old computer equipment at anything like its original cost, and bank loans or leases are a contractual commitment. After all of the fixed costs, the only solution may be to make staff redundant to stay solvent. This can be a very disturbing and unfortunate situation for the business. The staff lost represent training, skills and investment for the future. The computers that are left are depreciating fast, with little future value. Hence think carefully and deeply about the risks involved in any form of borrowing against the future, and make sure that they are worthwhile.

Direct purchase will reduce immediate profits and limit investment options, but does not store up possible problems for the future. It is well worth considering just how much of what is needed could be bought from more immediate sources of finance, or with short-term bank loans.

Renting computer equipment is another option, but is normally much more expensive if the equipment will be needed for several years. Where renting equipment comes into its own is with short-term project peaks of activity. Beware of buying or leasing extra equipment for which there is only a short-term requirement; it may prove an expensive white elephant when investment money could have been better spent elsewhere.

Always make sure that the people responsible for deciding the external prices of the products or services that a firm sells understand exactly what internal computer facilities are available at what price. It may be easy to provide a standard level of computer equipment at minimal cost, but sudden short-term increases in computer facilities to support particular products or production runs have to come from somewhere. If an organization is equipped for economy and efficiency, there will be little spare equipment. Taking equipment from somewhere else makes another part of the firm inefficient. Purchasing extra equipment which may not be needed in the future may create an unnecessary financial burden on the firm. Renting equipment is likely to be more expensive and must be allowed for in the prices for products quoted to the customer.

Management, support and other costs

Each organization has different support requirements. In a very small business with just one PC nobody thinks about support costs, but someone needs to take backups and pay for repairs when anything goes wrong. A larger business with several PCs probably needs a computer network, and someone must keep track of how much disk space is available and keep software versions up to date.

As soon as a business reaches a reasonable size, someone must consider investment policies and financing arrangements, and must organize some form of help desk for when things go wrong and set up maintenance agreements to make sure that any equipment which goes wrong is repaired promptly. Someone must take backups and make sure that all of the communications and network links are operating efficiently.

Then there are consumable costs: paper, ink toner cartridges, disks and so on. There are ongoing costs, such as fixed data links and telephone calls. Who pays for the office space and furniture for the central support unit?

Depending on the system and the level of support needed, it is quite possible for the recurring management, support and other costs to be several times the actual repayments on investment in equipment.

Service level agreements

Computer users usually expect an unlimited service and cannot understand why equipment takes time to repair, and why support help desk staff cannot instantly answer their particular enquiries. The problem is usually in the perception of the service that it is practical and economic to provide.

A very useful tool in managing both user and support service perceptions of what can be provided is the service level agreement.

First, leave behind any perceptions that this is just about internal contracts and additional bureaucracy. I have in the past found that some people become preoccupied with misconceptions about this before stopping to understand the importance of the concept.

The basic concept is quite simple. The computer users and the computer providers (the internal support service, external organization or whatever), sit down together to decide what service is needed in the knowledge of how much it will cost.

The computer support service can calculate a range of options for what can be provided: different computer specifications, different software configurations, different levels of network service and backup. They can offer different response times when equipment fails: does a computer need to be replaced within half an hour when it goes wrong, or should it be working again by the end of the next working day? What response is expected from the support help line: a reply within an hour or on the next day? Each different option requires a certain amount of spare equipment, standing idle in case something goes wrong, different costings for external maintenance services, and, importantly, different numbers of support staff with particular skills. All can be costed and considered.

The most important reason for doing this is so that the computer users become involved in understanding how much things cost and the level of service that it is reasonable to expect. It is no good paying for the worst level of service while expecting the best. All of the computer users and all of the support staff must be fully informed of the service level decisions that are made.

The great advantage of this approach is that the support service knows what is expected of them, and hence can plan and organize the service to suit. They do not need to try to guess what is expected – the computer users have decided what they want.

Of course, circumstances change, and the agreement of service levels must be a continuous dialogue – one with an understanding that there is a cost in making any changes, and that any changes will take time to equip, staff and implement.

That is the concept. How it is implemented is a business decision. Some firms will then commit everything to paper, defining service levels as an internal contract between the system users and providers, and even charging internally to projects and departments for the specific services provided.

Other firms may take a more relaxed team-oriented approach, seeing the main benefit of the exercise in internal understanding between everyone involved. Internal contracts and cross accounting are all extra internal costs which ultimately come out of profits, so the less internal bureaucracy the better. An amicable balance must be found, which allows costs to be tracked and understood without wasting effort.

Essential training

When adding up costs, don't forget about those costs implicit in any changes in the skills of either the computer users or the support staff. Training costs depend on training methods, and in Chapter 9 we saw some of the alternative approaches that modern technology can bring to training requirements. Just don't forget about it! And remember that training requirements will continue throughout the life of any computer system – there are always upgrades, changes and improvements to accommodate.

Upgrades and revisions

Another little extra which is easily forgotten is the cost effect of software upgrades. Even if there is a support agreement to provide version upgrades for free, they normally need time and effort to implement on every computer using the software. In other cases, particularly with lower cost software, version upgrades have to be purchased.

New software versions often bring with them particular requirements to upgrade operating systems and computer hardware. New versions need more memory, more disk space, and maybe new graphics or interface facilities. Disk files may need to be moved to different directories, or processed into new versions, all requiring extra effort and expense.

Older software may not run on new operating system versions at all, requiring a complete replacement of some software, with the associated costs. Be prepared for unexpected extra costs.

Archive or backup?

We have looked at the costs of preparing and maintaining current data, but what about backups and historical data?

Traditional backup regimes have been designed to allow restoration of a complete computer system in the event of a catastrophic failure. As the original versions of information are stored on computer systems rather than on paper, electronic archives to retrieve older information become more important.

Computer archiving systems are likely to become a significant cost in the future. Quite independently of the backups needed to recover from failures, an independent long-term archive of the final issued versions of documents will become a necessity.

This could lead to other minor savings and certainly process improvements. Many computer systems contain copies of issued letters, documents, pictures and drawings on local disk files for access in case they might be needed in the future. In practice, as soon as any of these are finished and issued, they will not change any further and do not need to be held in a form which can be modified. At the same time that a document is issued, it can be sent straight to archive storage, and registered and indexed for the future on an optical disk or other long-term storage, and on confirmation of successful archiving it can be removed from local storage.

The financial implications of this way of thinking are significant, because the archive becomes the principal record of the document and must be treated accordingly. The archive must be created simultaneously in at least two independent locations in case of unexpected total loss of one archive site. Network links must allow efficient transfer and rapid future retrieval. The archiving medium must be suitable for rapid searches and retrieval. But it is all possible.

The potential effect is for the archive to become the place where documents go as soon as they are completed, rather than somewhere to clear out old files to every few months when space runs short. The archive might no longer be a dusty forgotten corner to search as a last resort when other copies have vanished, but a modern, efficient, first place to look for a letter sent out yesterday, eliminating the need to keep lots of paper copies.

With mobile working and new office and working concepts, access to the firm's archive may become more important and more constant in the long term than the need for any particular office. It may be the only constant factor through a whole series of other business changes. So take a long-term view when considering costs and methods of archiving.

Hidden costs and unexpected benefits

To the accountant costs are always in black and white, something which can be quantified, manipulated, analysed and understood.

However, efficient computer investment is more of an art than a science. There are plenty of well-established strategies and approaches, but the territory of computer investment is a land of moving targets, quagmires and quicksands, where one needs to be observant, well-informed, imaginative and fleet of foot when needed. There are hidden costs and unexpected benefits in every venture, and it may not be worth analysing them in every detail as long as you are happy that you are going in the right direction.

One of the greatest unknowns is the people. How readily will they accept changes in working practices? Will the new computer system be seen as an excuse for everything that goes wrong, or a ray of sunshine leading to a bright new future? However much money is spent, it is people's attitudes which ultimately determine the success of a business.

Costs at the community centre

As the new community centre takes shape in our fictional market town, it is interesting to reflect upon how new technologies may have changed the costs and economics of the centre.

First of all, the project financing is likely to be rather complex. It was not an obvious commercial investment in the first place, so several different sources of finance will need to have been integrated to make the project work. Let us assume that a management company has been formed to operate and run the centre, with the majority of shares held on behalf of the local community by the local council, but with shares also being held by the main retail store, which has a major interest in the centre.

The retail store, with ready access to investment money, has agreed to act as financier, or at least to provide appropriate references and reassurances to a finance organization. In effect, the retail store will pay for building the centre, but in return will not have to pay any rent for ten years and will thereafter only pay a minimal rent to assist in running costs. The community centre will provide many services for the store (certainly car parking and the surrounding environment, and possibly even electrical power, water and other services) in return. After all, the community centre can generate revenue in various ways once it is built, but first it must find the money to pay the builders.

The local council has purchased or provided the land, and will take care of all of the road building and provision of electrical, water and waste infrastructure. One of the local Information Superhighway service providers has agreed to install all communication links for free, and then to charge for them dependent upon levels of usage.

The leisure centre itself will have to cover all of its own staffing and running costs, and make a contribution to the running costs of the other parts of the centre, but will not need to repay any of the cost of building the facilities. The theatre will be available at commercial rates for external organizations, but at the marginal cost of staffing, lighting and heating it to the local amateur dramatic society and the education centre.

The education centre will run a mix of educational courses, some at minimal cost and others at commercial prices, depending upon what the market can stand.

The permanent office space and shops in the shopping mall will be rented at commercial rates, but monitored carefully to attract local businesses. The flexible office space will also be available at commercial prices set at what is considered reasonable in such a community.

There will probably be a significant balancing payment from the local council, certainly to get the centre started, and set in consultation with the community against other financial priorities. The long-term objective must be for the whole centre to become financially self-sufficient and able to pay for all of its costs.

Computer programs have been used to model the finances of the whole project right from its initial stages until well into the future. This model has made it possible to assess the risks involved, and where appropriate to determine where it is best to insure against some risks. The model has also been monitored continuously during construction to make sure that costs will turn out as planned.

The virtual computer model of the project has also been used extensively by all of the design team and the construction team to minimize costs. This virtual project model allows long-term operating costs to be modelled in much greater detail than was possible previously, to see the effects of different forms of construction upon energy use, and to model long-term maintenance and replacement costs for all air-conditioning plant, surface finishes and other items of construction which are likely to deteriorate over future decades.

When construction is complete, the same virtual project model will be used to continuously check operating costs against these predictions and to study any potential refinements in operating procedures. The model will probably become an 'intelligent' model, actually monitoring conditions in the centre all of the time, and adjusting heating, air-conditioning and lighting to match the requirements of building use at any particular moment while also minimizing running costs.

The virtual building model has also been extensively used to study the best sequence and organization of construction, so that all of the contractors and subcontractors involved can coordinate their needs for access roads, lifting equipment, storage areas for materials and access to each area of the building as it is fitted out.

The ability to predict, monitor and control every aspect of the cost of constructing and operating the centre has become essential to the successful management of the project. Since long-term operating costs are critical to the financial success of the project, a long-term life-cycle

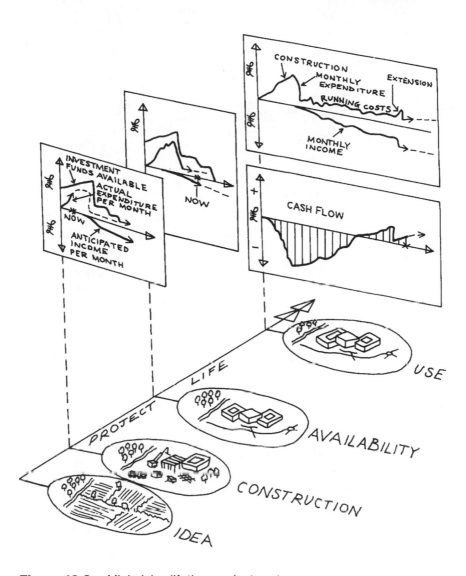

Figure 10.3. Minimizing lifetime project costs.

analysis has been used to look at total costs well into the future (Figure 10.3), rather than just minimizing immediate building costs without due regard for future operating and maintenance costs.

11 Culture or millstone?

Where are we now?

We have covered a lot of ground, but have we covered enough to start making some judgements about where we are and where we are going in the future? There is a great deal that has not been mentioned. How will information technology really change our daily lives, the ways we work, our leisure time, the way the government operates, the need for military forces and the whole living environment around us? Will it help to alleviate poverty and inequality, or will it make matters worse?

We can only conjecture, but hopefully as informed observers.

In this chapter we will debate whether we really are developing a new Information Society culture, or whether all of the changes and uncertainty are becoming a millstone around our necks.

Bursting the sales balloon

We seem to be surrounded by futuristic sales hype, trying to convince us to spend ever more money on new technologies which have shorter and shorter useful lives.

But it is not just technology. Every product we buy seems to be designed to wear out or become out of date sooner, so that we spend more and more money replacing it.

In the UK, the cars of the 1950s were designed to last for ever. All of the bearings and linings which could wear out were designed to be replaced. Then, salting of the roads in the winter led to the chassis of older cars rusting through, and then everyone got used to replacing their cars. New features started to appear every year. Most people now expect to change their car every few years. A couple of decades ago a fridge was expected to last 15 or 20 years. Now a fridge is beyond economic repair after only a few years – it is cheaper to buy a new one.

It seems debatable how long this trend can continue. Manufacturing industries are on a never-ending treadmill of having to sell more products to make more profits, using the global market-place to manufacture where labour is cheap and then sell into new countries to increase sales. All of the extra production means more environmental damage, hidden somewhere in the world. Everything has to be transported, with associated pollution, road-building and other environmental effects.

The world cannot sustain the environmental effects of extrapolating current trends for several more decades, yet if the international economy falters our standard of living is rapidly affected.

This dependency of the international economy on sales expansion is a millstone around all of our necks, in danger of dragging us either into environmental catastrophe or economic ruin over the next few years.

Sales horizons, business strategies and political manifestos have all become very short-term, more concerned with how to survive next year and how to beat the competition than with what needs to exist in 10 or 20 years' time, and how to get there. Somehow, it is easy to rationalize that any changes in the approach of one individual, one company or one government will have so little global effect that there is no point in trying. This is all down to attitude and education again, and someone has to have the courage to start soon.

The real breakthrough on the sales front will come when the top firms decide to tell all of us where they plan to go over the next ten years, and efficiently inform every individual and business of their best investment path to get there. Sales competition should not be about who can sell the brightest and fastest bells and whistles next year, but about who can sell the most coherent and comfortable vision of the future several years ahead. The future must become one of coexistence of parallel visions, rather than the instability of fighting for competitive domination.

This is perhaps a vain hope, but it would be good to see cooperation to find an environmentally sustainable future, rather than the competitive cut-throat business world where only money counts and the deeper problems of harmony with our environment can be either ignored or subcontracted to specialists to ensure legislative compliance with current laws.

Media at the crossroads

The whole media and information industry seems to be at a crossroads of deciding a new identity for the future. Long gone are the days of one or two television channels, or when reading one magazine or newspaper was enough to keep fully informed about all of the main events, discoveries and developments in the world.

First, communication technology brought more information more immediately to our doorsteps, through conventional newspapers and television channels. We all see the news as it happens, direct from where it is happening.

Then people's thirst for knowledge has been filled with numerous niche products: first through dedicated magazines, and more recently through specialized satellite and cable television channels.

Now add to this the new forms of transmission and presentation. Multimedia presentations and Internet publishing are developing very fast, giving unprecedented freedom of artistic presentation and visualization possibilities. Where will it all end?

I already sense a developing state of information inundation. Is all of this information useful and relevant, or are we just responding to a short-term fascination with access to it all? How much do we need, and how much would we really be better off without?

One interesting aspect of human nature is the constant need for change and progress. Most people assimilate a new situation, absorb what is relevant, reduce what they need to take forward to a reasonable minimum, and move on. Will multimedia be a passing fad or part of our future?

I certainly sense dangers in restricting the development and application of imagination. When reading a book or listening to the radio, the human mind is constantly creating images and feelings to help in interpretation. The television gives us the pictures as well, reducing the need for imagination. Virtual reality creates an illusion to fool the human brain into believing things that are not really there. Are we in danger of becoming machines ourselves, just processing information without the ability to fill in the gaps with our imagination unless the computer does it for us? Will exposure to new media develop or reduce our ability to think and communicate in terms of concepts and ideas? We do not know yet. But human nature is to progress rather than to stagnate, so we will move onwards to find out. We are all intelligent and adaptable – we can change course and reverse any changes as long as we have the depth of understanding to comprehend what is happening.

As Abraham Lincoln said, 'You can fool all the people some of the time, and some of the people all the time, but you can not fool all the people all of the time'.

The current bombardment with information from all directions has to mature and develop into an information environment that we can all fully understand. To succeed, the prices of new media services will need

197

to reduce to the level where it is logical to look at a multimedia source rather than to buy a newspaper or a book. Access to information must become as easy as switching on a television, and as readily available as a telephone. A whole platform of education must gradually extend right across our society, through school education, workplace training and political encouragement, to a point where most people understand what is available and how to access it, just as they use a telephone or buy a magazine.

Global freedom or hopeless dependence?

Is the globalization process giving everyone unlimited freedom to pursue a career of their choice? Is it improving the standard of living of countless people throughout the world? Or is it creating a complex chain of interdependence, like a house of playing cards where one card is balanced on top of the other, and any weakness could cause a complete collapse.

At the moment, the global market-place seems full of opportunities. But where someone gains, in most cases someone somewhere else must lose. Low-cost manufacturing in developing new economies has decimated established manufacturing industries in parts of Europe and the USA. Employment patterns are adapting, but it takes time. If the manufacturing boom should falter in response to a slow-down in international growth or changes in international attitudes and spending patterns, these new industries may go through further dramatic changes. As standards of living improve in the newly developing nations, other countries with lower wages also become more attractive bases for industry.

In the same way that efficient communications and low-cost transport have enabled various manufacturing industries to move around the world to the most cost-effective locations, information technology is progressively enabling other design and creative activities to redistribute themselves to the areas where the most cost-effective skills of appropriate quality are most readily available.

For the moment, globalization is creating many new opportunities for people all over the world. But is this another bubble which will eventually burst? Will environmental understanding lead to a move away from vast quantities of short lifetime replaceable goods towards smaller quantities of quality goods designed to last for many years?

How much education and entertainment can the world absorb? If clear international winners emerge in the race to produce the best media 'content', other established producers must suffer in other countries. Will people move on from spending money absorbing knowledge and watching passive entertainment to creating entertainment for themselves? Decades ago, most families and communities created their own entertainment, with singing and dancing and music. New technology makes it so much easier for anyone to be creative, whether playing music with the assistance of an 'intelligent' instrument, or creating drawings or virtual worlds with automatic assistance to create all of the tedious detail exactly as intended. Communications will allow people with common interests to meet and discuss with each other whenever they wish, without having to travel. Nobody really knows what direction people will take.

It is so important to understand the risks as well as grabbing the opportunities. Human nature, once again, tends to march ahead within the knowledge of what is obvious, correcting mistakes later when side-effects become apparent. Globalization makes the speed of change and the extent of any effects greater every day. Celebrations of successes could turn sour very quickly.

Dancing with thieves

Another interesting effect of the new Information Society is the ability to communicate very easily with people whom we know nothing about. Conventionally, there is some point of reference within which you meet someone that gives you some confidence and knowledge that you are dealing with the right person. It might be that you meet in the person's office, and make a subconscious assessment of how his or her business is organized. Or you might have an introduction through a friend or business associate who has done business with that person before, which will reassure you that all is well.

In the electronic world, all you have is an electronic address. It might be redirected to anywhere in the world. The people that you are dealing with could have created a whole electronic facade (such as pages on the World-Wide Web or electronic addresses for referees who aren't real at all) to make them appear to be something that they are not. All very credible.

Along with the opportunities offered by the new international communication freedom must come a wary respect for what we can not be sure of. International customers may not be quite what they seem. They might be testing our security or our gullibility, with a view to extracting money by dishonest means. They might be competitors in disguise, checking on where we are doing business and how we advertise ourselves. Electronic communication opens up new opportunities for deception, and makes it possible for the perpetrators to hide, invisibly, almost anywhere in the world.

Throwing away the safety rope

Having sounded a word of caution, I would also like to put in a recommendation to be prepared to jump in and swim with the tide when the climate is right. We cannot hang on to the past forever, and there comes a time when it is better to look forward to a new culture and a new way of working and concentrate on getting there rather than continually checking how to retrace our steps into the past.

I remember once going on an activity holiday with all sorts of outdoor pursuits. I tried climbing a relatively easy low rock face, but I kept coming to a standstill. I couldn't understand how other people managed to climb the same rock face so effortlessly. I had not done such climbing before, and had a safety rope pulled fairly tight on a harness, as I was sure that I would fall off. Two hands, two feet – I kept three good foot- or handholds and then cautiously moved the fourth to a new hold. But there were never sufficient good holds near enough, and I just could not get up that rock face.

Then I watched more carefully how the others made it look so easy. They concentrated upon where they were heading for, looking ahead for a route with good holds but without checking all the way ahead in detail. They kept the safety rope slightly slack, so that it didn't interfere with their climbing. But most of all, they kept moving. They used their momentum to drive them forward to the next hold, reaching further, changing in an instant if one hold proved too far away or insufficiently secure, and stopping just for a moment to take an alternative route. I tried the same technique and it worked.

Look to the future, aim for something worth going for, and keep moving and adapting as you go. Keep safety in mind, but do not let it become an intolerable constraint.

Bringing civilization to the frontier towns

Today's information technology is in the frontier towns of new territory. The rule of law is haphazard and dependent upon people's individual values rather than upon a carefully debated and drafted constitution and legal system.

The Information Superhighway is bringing a reliable and integrated transport system to the frontier, like railways and roads throughout the territory. Once communications exist, civilization can develop. Nobody can then operate within the territory without understanding the values and behaviour expected. The society becomes self-regulating as it becomes more established – it suits everybody to live within agreed laws, and to keep an occasional eye on each other to ensure compliance with the letter and the spirit of accepted values. Legal processes become established and communications ensure that no-one is too remote to be beyond the law.

As a frontier territory changes to a civilized society, so people's individual priorities change. Safety and security become expected norms, rather than a daily challenge. People start looking to improve their standard of living rather than just survive, and social and leisure activities develop.

This is the transition that must occur on the way to a successful and beneficial Information Society. At the moment, technology may appear more like a millstone, holding us back as we fight to survive in an uncertain world surrounded by hostile new technologies which most of us do not fully understand. But as we learn and adapt we will undoubtedly develop a more stable and comfortable Information Society culture in which we should all feel more secure and confident about the future.

The millstone of the past

So, if there is a millstone, it is not so much the technology itself, but more our individual perceptions and understanding of it (Figure 11.1).

Yes, there are legacy computer systems in some organizations which are proving very costly to update and develop into suitable systems for the future, but why have these problems occurred? If someone buys an old truck instead of a sports car, and then complains that it won't go very fast and is impossible to park, we don't blame the truck, do we? We ask ourselves how they could have invested their money in something which was not suitable for what they intended to do with it.

When the computer system is completely unsuitable for today's working environment, why do we blame the computer? Someone, somewhere made a bad investment decision. There may well have been a computer system salesman to blame somewhere as well, more concerned with immediate sales commissions and profits than with the long-term usefulness of the system to the customer.

201

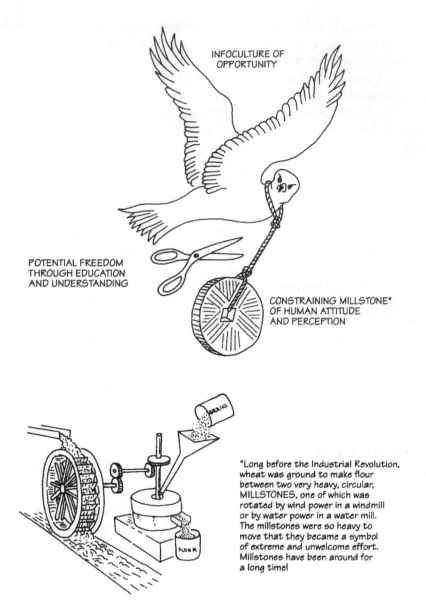

INFOCULTURE OF OPPORTUNITY

POTENTIAL FREEDOM
THROUGH EDUCATION
AND UNDERSTANDING

CONSTRAINING MILLSTONE*
OF HUMAN ATTITUDE
AND PERCEPTION

*Long before the Industrial Revolution,
wheat was ground to make flour
between two very heavy, circular,
MILLSTONES, one of which was
rotated by wind power in a windmill
or by water power in a water mill.
The millstones were so heavy to
move that they became a symbol
of extreme and unwelcome effort.
Millstones have been around for
a long time!

Figure 11.1. Taking off the handbrake.

We go back, yet again, to those two key factors: people and education. How can we really blame the salesman if he had no idea about the chief executive's future plans for the business? Did anyone really know how technology was going to change? Could anyone really have predicted changes in the market-place and in business practice? It is always easier looking backward than looking forward, but we must look forward and we cannot afford to make many mistakes. We need to mobilize everybody's ideas, and to have an open and informed opinion about the future.

The other part of the millstone is attitude and motivation. If people don't believe, or don't want to believe, that a new system will work, it is unlikely that it will. If workflows and jobs have been rearranged to improve efficiency, with associated job reductions, there is bound to be some resentment, fear and concern about the future unless staff have been fully prepared for the changes and involved in making them happen. The most brilliantly conceived system is unlikely to work without a positive attitude to using it by the people that it affects.

A few other problems

This whole book has concentrated upon information technology and the culture changes associated with new developments and ideas. I have conveniently ignored many other problems that the world is facing, any of which might dominate our thoughts and push technology developments into the background if international circumstances or attitudes were to change.

Quite apart from the whole subject area of environmental stability, there is the need to properly address the problems caused by the expanding populations of many countries, and the devastating effects of recurrent food shortages and famines in various parts of the world. A disturbingly large proportion of the world's population still lives in poverty, and new technology may do little to help them.

The world seems to suffer from continual territorial conflicts, using ever more sophisticated technology, which are continually in the news through media communications. I have not discussed the effects of technology upon military activities, but I do hope that the current shift towards peacekeeping activities and away from the threat of major conflicts will continue.

A major natural disaster could at any time hit a large population centre anywhere in the world, putting technology developments into the background, but hopefully benefiting from existing technology to minimize injuries and assist in restoring order and comfort.

However important it may seem, information technology is only one component of the complex lives that we lead.

THE NATURE RESERVE

THE SHOPPING MALL

THE SWIMMING POOL

THE THEATRE

THE OFFICE CENTRE

THE EDUCATION CENTRE

THE LAKE

Figure 11.2. The community centre in action.

The culture of the future

I will leave you to judge for yourself whether the Information Society is actually a new culture in itself, or just a natural progression of changes as part of human development. In a decade or two the historians will draw their own conclusions.

The community centre in action

The community centre in our fictional market town in England is now in full operation (Figure 11.2). Many different sections of the community benefit from its existence every day – it has become very much part of the town.

Many assumptions and simplifications have been made in developing this example, not the least of which is assuming the ease with which finance might be found! But the intention was to trigger thoughts and ideas to stimulate your imagination about what might actually happen in the future. You will make your own judgements here as well.

The most important effect of any project of this sort is to increase people's feeling of security in their own community and their confidence in the future. As well as providing services and entertainment, the completed centre has had a localized effect upon employment patterns and opportunities. More people can work closer to home. Education is more readily available to everyone, and at any level right up to advanced postgraduate education. People working through the community office centre can change jobs more easily to develop new career paths as older industries contract. Hopefully, everyone has gained a greater appreciation of the opportunities for the future.

12 Gazing at the horizon

A little stargazing

Nobody really knows what the future world will look like, how we will live, how we will work, or how we will think. But the future is not just an empty vacuum of frightening unknowns – it will be a combination of everyone's hopes, wishes and aspirations, constrained by practical and financial limitations, and hopefully tending towards some form of harmony with the natural environment around us.

In this chapter I want to paint a few thoughts and ideas on the wall of what may be hidden over that horizon of the future. We must look forward to the future in order to shape the world in which we all want to live. Everyone must have their own dreams and ambitions, and we must hope that the international framework of the developing Information Society can create a world in which more people can fulfil many of their ambitions.

The following sequence of science fiction interludes is intended to trigger ideas and assist in forming opinions – is this the type of world that you would like to live in?

Early morning at home

Let us imagine that we have just woken up in the household of the future. It is a living space, somewhere that the individual or family is comfortable and relaxed, perhaps in the countryside in a small community or possibly in an apartment in the bustle of a metropolis.

The first notable difference is that the technology in the domestic environment has matured to eliminate all of those disorganized boxes and units, cables, connections and switches that are progressively cluttering up the domestic living spaces of the 1990s. The television, the hi-fi, the computer unit and keyboard, the answerphone and the remote control units all seem to have vanished. We seem to be in a pleasant room tastefully furnished and decorated, but where has all of the technology gone? Puzzling.

Look again. All around us are information surfaces (Figure 12.1), like giant flat-screen televisions, but at a resolution that can show a printed page at its normal size. Large areas of information surface may cover most of some walls. Smaller areas are arranged in conveniently viewable parts of different furniture units, such as the flat surfaces of desks, vertical or sloping surfaces which can easily be viewed when sitting down comfortably. Perhaps by then we might even see the holographic images in thin air favoured in the science fiction movies, but they are not essential for this vision.

Visible on each of these surfaces is anything that we might have decided that we want to see: well-known paintings from the past; modern moving electronic artwork; a live picture of a busy street in a major city, or the countryside at a well-known beauty spot; and pictures of friends and family, perhaps static shots with particular memories attached or maybe moving pictures recorded a few hours before in a different time zone.

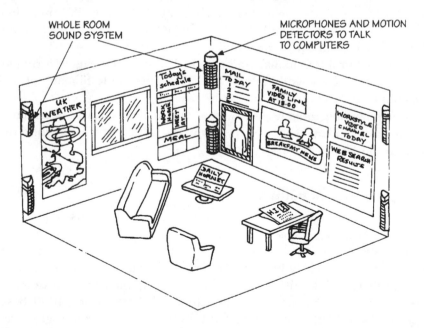

Figure 12.1. The information surface living room.

Anywhere on the information surfaces there may be windows of information: a picture taken a few minutes ago from space showing the local weather patterns, and the latest weather forecast for where you are expecting to be today alongside it; a list of electronic messages waiting for you to read them, like the letters that used to arrive through the letterbox; or any number of television screens, showing programmes of news, information and entertainment at particular times that you have requested, or on demand when you want them.

Also visible, of course, are absolutely any pages of information from anywhere in the world on the Internet or on whatever the Internet develops into: the latest sports information, news stories, or perhaps a game of chess or a computer game in progress with a friend on the other side of the world.

There may be virtual worlds which you are currently exploring, perhaps looking at developments planned for a nearby city or planning a holiday for next year. There could be a diary and scheduler for today for yourself with family and friends interlinked so that you know when you are likely to see them. The diary is adaptive and flexible: if you change your plans to do something else, the system will just let you know the consequences and inform the other people involved.

And then there is sound. In every room there is a sophisticated sound system which can create a sound image in any location around you, so that sounds can come from the direction in which you see a particular picture. Loudspeakers, or their future equivalent, are discreetly built in to the corners of the room or in fixed items of furniture.

How is it all controlled without remote controls and keyboards? By sound and movement. Sound recognition has advanced to the point where you just tell the room what you want to see or do, and it does what you ask, just like asking someone else to change channels or adjust the sound on the television. And it can remember things too, so when you find an arrangement of information you like, you ask the room to remember how it looks so that it can be restored at any time in the future.

It may all sound exorbitantly expensive, but the average motor car is pretty expensive in the 1990s. Rather than buying countless different electronic units to do different things, why not just make a comprehensive investment once in a while, like putting in central heating or refitting the kitchen? There will be running costs, of course. Just as heating costs money, so will information cost money, but there will always be a choice in how anyone decides to spend their money.

The whole home environment has become an interface with the world of information, as local or as international as an individual or family desires, completely within their control. And only the interface is visible – everything else, all of the boxes of electronics and cables and controls have been tucked away out of sight. None of that needs to be visible.

Where shall I work today?

The next question is: where will I be working today?

'Work' covers an incredibly diverse range of activities. The trend to automate and mechanize is bound to continue, reducing the extent of repetitive manual work needed in the world. However, there will always be many jobs close to the land in agriculture and construction, or the seas in shipping and fishing. There will be manufacturing industries, service industries and entertainment forms which need people to be in particular places to work directly in physically immovable locations or to interact directly with a particular group of people.

But an increasing proportion of working activities will become less dependent upon physical location. Traditional office work is likely to disperse closer to home, and a lot of business travel is likely to be replaced by electronic communication. Creative activities look set to increase, as improved standards of living and increased leisure time give people more opportunity to create individually tailored living and working environments.

Office blocks may give way to community working and leisure centres, as cities disperse into the suburbs, both to reduce travel time to work to suit individuals and to reduce office costs to suit businesses.

For many people, there will be a choice of working environments on different days, with greater individual management of working location and working hours. For office production activities, many people may have a fully equipped personal office at home, from which they can instantly link themselves into a corporate office network anywhere in the country, or in the world, and immediately be in communication with all of their working colleagues and business associates, with full electronic access to all of the archives and files that they need. It will be possible to connect and disconnect at will, as if with a transporter beam – one moment at home isolated from work, the next moment fully connected and immersed in the office electronic working environment. Working hours can be determined to suit family, leisure, educational and professional activities, dynamically planned to fit with working colleagues around the world and customers and clients. The working day is likely to lose specific bounds of starting and finishing times – it will be more a matter of achieving all of the communication that is needed with others at mutually acceptable times and then fitting in appropriate work production each month.

One person may have several different jobs, connecting to different office environments on different days or at different times of day. As workload varies, this flexibility (Figure 12.2) may suit employers as much as it suits employees, allowing individuals to pursue other money-earning opportunities when work is short.

As well as fully equipped home offices, there are likely to be community working centres, with similar working stations which can be rented by the hour on demand and connected to any office in just the same way. Just as the home office may suit the young family, the community office will offer social interaction similar to a more conventional office environment to younger people and anyone preferring to work in an environment of other people but not wishing to travel far. The community office will also have meeting rooms and other facilities which it is impractical to provide at home.

Then there will still be the more conventional corporate and regional offices, but probably rather more compact than in the past. Such offices will be the anchor points of organizations, the physical bases through which all activity is linked. But nearly all of the people, the executives and managers and producers, may actually be working at their home or community offices.

As everything becomes more electronic, it will be essential to maintain and introduce appropriate forms of social interaction. In a conventional business, conversations over lunch and at the coffee machine often have an essential role of providing additional routes of communication, understanding and reassurance, allowing innovative ideas to short-circuit conventional hierarchies and defined communication routes, and enabling clarification of ideas and correction of misinterpretations. Perhaps there will be defined office days, when groups of people make a definite effort to be in the same place at the same time, with part of the day set aside for informal meetings. Or perhaps company social and sporting activities will become a recognized part of the working week, taking the firm's social communication outside the working environment altogether.

Working with anyone, anywhere

The changes in the working environment will involve more than just technology. Increasing pressure to reduce costs and streamline activities must lead to flexible, process-oriented teamworking environments, rather

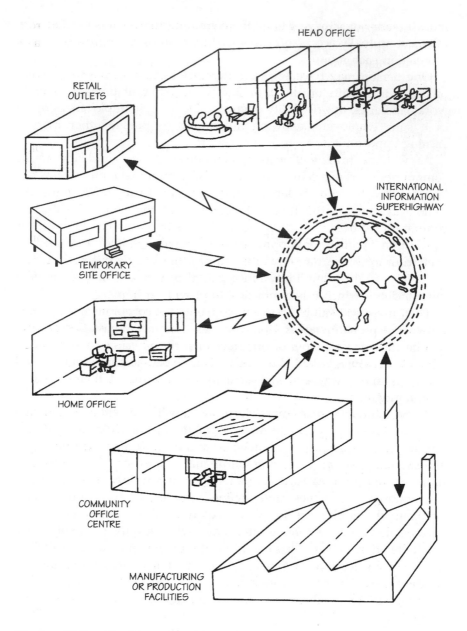

Figure 12.2. Flexible, adaptable working patterns.

than authoritarian and inflexible hierarchies commanding and controlling their dominions. Anybody who makes a contribution should have the right to appropriate payment in return, with much greater visibility

212

within an organization of where the money is coming from and where it is going, and greater consciousness in everyone of the social and environmental implications of every aspect of their work.

There is likely to be much less chance of finding a single career with one firm for a working lifetime. Young people will start out on their working careers with a much greater awareness of where career opportunities lie, developing alternative threads and plans to suit different circumstances. For anyone with ambition, the need for a plan for acquiring skills and continuously learning and developing throughout their career will be well understood.

Many working environments will involve linking electronically with a team of co-workers distributed around the same town, or the same country, or around the world, depending upon the situation. Long-distance communication costs will have reduced so much that physical location is almost irrelevant, but time zones for meetings and discussions will obviously be a consideration.

An obsession with contractual obligations and minimizing costs will hopefully have diminished. Businesses which have not adapted to the new financial and working culture regimes will sink below the surface as the battle to survive ceases to be worthwhile. Businesses which develop a working culture properly compatible with the Information Society will flourish as they develop confidence in their ability to swim strongly in the new environment and simultaneously gain respect from their clients for the quality and value of the products and services that they provide. Mutual respect between employees of all ages and abilities will become far more important than any implicit or actual authority.

The boundaries between different firms will soften, as teamworking and integration become the normal approach to any business situation. On any project, the firms will work together to maximize the overall profit while also minimizing, managing and insuring against any individual and collective risks that they can identify.

Technology will play a crucial role in this new working culture, not just by allowing efficient and rapid communication between anyone anywhere on a project to eliminate misunderstandings and reduce mistakes, but also by allowing efficient and rigorous separation of information where needed, for instance keeping information about projects for two different clients quite independent of each other. Vital cost and progress information will be continuously tracked and monitored by knowledge-based systems to bring any problems to everyone's notice as soon as the first signs are identified.

Many businesses will be able to reduce their long-term commitment to fixed costs, giving them more freedom to adapt to market conditions and respond to changing customer expectations. If a significant proportion of the office space being used is actually in people's homes and being rented by the hour from community office centres, there is much less long-term fixed commitment. Manufacturing facilities will be designed with flexibility in mind, to allow rapid adaptation to producing different products tailored to individual customer requirements as the market changes. Recognizing the need for more flexible career paths to ensure long-term employment, many employees will accept short-term rolling contractual arrangements, enabling them to move on to other firms or to change career direction as the market shifts, rather than hanging on to the bitter end on a long-term contract as the salary bills and other fixed costs drag a firm into insolvency. Changing employment to avoid the uncertainty of a diminishing business will become more like taking an alternative road to avoid a traffic jam. Many more people will plan alternative skills and be prepared for such changes.

At the same time, good teamworking in businesses should actually reduce the chances of unexpected job reductions. Everybody should know the state that a business is in, and job reductions should become a mutual decision between employer and employee in both of their best interests. If job reductions are inevitable, an employer may actively participate in finding alternative working or educational opportunities in the hope that the employee will return when conditions improve.

A meeting with a few friends

Everybody has groups of friends with common interests, but the pressure of time and the need to earn money have gradually reduced the time available for informal meetings and discussions in much of the developed world. This is in sharp contrast to many so-called less-developed countries, where the need for discussion and relaxation to maintain a balanced outlook may well be better understood.

The main problem has been finding mutually convenient times to meet in the midst of increasingly complex working and social calendars. This is compounded by the continual geographical relocation of different people to suit working, family and leisure pursuits. An individual's circle of friends may no longer live locally, and why should they?

There is no substitute for an occasional meeting with friends for a social or entertainment event. But there will no longer be any need to lose touch for months or years in between. Just send an electronic message to your friends suggesting a virtual meeting. The computers will compare your diaries and schedules and suggest a suitable time and place for each individual – maybe after breakfast at home, or mid-morning at the office, wherever that might be, or in between entertainment at the leisure centre. All the organization will just be taken care of.

And then you meet. It might be a face-to-face video conference, or all relaxing in a common virtual room. You might have a common presentation area in your virtual meeting place to show recent video film to discuss, or diagrams, or to sketch thoughts on a whiteboard. One of you might make a presentation or a speech. You might all arrange to have a cup of coffee or a meal at your current location. The format is up to you.

An education break

Mixed into your working, social and leisure time, there is also very likely to be a significant component of learning and education to develop new skills, whatever your age or occupation.

A whole range of learning options will be available. You might opt for self-managed local learning in a multimedia environment or an Open University-style distance learning course for a diploma or a degree. In addition to recorded television lectures and individual learning exercises, it will be possible through video conferencing to attend live lectures, participate in discussion groups and have individual meetings with your tutors, just like a conventional university of the past.

Many offices are likely to have an education corner, where people gather at agreed times to extend their general education through electronic media and communication. There is also likely to be corporate education, reinforcing a common culture and ideals across the workforce, either through group activities at main office locations or individually at the home office or community centre office.

Research will become far more integrated with working activities. There will still be plenty of dedicated research institutions, but working individuals may also elect to spend a proportion of their time on advanced research activities. From their home or working desk they will have full access to documentation of all past research activities of any institution in the world. They can schedule discussions with other researchers anywhere in the world, or with a research supervisor thousands of miles away. They can organize debates and meetings, and attend conferences electronically, integrating research activities into their world to suit their lifestyle. From the other direction, research workers in research institutes may elect to spend a proportion of their time working, perhaps just to supplement their income, but in many cases also to keep in close touch with real problems rather than just becoming lost in a world of theory.

Participating in the community

Everybody will choose their own methods of staying in touch with world, national and local events. Some people may avidly read whatever form the newspapers of the future take, a selected digest of the most important news of the day according to the formula of a particular editor. Others may watch the equivalent of television news channels. Some people may decide not to bother to read or watch anything, and just rely on conversations with their friends to keep them up to date with anything important.

There will be much greater opportunity for tailoring a personal electronic news and information service to suit individual wishes and needs. Information about particular sports or communities, or about certain types of activity in the local district, may be assembled and presented automatically, highlighting specific topics.

There will also be much more opportunity to feed back opinions on policies and political developments and to participate in debate about the development of the local community. Public opinion may no longer be something which is tested every few years in a general election and monitored in between by public opinion polls. It will depend very much upon individual interest and commitment, and on the attitude and culture prevalent in our society, but it will become possible to feed back instantaneous thoughts about developments in the news and to participate in local discussions and meetings without leaving home. The conventional barriers to participation of finding the time to travel and attend meetings or to visit offices at fixed times of day, which conflict with working and family commitments, may steadily be broken down to a point where anyone can participate quite efficiently in getting things right, making it inappropriate to just complain about what is wrong.

The fictional community development described at the end of the preceding chapters is intended to illustrate this view. The 'us and them' of the government and the people must progressively be replaced to a large extent by just the 'us' of the community. Everybody must take an interest in the place we live in and the ways that we all live, and in the choices about our environment and our future.

Professional development

Our world relies upon many established and developing professions and professional bodies to maintain appropriate standards of conduct and competence among specific groups of skilled workers, and also to develop the deeper and wider thinking activities of maintaining morale and respect for each other. These professional bodies must keep a solid presence among the shifting tides of new ideas, making sure that vital shortcomings are not overlooked in the rush to change and take advantage of new ideas. They must also cross-fertilize new ideas to take society steadily forward for the betterment of mankind. The actual shape and size of groupings of skills falling within each professional society may change, but the need for professional bodies and learned societies to maintain a deeper understanding and apply a steadying hand through stormy and turbulent new developments is unquestionable.

Once again it often comes down to a question of time and money. The best minds are also often the most commercially useful minds. Agile perception and depth of understanding are valuable assets, to be put to commercial use to earn money, both by an individual and by the employer, if any. Meanwhile, people earlier in their careers who should be learning from the experience of older skilled professionals are bombarded with other priorities for their time.

Information technology to the rescue again. There is quite a parallel with education, as professional skill development and the development of intellectual knowledge through education are very closely linked. That same education corner at the office or electronic workspace at home can be used to link to regional or national professional meetings, to watch presentations and to participate in the discussions which follow. If people cannot travel to a meeting at a particular place and time, they might be able to participate on a video conference link to the meeting.

All of the papers and discussions of a learned society can also be made available through electronic means, instantly searchable from anywhere, making it possible to read through a history of best practice and perhaps see video recordings of recent meetings to assimilate a better under-standing of a subject and to make decisions in a new situation with the benefit of much of the experience of what has gone before.

Travel for pleasure

It will be interesting to see just how, and why, people travel in the future. In the past, the principal reason for travelling has usually been for business and working purposes, either to meet people or to travel to a different location where work takes place. Leisure travel has been a secondary activity, made possible by the trains, cars, ships and air travel originally created to support commercial activities.

There will never really be a true substitute for a face-to-face meeting, with the associated opportunities to watch each other's body language and for the social interaction of having a meal together or meeting other people unexpectedly. But there are several strong pressures to reduce business travel. The strongest will probably ultimately be cost. When the cost of a video conference discussion with someone drops to a tiny fraction of the travel cost to meet, and it is available as instantaneously, on demand, as making a telephone call, business economics will apply strong pressure to meet by electronic means most of the time. Individually, many people will also prefer to have more control over their time by spending less time travelling. And environmental pressure to spend less money building new roads and to reduce air pollution will apply yet another strong pressure to minimize business travel as part of normal working practice.

So travel may become more of a social and leisure activity, rather than a business need. With dispersed families and friends, people will want to concentrate the travel that they do make upon meeting people that they really do want to meet, and going to sporting, social and entertainment events to share experiences with other people.

The future balance between private and public travel facilities is also very difficult to predict. The main arguments for private motor cars are individual freedom and convenience, compounded by the inability of public transport to provide either at an acceptable level. But these problems are closely related to communication and perceived economics. In the past, public transport operators have never known exactly who wants to travel when, and as a consequence services never quite match the travellers' requirements. In the new communication age, an individual's travel requirements can be checked and optimized to give an integrated travel service. A local taxi or minibus pickup in a few minutes at home may one day synchronize with a bus or train linking through other services right through to a destination. Transport could become much more demand-led, running services at the optimum timing for the most people at any particular time, providing an overall total travel time between starting and finishing points rather than lots of independent fixed-time services. Luggage would work its way from start to destination just as on a connecting series of airline flights today. Comfortable travelling positions with integral information surfaces might allow conversations, education or entertainment to continue throughout each stage of the journey.

Perhaps the coordination involved is too far-fetched to imagine for several decades, but it is not technologically impossible, so it might happen. Once again, the pressures for change are very strong, with increasing problems of air pollution and environmental destruction in all of the major populated areas of the world.

Going shopping

Where will we go shopping? The popular myth is that we will all just sit in our armchairs at home and order everything from electronic virtual catalogues displayed on the wall. But perhaps this might get rather tedious and predictable after a fairly short period of time.

The large out-of-town stores in Europe, the USA and other countries, and modern shopping malls full of unexpected varieties of unusual goods, illustrate just how much shopping has developed from a necessity of existence into an everyday exploration and social activity. Once the routine shopping is taken care of, there is always the opportunity to go to particular shops which normally have interesting things to buy, for clothes, household goods, furniture and hobbies. Shopkeepers in turn try to make shopping interesting by finding new products to display to stimulate ideas and draw us into making unplanned purchases.

Let us look at another scenario. The world of products available on the developed Information Superhighway will rapidly expand to unthinkable proportions, where nobody can really expect to fully understand the whole range of what is available. It will be difficult to know where it is best to look, let alone where it is best to buy. There are bound to be advice services on the Superhighway, clamouring to tell us where to buy, where each such service has unknown commercial links, but wouldn't most people prefer a more personal service?

Local shops in many cities and villages have closed in the past because they just could not compete with the ranges of goods that the larger stores offered, and could not compete with the prices that large chains of stores could negotiate for bulk supply contracts. But what if new technology reverses this situation? With electronic communication, the local corner shop can become an outlet not just for the limited range of one large chain of stores, but for every store in the world on the Superhighway (Figure 12.3).

The difference from just shopping at home on your own is that finding and obtaining articles to purchase will become quite a complex skill in its own right. And shopping can also become much more of a social activity again. The local dress shop can become a knowledgeable adviser on the latest Paris fashions, but with a professional knowledge of where in the

Figure 12.3. The international corner shop.

world you can best obtain similar materials, and a working contact with an excellent skilled dressmaker somewhere in Asia who can create a dress to your specifications at an affordable price for delivery next week. You can create a virtual model of the dress to see how it will look, and send this as part of the specification.

If you want to rearrange the interior of your house, the local interior designer will have access to an immense range of products and ideas from all over the world, and will be able to build a virtual model before you buy and then assist you in tailoring the materials and quality of finish to balance between your expectations and the money that you want to spend.

This particular vision requires rather a significant shift of values, away from do-it-yourself cheapest solution self-reliance to accepting that, with a little professional help, you might end up with a more pleasing solution, and that you might benefit from someone's advice about where to find the best prices. Such service shops will need to take payment to give their proprietors a reasonable living, and the people using the service must show long-term commitment to supporting this approach. There are different reasons why different people may support the idea – some will like to pay a little extra for real quality, while others might value their own time and prefer to get professional assistance in finding the best prices and value. Others may just feel that they would like skilled assistance rather than being constrained by their own limited knowledge. But the net effect would be to supplement the large shopping malls and megastores with some local community shopping activity as well.

Local service opportunities

It might appear that there will be far fewer employment opportunities in this high-tech world; especially for less-skilled younger people, but think again!

If people start to appreciate much more the value of their time, and the choice of what they do with their time, they will naturally look to eliminate the activities that they would rather not do. Some people enjoy cooking. Others would rather be enjoying entertainment with their families or doing a short course of education to enhance their skills and pay. But everyone is becoming increasingly aware of the need to eat a balanced and healthy diet, with nourishing and well-presented food. Some people enjoy gardening. Others would like a beautiful garden to sit in on a summer's day, but without the effort of creating and maintaining it. Some people enjoy going to the shops for their everyday needs. Other people just wish that the fridge, the food shelves and all of the consumable household items, from the toothpaste to the light bulbs, were always fully stocked and working.

These are all business opportunities for enterprising people. They are not menial tasks for low wage earners. These are all skilled activities requiring training and understanding, which could be available at a price. The main problem, once again, is one of attitude. People don't like spending money on things that they think that they could do for themselves. But do they really have the time? Would they really rather be doing something else?

If this type of local activity were to develop, it would also develop and restore some of the community and social activity which the commuter dormitory towns and villages of the industrial age have tended to destroy. It is also more possible to see how some people might choose to start their career in a local enterprise, earning money and developing business and social skills, while simultaneously using part of their time to develop the next stage of their skills education in another field for a different career in a few years' time.

Entertainment

What about entertainment, which with increasing leisure time is already becoming a major component of many people's lives?

There is intense effort from many media organizations to shape our leisure time in terms of non-stop films, television programmes and computer games. There is little doubt that, in due course, we will have almost complete freedom to watch and interact with whatever we want, whenever we want. We might choose any film that we like, or decide to watch a particular series of documentaries over a period of weeks. There will be endless virtual worlds to explore on the Information Superhighway, and seemingly limitless knowledge to explore through presentation techniques pioneered through the development of the Internet.

There will be opportunities to attend concerts, drama and sports events electronically as they happen, and to take an active part in discussion groups and clubs and societies. It will be possible to participate in international electronic games, quizzes, challenges and debates.

The sound system will be able to instantly retrieve and play any recording of any piece of music. For many types of music it will be possible to create your own interpretation, becoming the conductor of the orchestra as the sound system plays all of the individual instruments directly from the electronic score.

The future of books and reading will be interesting to watch. Somehow, a flat electronic screen just does not feel like a book. You cannot turn the pages, see how far you have got and how much there is left to read. You cannot instantly refer to another chapter to check something, or turn to the index whenever you want to. Electronic publishers will probably try to create all of these effects, but we will see if they succeed. Perhaps books will still exist, but eventually in an environmentally friendly rewriteable form. A standard domestic unit might download a book from the Superhighway, print all of the pages, bind it together and give you a book to read. But when you have finished reading it, the same machine will dismantle the book, extract the ink from the surface of each page, and stand ready to create another book whenever you want – a rather sophisticated version of taking a book out of the library. Perhaps it will never happen; we shall see.

There will, of course, still be a complete range of conventional leisure pursuits: modelling, painting, playing real musical instruments, playing games made of real wood, plastic and paper, and all of the sports and other leisure activities that we have today. There will also be a complete range of real entertainment outside the home, and some people may decide that they prefer to leave their electronic homes and go out to watch a play in a theatre or a sports event in a stadium fairly often.

The main challenge will be to decide and manage how we use our leisure time. We will all have to avoid the human tendency to become passive vegetables, just sitting watching images on a screen, and maintain a constructive balance of creative activities and challenges to make our lives enjoyable.

Exercise, sport and health

The need to maintain physical health through regular exercise and sporting activities is becoming much better understood, and all forms of sporting activity are likely to become more readily available.

The main effect of technology is likely to be the availability of regular monitoring and planning of sports activities to suit the particular needs of every individual. Simple measurements of all of the body's key parameters may be available at the home, from which a computer can diagnose the best exercise or sports regime for the next few days and months. Diet may be automatically adjusted to compensate for intensive periods of sporting activity.

Any irregularities in normal body rhythms and parameters will automatically be picked up very quickly, leading to early diagnosis of any illness and referral to specialist treatment if needed at the optimum time.

Civil engineering in the infoculture

So what will civil engineers like me be doing in this dazzling new world of technology?

Well, as it happens, people will still need places in which to live, places to work, places to shop, leisure and community centres, manufacturing installations, transport systems, water, electricity and waste disposal alongside the new information infrastructure. There will be urban settlements and rural communities. There will still be floods, earthquakes and other natural disasters to plan for and protect people against as far as is possible.

The buildings may change, the transport systems may change, and the organizations which design, construct and maintain them may adapt to a different working environment. But the same basic skill of understanding how to fit human habitation and all of its requirements into our complex natural environment will still be needed more than ever.

Planning for the future

I will leave you to draw your own conclusions for the future. I hope that I have given you some food for thought. I am quite sure that human attitudes and understanding will be the main constraints or accelerators controlling future changes, regardless of what technology is actually available.

Do you like the idea of the sort of world that I have presented here, or do you really want to see something quite different? Either way, watch for signs of changes happening around you and add your opinion to the debate. If it is right, get on with it; if it is wrong, change it! Right and wrong become a little less clear and down to individual opinions when it comes to lifestyles and individual freedoms, but the more you know the better you can argue the case.

Figure 12.4. Heading for the future.

Whatever the future might be, try to form your own opinions and plan to be part of it. Try to understand how other people feel and what they are thinking. A culture is formed from the complex interactions of many different people with the environment in which they find themselves. Information and information technology have become part of our living environment, and hence part of our culture. We expect information to be available, and we expect technology to supplement and support human capabilities.

We need to make quite sure that we are in control of our destiny if we want to be, rather than just becoming swamped by an ocean of haphazard forces and influences. Just as sailors perfected the art of steering their ships through the stormy and uncertain environment of the world's oceans, in the face of immense power and many unknowns, we must now chart a course through the turbulent waters of the infoculture ocean.

Individual freedom, global harmony

My own hope is that the changes ahead will support two important cornerstones of the development of human civilization: an increase in the freedom of individual people to live their lives as they would like to live them, and an improvement in all aspects of global harmony, both through people understanding each other's views through communication and through more widespread and comprehensive understanding of our natural and built environment and how every one of our actions affects them.

To turn to philosophy for a moment, it is intriguing to realize that humankind must develop or it will stagnate and die. There is no perfect solution, no final stage of development where we will have reached utopia and there is no further development that can improve our lives. What would we do if there were? There would be nothing to work or strive for, nowhere to go. When a mountaineer reaches the top of a mountain, where is there to go next? Up another mountain of course – a new challenge, new unknowns, otherwise why live?

So there is no final stage of human development that is just around the corner, no comfortable place to stop and live out the rest of our lives without having to think any more. The complexity of the world will not let that happen. But hopefully there will be a few ledges on the way up the mountain to catch our breath, and maybe a few towns, villages and leisure resorts on our travels where we can stop to recuperate and plan the next stages of our travels toward the world of the future.

Sustainability must not mean stagnation either. The world must live and breathe and develop and progress, but with rather more understanding of the consequences for future generations. The natural world around us has not stopped developing. Where civilization and nature meet, both sides adapt to new circumstances. The trick is to find a little more harmony and balance.

If personal freedom does increase significantly, giving everyone more choice in what they do with their time, we will all need to develop a conscious skill of how to use our time constructively. The world will have little sympathy for those who just take everything that the present can offer without thinking about the future. When times are good, we will need to spend part of our time learning and developing new skills to take us through leaner times ahead, rather than just indulging every minute that we can in our favourite leisure activities. We will all have to take a little bit more control over our individual destinies.

One of the greatest strengths of the world is the immensely rich cultural diversity between different continents, nations and communities. We must take care that the pressures for change in our infoculture of the future to not swamp and drown much of the existing cultural differences and qualities in every corner of the world.

When we have watched every film ever made, beaten the challenges of the most dazzling computer games, and saturated our minds with technical knowledge through multimedia education, we might start looking for a little more depth in our thoughts to find peace and harmony with our inner selves.

Quite a few civilizations worked through this need for inner wellbeing a long time ago, and found it without waiting for the wondrous world of information technology. Perhaps, in due course, we will all slow down a little, and use the new technologies to communicate with people all over the world who we had never dreamt of talking to, as we each search for individual peace and harmony with our world.

Appendix A: Webspace

http://www.infoculture.co.uk

There is a World-Wide Web page on the Internet linked to the publication of this book, maintained by the author.

Unlike the printed page, the Web is dynamic, and pages on the web can be revised and extended at any time. Hence, a web page can contain updates, examples, comments, feedback and links to other interesting areas of the Web.

If you have access to the Internet, or visit a friend who has, or come across a Cybercafé or any other means of looking at this page, please take the opportunity to do so.

Appendix B: Events and people

My knowledge and experience have been shaped by all sorts of events and meetings; talking to many colleagues, friends and researchers; and many, many chance meetings with people from all walks of life. It would be impossible for me to acknowledge everybody individually, but I would like to extend my heartfelt thanks to everyone who has taken the time, at some time over the last 30 years, to explain things to me and to debate and explore the potential of new ideas.

At places in the text I have made reference to just a few of these events, and below is a sample of some of the events and people who have played some part in the background to this book.

1. (Chapter 1) The concept of the analogy between the motor car and the computer – From one of the keynote speeches at an Esprit conference in Brussels in the late 1980s or early 1990s.
2. (Chapter 1) The Information Society – initially from the IT Forum debate of the annual Esprit and European IT conferences in Brussels, which I attended several times at the end of the 1980s and during the 1990s. Brought up to date at the People First symposium in Dublin, September 1996.
3. (Chapter 2) Understanding technology trends – supporting and later managing UK computer facilities for Scott Wilson for various periods between 1985 and 1996.
4. (Chapter 2) Artificial intelligence, voice recognition, neural networks – A whole series of computer-related conferences and meetings. These started with a UK Alvey conference in the 1980s, continuing through several Civil-Comp conferences, and a European meeting in Aix-les Bains in the late 1980s. This knowledge was also extended by another series of meetings in Paris, Amsterdam and London to

develop the Esprit Computer Integrated Building exploratory action report 1990/91.

5. (Chapter 2) Traditions in construction – working in design offices and on construction sites 1977–1996.

6. (Chapter 3) Concepts, objects and data – thinking developed for a presentation at an SERC funded N+N international research meeting at Armathwaite Hall in the Lake District in 1993.

7. (Chapter 4) The infoperson's toolkit – idea developed for UK Television Education Network programme in 1996.

8. (Chapter 5) Understanding the Internet – encouragement and assistance from countless people, some of whom I only ever communicated with by e-mail, to understand what the Internet is all about.

9. (Chapter 6) The Ordnance Survey – presentations given by the Ordnance Survey to various professional groups.

10. (Chapter 6) Locational independence and teleworking – some ideas resulted from attending meetings organised by UK Derbyshire Enterprise Board as part of an initiative to develop new employment opportunities in the coalfields in the early 1990s.

11. (Chapter 6) British Telecom – changing working methods to reduce office space overheads, talking to Frank Shepherd who gave a presentation at a meeting about Paperless Civil Engineering at the Institution of Civil Engineers, October 1996.

12. (Chapter 7) Experiences installing a PC in Uganda (i): the design office – with thanks to John Walusimbi and others at Associated Consulting Engineers in Kampala for reminding me what civil engineering is really about.

13. (Chapter 7) Experiences installing a PC in Uganda (ii): repairs – with thanks the electronics engineers in Kampala who repaired the uninterruptible power supply for showing me what a little ingenuity and understanding can achieve.

14. (Chapter 7) New approaches to management and work organization – with thanks to Chris White of Scott Wilson, who, through organizing a provocative and stimulating internal management course in 1993/1994, set me on a voyage of discovery through all sorts of different books and learning opportunities.

15. (Chapter 7) Business process re-engineering and Total Quality Management – initial understanding of the importance of these concepts at a fringe session of the European IT conference in Brussels in 1994.

16. (Chapter 7) Business process re-engineering – a better understanding of the implications and opportunities through meetings with Michael

Cleary and Charlie Ericson at Lansing in Michigan in January 1995.

17. (Chapter 7) Understanding that the best leader may not be the most senior member of the team, and other management concepts, through discussions with my brother Geoff Vincent back in the 1980s – see *Taming Technology* in My Bookshelf.

18. (Chapter 8) Understanding what can go wrong – from my years of working with computers at Scott Wilson.

19. (Chapter 9) Understanding the future individual responsibility for learning – with thanks to Chris White at Scott Wilson for explaining the importance of this to me several years ago.

20. (Chapter 9) The learning culture – through the European debates and conferences already mentioned above.

21. (Chapter 9) New learning needs and learning methods – A series of meetings over dinner with Tim Cornick and Jeff Wix at the Jade Cottage in Thatcham, where we debated new education needs in the construction industry. Also with thanks to James Mather for turning some of these ideas into components of practical short courses organised at the University of Reading.

22. (Chapter 10) Computer costs – while managing the computer facilities for Scott Wilson's UK offices 1993–1996.

23. (Chapter 10) Strategies of evolution or revolution – my own interpretation of a meeting at the Institution of Civil Engineers October 1994, the particular speakers were David Jones of John Laing and Peter Rutter of Scott Wilson.

I would also like to extend particular thanks to friends and family who took the time to read through and comment on the draft of this book, and in particular to Derek Hadden, Viv Vincent and Mike Vincent for their detailed comments and suggestions. Also, special thanks to my wife Margaret, and my son James, for their assistance and support, often from thousands of miles away by e-mail.

Appendix C: My bookshelf

I do not keep systematic records of the source of every item of knowledge that I acquire, but I find it fascinating, as I finish writing this book, to look at the row of books on my bookshelf that I have read all or part of over the past few years, all of which have played some role in forming my views.

This is not an exhaustive reference list, and I do not necessarily support all of the views expressed in the books in the following list. However, for anyone looking for further interesting reading material, it may be useful to look through some of these books in your local library or at your local bookstore to see whether they spark your interest.

A Brief History of Time. Stephen Hawking, 1988. Bantam Press.
Atlas of Management Thinking. Edward de Bono, 1981. Penguin.
Beyond National Borders. Kenichi Ohmae, 1987. Dow Jones-Irwin.
Beyond Workplace 2000. Joseph H. Boyett with Jimmie T. Boyett, 1996. Penguin.
Communications, Technology and the Development of People. Bernard Woods, 1993. Routledge.
Computer Integrated Building Design. Tim Cornick, 1996. E&FN Spon.
Earth in the Balance. Al Gore, 1992. Earthscan.
First Things First. Stephen R. Covey and A. Roger Merrill, 1994. Simon and Schuster.
Isambard Kingdom Brunel. L.T.C. Rolt, 1957. Penguin.
Making it Happen. John Harvey Jones, 1988. William Collins.
Management of Design Offices. P.A. Rutter and A.S. Martin (eds), 1990. Thomas Telford.
Reengineering the Corporation. Hammer and Champy, 1993. HarperCollins.
Taming Technology. Geoff Vincent, 1988. Kogan Page.

The Age of Unreason. Charles Handy, 1989. Business Books.

The Borderless World. Kenichi Ohmae, 1992. Harper Collins.

The Demming Management Method. Mary Walton, 1986. Dodd Mead and Company.

The Prince. [1532]. Machiavelli, 1979. Viking Press.

The R Factor. Michael Schluter and Davis Lee, 1993. Hodder and Stoughton.

The Teleworking Handbook. Imogen Bertin and Alan Denbigh, 1996. TCA.

The Way Forward: Beyond Agenda 21. Felix Dodds (ed), 1997. Earthscan.

Thriving on Chaos. Tom Peters, 1988. Macmillan.

Total Quality Management. Oakland, 1989. Butterworth-Heinemann.

Troubleshooter 2. John Harvey Jones, 1992. Penguin.

Troubleshooter Returns. John Harvey Jones, 1995. Penguin.

What They Don't Teach You at Harvard Business School. Mark H. McCormack, 1986. Fontana.

Whose Reality Counts? Robert Chambers, 1997. Intermediate Technology Publications.

Index